Bobbi & Jim —

You folks are two super-courageous
people that make it all feel so very
natural and right. Here's to the very
best to both of you and lots more
courage in the future —

with love & affection

Rab

Praise for The Courage to Act

"*What we search for as leaders is a compass to guide our decisions and our actions when we're ambivalent or uncomfortable, and when we're getting conflicting data and pressure to act decisively before we're ready. In their five-part formula, Klein and Napier offer such a compass.*"

RON ROBISON, SENIOR VICE PRESIDENT R&D AND CHIEF
MEDICAL OFFICER, SOLVAY PHARMACEUTICALS, INC.

"*The real value of* The Courage to Act *isn't in the wisdom you'll find in its pages. It's in the way it shows you how to apply that wisdom to the challenges testing your courage and the courage of the people around you.*"

FREDY-JO GRAFMAN, DIRECTOR, HUMAN RESOURCES,
ELAN MEDICAL TECHNOLOGIES

"*The five-factor model shows how leaders at all levels can get themselves and their teams over the hurdle to drive results and to establish trust—something that is a critical business imperative today.*"

RON ESPOSITO, PROFESSOR, NEW YORK UNIVERSITY;
MANAGEMENT AND ORGANIZATION EFFECTIVENESS
CONSULTANT

"The Courage to Act *is extremely thought provoking. It's written in a way that provokes action on the reader's part. A book that should be read!*"

BILL M. WILLIAMS, PH.D., C.T.A., AUTHOR OF TRADING
CHAOS AND NEW TRADING DIMENSIONS

THE COURAGE TO ACT

The
COURAGE
to
ACT

5 Factors of Courage to Transform Business

MEROM KLEIN AND ROD NAPIER

Davies-Black Publishing
Palo Alto, California

Published by Davies-Black Publishing, a division of CPP, Inc., 3803 East Bayshore Road, Palo Alto, CA 94303; 800-624-1765.

Special discounts on bulk quantities of Davies-Black books are available to corporations, professional associations, and other organizations. For details, contact the Director of Marketing and Sales at Davies-Black Publishing; 650-691-9123; fax 650-623-9271.

Visit the Davies-Black Publishing Web site at www.daviesblack.com.

07 06 05 04 03   10 9 8 7 6 5 4 3 2 1
Printed in the United States of America

Library of Congress Cataloging-in-Publication Data
Klein, Merom and Rod Napier
        The courage to act : 5 factors of courage to transform business /
        Merom Klein and Rod Napier.— 1st ed.
            p. cm.
        Includes bibliographical references and index.
        ISBN 0-89106-178-9
            1. Business. 2. Industrial management. I. Title.
HD57.7 .L575 2003
658.4′092—dc21
                                                                2002025600

FIRST EDITION
First printing 2003

To my wife, Louise Yochee, and the courage we inspire in one another to continue to live the dream; to my daughter, Elana, who continues to amaze and delight us with her courage; and to Abilgail, who walks the fine line between courage and chutzpah
—Merom Klein

To my wife, Julie, who knows the work of love; and to Burke O'Brien, forever a hero
—Rod Napier

CONTENTS

PREFACE

To see what is right, and not to do it,
is want of courage or of principle.
CONFUCIUS

Our fascination with courage is nothing new. Since the dawn of time, we have been drawn to those who courageously face extraordinary moments of truth or who create moments of truth that change the course of history. We are fascinated by those whose lives seem larger than our own, those who face the same struggles and the same everyday moments of truth that confront us all but who manage to beat the odds, live the dream, and achieve the unachievable.

In the early days of the Courage Institute, when we first started talking with work groups about courage, the concept appealed to only a small group of adventurers, the outliers in organizational life, who were inspired rather than put off by innovation, empowerment, and personal initiative. Now, of course, with different business realities, we see that more and more of the workforce needs courage.

Living on high alert, in a constant state of vigilance and readiness, is no longer confined to those of us who live in war-torn countries. In the current work environment worldwide, we all live with the threat that the rug can be pulled out from under us at any time. In business, there is prevailing uncertainty and insecurity about the next merger, reorganization, or quarterly announcement. Because of the value that is placed on initiative and empowerment, people feel they have the license to encroach on others' territories and challenge official, formal authority. We're being held to higher and higher standards of ethics and fiduciary responsibility. The more advanced our own technical expertise is and the more sophisticated our enterprise becomes, the more we are dependent on the knowledge, values, and cooperation of others. Such dependency requires courage.

If you've ever lit a fire from just a spark, you know it takes a lot of energy to create a flame. The same is true of those who inspire the courage to embrace an embryonic change, breathe life into it, and persevere through the trials and difficulties that follow. It takes courage to swim against the tide of convention and peer pressure in order to capture the interest and imagination of those at higher levels of the organization. And it takes courage to follow leaders who offer a vision of something that hasn't been tried before or that hasn't been successful in previous attempts.

In the Hebrew language, there are two versions of the English word courage. One is *chutzpah,* which has a decidedly negative connotation. With *chutzpah,* you push other people out of the way to get where you want to go. It's an exercise of power that makes others say "Ouch!" or at the very least makes them wonder what you're up to and whether you can be trusted. *Chutzpah* puts people on edge and raises their level of fear.

The other Hebrew term for courage is *ometz lev,* which means "strength of heart." *Ometz lev* draws other people in, brings them up to your level of strength, and creates a level of synergy that achieves more than either partner would achieve alone. *Ometz lev* is an exercise of power that leaves others feeling affirmed and appreciated, challenged and excited. *Ometz lev* may not make the fear go away, but it makes you willing to face it, deal with it, and help others do the same. The five-factor model of courage—including candor, purpose, will, rigor, and risk—that we'll present in this book is about what it takes to instill *ometz lev,* and not *chutzpah,* from the top of the organization down, from the bottom up, and from your sphere of influence outward to colleagues at your same level of the organization.

In today's world, courage has become a mainstream business concept, not a curiosity or an exotic "nice-to-have" feature. Courage Institute programs are now offered to more than the adventurous few and are often conducted far away from our base in Israel. Indeed, our faculty are now teaching the five-factor model to scientific, engineering, and accounting teams in many of the world's leading corporations and government agencies. Courage has been added to the list of competencies for executives, to be sure, and also to the list of qualifications of anyone who's expected to provide expertise and leadership.

A Historical Perspective

Of all the revered historical figures we might have chosen to write about, few exemplify the five courage factors like King Sejong the Great, the ruler of Korea from 1418, when he was twenty-two, until his death in 1450. He inherited a country with no written language and a literacy rate pitifully lower than that of any other Asian country. For his predecessors, that was simply the way things were. For King Sejong, however, that reality was a "moment of truth"—a challenge that he could choose to accept, and change the history of his people, or avoid, and leave things as they always had been.

King Sejong embraced the challenge, leaving behind one of the highest literacy rates in the world, one that is still the envy of other Asian countries. His legacy included a wide array of technological and scientific advances, developed centuries before Europe would make the same discoveries.

At a time when the power of the king was absolute and his subjects could be held in submission by ignorance, poverty, and fear, King Sejong the Great was driven by a vision of education, prosperity, and empowerment for the citizens of his country. He saw what Korea could be. But, as we all know, change doesn't take place just because the person at the top has a vision and knows what's strategically important—even if he is a king ruling a feudal society.

In the insular world of his palace, King Sejong invented a written alphabet for the Korean language and tested it with groups of children. When he was satisfied that his Hangeul system was easy enough for even the simplest of his subjects to learn, he rolled it out throughout the kingdom. He expected his subjects to embrace the new symbols and understand the value of being a literate people. But he had a tough time getting his subjects to learn to read and write using the symbols he had invented and tested. Until King Sejong created this moment of truth for all of Korean society, only the elite could read and write, and they did so in Chinese, not using a Korean alphabet.

According to the legend of King Sejong, as told in *The King's Secret* (Farley, 1997),

> [I]mportant people in all the cities and villages looked at the symbols and whispered among themselves. "We cannot use them," they told one another. "King Sejong is great, but the gods are even greater. Koreans have always used the Chinese way of writing, because the gods will it."
>
> Many weeks later, [Royal Minister] Chong-In-ji told the king the sad news. "People don't like the new alphabet. They say the gods have blessed only the Chinese way of writing."
>
> "The gods can bless more than one way of writing!" King Sejong declared. "We must think of how to show people this truth."
>
> But no matter how hard he and the scholars of his court tried, they could not think of a way to do this.

Thus was born a monumental change management dilemma.

Even today, it isn't easy to teach adults to read. And for those who have already mastered one alphabet and must learn to navigate with a new one, becoming literate in a second language can be a frustrating task. Today, those who don't know how to read and write recognize that they are operating at a disadvantage. But in King Sejong's day, there was safety in numbers. Those who couldn't read and write with the new Hangeul alphabet could take refuge in the fact that most of their fellow countrypeople couldn't either.

As Korea's monarch, Sejong had the power to demand that his subjects learn the new language. But he was wise enough to know that forced compliance wouldn't work. Even if he got the people to learn a new written language, he couldn't force them to use it. He understood that this societal transformation couldn't be ordered or decreed.

If the people didn't have the courage to confront their illiteracy and embrace the change, he knew that his literacy initiative wouldn't succeed—let alone take root in society and outlive his reign. If they didn't have the courage to transform their view of Korean culture vis-à-vis the revered Chinese language, the new symbols would be dismissed as the ravings of a self-impressed monarch rather than embraced as a gift to the people. What's more, King Sejong knew that very few of his subjects would have the courage tell him the truth, as Chong-In-ji had done, and would create the illusion that the new alphabet was taking root, lest the king be displeased and dishonored.

With benefit of hindsight, we can see that Sejong's experiment was indeed a success. The Hangeul alphabet is still in use, and the literacy rate in Korea is among the highest in the world. And, far from sowing the seeds of the overthrow and destruction of the Choson dynasty, King Sejong built the foundation for a ruling dynasty that would endure for more than five hundred years.

But no courage is required to look at a success in retrospect. Looking forward from 1443, when Sejong introduced the Hangeul alphabet, or from 1446, when the script was promulgated, the experiment looked much more tenuous. From what we can piece together from historical documents and Korean folklore, it looks as if King Sejong the Great had all five courage factors firmly in his mind and in his heart.

- **Candor: the courage to speak and hear the truth.** King Sejong knew that the common people—the very subjects he most wanted to reach—would not dare to tell him the truth if it were something he did not want to hear. So he disguised himself as a commoner and went among the people to hear firsthand how the new alphabet was received and learn of the difficulties and skepticism that would have to be overcome. Armed with direct, honest feedback, King Sejong convened meetings of his inner cabinet to deal with the problems and find solutions.

- **Purpose: the courage to pursue lofty and audacious goals.** "The sounds of our country's language are different from those of the Middle Kingdom [China] and are not confluent with the sounds of characters," King Sejong is reported to have said. "Therefore, among the ignorant people, there have been many who, having something they want to put into words, have in the end been unable to express their feelings. I have been distressed because of this, and have newly designed twenty-eight letters, which I wish to have everyone practice at their ease and make convenient for their daily use" (Key and Renaud, 1991). Everyone. Daily use. Lofty and audacious? You bet.

- **Will: the courage to inspire optimism, spirit, and promise.** According to the legend of King Sejong, there were times in the change process when even he was discouraged and lost heart. He expected the new alphabet to be embraced enthusiastically as his gift to a grateful nation. He tested it to make sure it could be easily learned. Still, it was not embraced and few had the will to overcome their illiteracy. Legend has it that, until the symbols were seen etched in the bark of the trees of the forest and those etchings were taken as the will of the gods, neither the "ignorant people" nor the noblemen in King Sejong's court were willing to endure the frustration of learning and teaching the new language.

- **Rigor: the courage to invent disciplines and make them stick.** Institutionalizing the Hangeul alphabet took more than a royal decree. For the letters to be more than a handwritten curiosity that was out of the reach of the common people, King Sejong also had to invent a way of transforming the language from calligraphy to reproducible type. Printing with wood blocks was impractical because only twenty to thirty copies could be made from a single woodcut. Unless typography could be improved to meet the demand for a greater number and variety of printed texts, Sejong reasoned, the language would not endure. Thus, he assembled a brain trust of technicians and charged them with the task of improving the typeface and moving from wood to metallurgy. The advances in metallurgy brought fifteenth-century Korea to a level of industrial development—in tools, farm implements, and printing—that Europe wouldn't achieve for another three hundred years.

- **Risk: the courage to empower, trust, and invest in relationships.** Many of the senior ministers in King Sejong's court warned of the dangers of universal literacy. If the masses are able to express their true feelings and articulate their thoughts freely, the ministers argued, how can we maintain our power and control? Encouraging widespread literacy was a radical, unprecedented experiment and required a giant leap of faith. Who knew what people would do with their newfound power and independence once the written language took on a life of its own? To mitigate the risks and truly empower the people, Sejong instituted a series of land reforms and tax reforms that were commensurate with the freedoms that a literate and educated people should enjoy. He introduced the first system of health care reform as well. Rather than underestimate or shrink from the risk of literacy, King Sejong embraced it and prepared society for its newfound power and independence. He strengthened the authority and legitimacy of the Choson dynasty by building the Korean national consciousness and raising it to an unprecedented level of freedom and democratic achievement that would remain unmatched for many centuries.

In modern times, we also are impressed with leaders who strengthen their own power and influence by enabling and empowering their followers, rather than subjugating them. We admire the candor, purpose, will, rigor, and risk of leaders like Yitzchak Rabin, Anwar Sadaat, and Shimon Peres, in contrast to those who speak of peace but continue to exploit their people and generate fear rather than opportunity and liberty. We admire the integrity of military heroes like General Norman Schwartzkopf, who, even before he was a general in Vietnam, took a zero-tolerance stance toward the racism that he saw in some military circles and had the courage to stand by his convictions. We admire the courage of heroes like Ernest Shackleton, who refused to abandon his shipwrecked crew in the wasteland of Antarctica and did whatever he could to imbue his ill-fated team with the candor, purpose, will, rigor, and risk to survive the hardships, even when it would have been easier to admit defeat and return to the warmth and comfort of England.

With twenty-twenty hindsight, we know that the corporate officers of Johnson & Johnson were right when they had the courage to pull the entire supply of Tylenol® off the shelves and take the hit on their bottom line. We know that the officers of Enron and World-Com were wrong when they refused to admit that their companies were losing money and instead posted a healthy profit. We know that Nordstrom was right in betting on the initiative and entrepreneurial spirit of its employees, building a foundation firmer than that of companies who treated workers like expenses to be managed and cut whenever possible.

Again, this is courage viewed in hindsight. The officers of Johnson & Johnson refused to compromise their candor, purpose, will, rigor, and risk in the face of a moment of truth that no one would willingly encounter. They didn't know how it would turn out, any more than General Schwartzkopf knew whether turning away from an officers' club that denied entry to South Vietnamese army officers would redline his military career—or any more than King Sejong the Great knew how his subjects would handle the freedom and responsibility that came with literacy and reform.

Few of us face the awesome responsibilities of a head of state, a king, a general, or the CEO of a major corporation. In a past era, these were the figures who needed courage. The rest of us were the benefactors who followed the course that they charted.

But new freedoms, knowledge, and opportunities require new courage. Those who grew up in a literate Korea needed a higher level of courage than did those who grew up as "an ignorant people." It wasn't just King Sejong who needed a higher level of candor, purpose, will, rigor, and risk. It was the common fifteenth-century Korean who also needed a higher level of

- **Candor:** to speak and hear the truth in order to get help with the new alphabet, to provide feedback, and to help the technical advances take on a life of their own

- **Purpose:** to pursue the lofty and audacious goal of becoming literate and helping others do the same, one family and one village at a time

- **Will:** to inspire optimism, spirit, and promise in the face of frustration, to persevere until they had learned the Hangeul alphabet and could use it fluently

- **Rigor:** to invent better disciplines and make them stick, by reproducing the characters of the alphabet faithfully and creating new reading materials, and sharing those reading materials with other family and community members

- **Risk:** to empower, trust, and invest in relationships and embrace new freedoms with a sense of civic pride and responsibility rather than using them as a weapon against those who were helping to build a different partnership between the king and his people.

What Can We Learn from King Sejong and His People?

Not everyone is lucky enough to work in the shadow of an executive team or a CEO as visionary, enlightened, and benevolent as King Sejong the Great. Still, it's hard to imagine any modern organization in which workers don't have new freedoms, new knowledge, and new opportunities. By necessity, matrix and team structures are replacing or at least supplementing chains of command and hierarchies. Those at the top don't necessarily know more than those in the trenches. We have the power to capitalize on opportunities for our organizations or allow them to get away.

Followers rely on their leaders for vision and inspiration. That is as true today as it was in King Sejong's time. And, now as then, we still suffer the consequences when our leaders aren't enlightened and responsible, when they abuse their authority and discretion (as the employee-shareholders of Enron and WorldCom will attest).

Leaders are also dependent on their followers. A new alphabet is useless if people don't learn it and use it. In modern corporations, more sophisticated technology and more complex partnerships are worthless if they are not embraced at the grassroots level. Changes happen quickly and require too much knowledge and problem-solving skill for all practices and procedures to be mandated or controlled from the top down. Stock options have no value if people don't sign on to the program and see hope for the future.

In fifteenth-century Korea, the partnership that had to be forged between King Sejong and his people was truly extraordinary. Without such a partnership, and the courage it inspired in all walks of life, none of Sejong's great accomplishments would have been possible. In twenty-first-century corporations, we need the same kind of partnerships—and the same level of courage. We need to make the extraordinary

ordinary. Even in organizations such as the FBI, we have seen what happens when people who have mission-critical information are too fearful to speak up, and when pandering to those in power is more important than achieving the greatness to which the organization purports to be dedicated.

In corporate failures such as those we witnessed at Enron, World-Com, ImClone, and Arthur Andersen, among others, there was too little courage too late. The monarchs claimed they didn't know what was going on in their royal courts. King Sejong, in contrast, didn't wait for the truth to come to him. He knew that his royal ministers had too much at risk to bring him news that he might not want to hear. So he dressed himself as a commoner, went out to manage by walking around, and then revealed himself to be the king, in a public display that said, "I want you to have the courage to be real with me, tell me what you think, and work with me to face problems and solve them together."

Even in the presence of a King Sejong, embracing new freedoms and opportunities requires courage. The royal elite, who could already read and write in Chinese, faced moments of truth that were different from those of the newly empowered commoners. We also face moments of truth when we see things in our organizations that aren't congruent with the vision or the professed values; accounting or business practices that are questionable or misleading; opportunities that aren't yet being seized and value that isn't yet being leveraged as effectively as it could be; and groups that are disenfranchised or treated as if they are incapable of thinking and acting like active partners, even though they draw a paycheck from the organization.

In a time when we all have more discretion and more mobility and our judgment has far-reaching consequences for the success of our enterprises, we all need more courage. We need to find it within ourselves and inspire it in those around us, whether they are below us or above us in the organizational hierarchy. What we say and what we intend is less important, in this environment, than what we do and how we act. If we don't have the good fortune to look up the hierarchy and see a King Sejong the Great, the imperative is even stronger and more compelling.

We hope this book helps you find more of the candor to speak and hear the truth, a greater sense of purpose, a more optimistic will, a more disciplined rigor, and a greater inclination to trust and risk.

ACKNOWLEDGMENTS

We would like to acknowledge the contributions of those who have sustained us and kept the spark of courage alive within us to see this project through.

First, of course, we appreciate the moral support and guidance we received from our wives and colleagues, Julie and Louise Yochee.

We appreciate the many contributions of Christine Cavalieri, who helped us keep our eye on the ball through the many iterations of this project. Thanks also to our capable editors, Karen Kozek and Sylvia Burlin.

We are indebted to Connie Kallback, Acquisitions Editor at Davies-Black, who is everything a writer could hope for—a kind, honest, and supportive cheerleader and advocate when one was most needed.

Thanks to Karl Weber, who provided the mature insight and wise guidance only a remarkable literary advisor could provide; and to David Baum, who offered guidance on early drafts of our manuscript.

And thanks to the partners and collaborators who have sharpened our focus on courage, pointed us in the right direction, and kept us going, including Steve Rhodes, Todd Dollinger, and the entire team at Trendlines; Ron Resnikoff and his staff, who got us started; Steve Krupp and Beverly Burton of Key Management Strategies, where we pioneered our work on courage; Robert Atkinson, Fredy-Jo Grafman, Linda Symons, Larry Brower, and George Scurlock, who have brought these concepts to life as client/sponsors and pushed us to see this project through; Joel Katz, who provided much-appreciated support and advocacy; Ken Victor, our partner at Edgework Leadership Group; and Robert Lazar, Elissa Lewin, Elliott Rotman, and Gary Weinman, who gave us wind under our wings and an infusion of courage when we most needed it.

ABOUT THE AUTHORS

Both authors have owned successful businesses, consulted with a wide range of clients, and written extensively. More important is their commitment to the understanding of how groups and teams function. They have worked on assignment in several dozen countries on four continents. From these experiences they have derived the principles framed in *The Courage to Act*.

MEROM KLEIN

Merom Klein spent fifteen years as CEO of Key Management Strategies, a U.S.-based training and consulting firm that piloted groundbreaking research in the essential elements of his Courage Index. The worldwide distribution of his state-of-the-art training simulations has provided further understanding of what it takes to imbue teams with courage and enable them to apply their experiences to their back-home challenges. More specifically, Klein's research has revealed the differences between resilient and nonadaptive teams and how to increase any team's effectiveness.

Klein founded the Courage Institute in Israel, where he has established an international network of behavioral science professionals with clients in North America, Europe, Asia, and the Middle East. His clients have included numerous organizations that have transformed themselves into flatter, team-based matrix organizations in a variety of industries. He has worked with ARAMARK, Sunkyong, NASA, Illinois Tool Works, Amersham Health, Exelon, Bayer, Rafa'el, Lockheed-Martin, KeyCorp, ING, Elan Pharmaceuticals, PowderJect, CIGNA, Millennium Pharmaceuticals, and operating divisions of Merck, GE Capital, and Intel, among others.

Klein earned his Ph.D. degree at Temple University. In addition to his extensive consulting and training, he has been invited to lecture and has run his simulations on change management, bridging cross-cultural differences, and courage at Wharton, Drexel, Temple, Loyola, and University of Haifa. He regularly speaks at international conferences in the areas of leadership, change, and team development.

ROD NAPIER

Rod Napier is coauthor of the seminal text in the field of group dynamics, *Groups: Theory and Experience* (Napier and Gershenfeld, Houghton Mifflin, now in its seventh edition). He has devoted his career to the study of how groups and teams function and their relation to the success of larger organizations. While a professor at Temple University, he pioneered the concept of 360-degree feedback and developed the widely used practice of performance hiring. The question he continues to study is how to develop applied theory that can be translated into skills and actual behaviors for leaders in every aspect of organizational life.

Since leaving Temple, Napier has divided his time between consulting and writing (ten books, including *Making Groups Work* and *Tools and Activities for Strategic Planning*). He has worked with a broad array of clients, including CBS, Exxon, the United States Army Corps of Engineers, the United Nations, the New Israel Fund, Merck, and Becton Dickinson. In addition, he has been engaged in issues of planned change with a variety of colleges and universities, including Wellesley, Swarthmore, the University of Pennsylvania, the University of Virginia, and Cornell University. Napier is a teaching fellow at the Wharton School, and he is a skilled presenter to large and small audiences at a wide range of conventions, seminars, and colloquia.

Why
COURAGE
Now?

WHY COURAGE?

A Time of Uncertainty, Challenge, and Conflict

Courage is a special kind of knowledge. It's knowing how to fear what ought to be feared and how not to fear what ought not be feared.
DAVID BEN GURION

Less than a decade ago, we would have looked at the difficulties and adversities that the average team encounters and concluded that they were symptoms of mismanagement. Quick turnarounds and around-the-clock availability would have been considered oppressive or unreasonable. If plans had to be scuttled and reworked in the midst of execution, we would have assumed that someone didn't have his act together. If teams were pushed to the edge, beyond their comfort zone, they would have had a built-in excuse for mistakes in judgment or execution.

But today the very same conditions are considered normal and inevitable. There are competing priorities. Conflicts arise when there is no one at a higher level to smooth things over, reallocate resources, or adjudicate fairly. It isn't easy to make your voice heard and have your

3

expertise taken seriously, even when you are the bona fide expert and know what you are talking about. And job security? Even in Japan and Scandinavia, it's an anachronism. You're only as good as your last performance.

Sweeping changes in the way most of us work have created a new wave of fear, uncertainty, and ambiguity. The changes didn't come in a sudden attack. No one planned or orchestrated this coup. It just happened. Like other revolutions, this one has freed the masses, in this case from rigid hierarchies, lockstep career paths, and stifling petty bureaucrats. But newfound freedoms, opportunities, and empowerment haven't made life easier or simpler. Instead, they have generated fear, pressure, noise, and contentiousness—and no kings or higher powers to ameliorate the concerns, steady the course, clarify the priorities, or resolve the conflicts.

A New Kind of Team

Working in teams is nothing new. After decades of planning teams, project teams, executive teams, review teams, quality circles, and task forces, virtually everyone has been part of a team at some point in his or her organizational life. But the teams of today can't be compared to the teams of ten or twenty years ago, any more than raising a family today can be compared to the lifestyles of Ozzie and Harriet or June and Ward Cleaver or the fight against terrorism can be compared to battles in Korea or Vietnam. The pressures, responsibilities, diversity, pace, mobility, and outside influences are dramatically different. Semiautonomous cells, virtual partnerships, and loosely connected networks nest within organizational hierarchies. The bar is always being raised; there is always more to learn, no matter how close you feel to the top of your game.

Very little has prepared team members or leaders to deal with these pressures. Some of us remember when managers were paid handsomely to plan, organize, direct, and control. We may feel bewildered or resentful when we're given an assignment whose parameters keep changing and we're expected to figure it out for ourselves. We want to be able to ask a straight question and get an answer other than "It depends" or "I can't find anything about this in the manual." We want to feel appreciated for what we've knocked ourselves out to accomplish—not knocked for what hasn't been achieved.

Inside the team, we expect a world that's benign, collegial, egalitarian, and supportive. But the proliferation of teams has not magically done away with the competitive, dependent, turf-protective, risk-averse attitudes that have prevailed in many organizations for many years.

Molecules Within a Hierarchy

Team structures belie a schizophrenia that's embedded in most post–Information Age organizations. We still draw the same old organizational charts (see Figure 1) to depict who sits where and who reports to whom, who earns the big bucks and who should be satisfied with a cost-of-living increase in pay. Some people have gotten cute with the pyramid and inverted the chart, but turning the drawing upside down doesn't change where the authority lies. Fourteen levels of hierarchy may have been reduced to five, but we still want to know where we fit and how close we are to the top of the house.

Despite the fact that we still draw our charts with boxes, silos, and pyramids, we're supposed to solve problems and seize opportunities as though the hierarchy didn't really matter. We're supposed to solicit and listen to know-how, wherever it resides. We're expected to coordinate our work with that of colleagues in other departments and other divisions so that the ultimate enterprise-wide objective takes precedence over narrow parochial orders or policies. You can't order someone to do something when she doesn't reside in your pyramid or silo on the formal hierarchy; so you have to explain your logic, build relationships, and rely on trust and influence rather than command and control.

On paper, it's easy to see the potential benefits of flat and flexible organizational structures (see Figure 1). It's easy to see how much more can be accomplished when the right brain trust is assembled, when we pay more attention to competencies and interpersonal

FIGURE 1

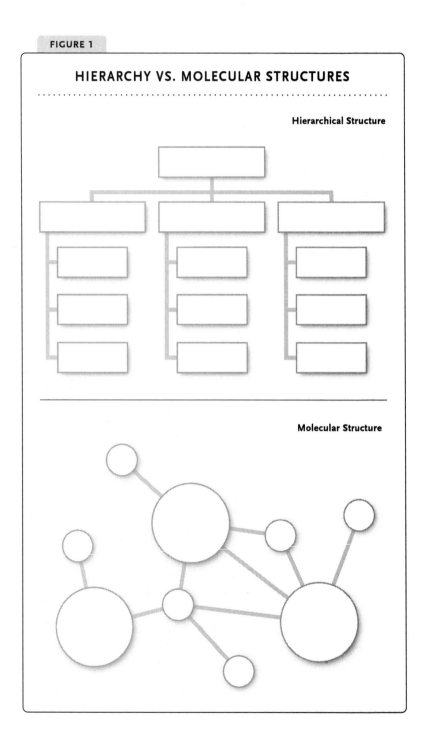

HIERARCHY VS. MOLECULAR STRUCTURES

Hierarchical Structure

Molecular Structure

chemistry than to whose pyramid owns the talent or gets the credit. Problems are solved faster and better when team members are less concerned about what's politically expedient and, instead, are more concerned with doing the right things, telling the truth, pushing the boundaries of the status quo, and pitching in to help, teach, and learn from one another. Layers of bureaucracy, as well as redundant checks and double-checks and their attendant costs, can be eliminated when people take their time lines, budgets, and accountabilities seriously and when they manage themselves accordingly. Resources can be leveraged and deployed better when people have the flexibility to serve on more than one team and work on more than one project.

But what's on paper doesn't necessarily change what's in people's hearts and minds. We know the benefits of working in teams. In a few places, we may have seen those benefits come to life. But just because the right people are thrown together and told to behave like a team doesn't mean that egos, power and control needs, individualism, and unbridled ambition or professional rivalries are any less present. Just because people have the right know-how doesn't guarantee that they'll show or share what they know. Just because the measures and time lines are visible doesn't guarantee that people will accept accountability. The results, all too often, are teams that are given a mandate to be flat, agile, empowered, and collaborative but lack the courage to act differently when they are put to the test.

Will the Real Fast Companies Please Stand Up?

If you think the shift to teams and matrix structures is confined to a few fast companies in the high-tech, scientific, or dot-com world, think again. ARAMARK Corporation is the antithesis of this profile. Started as a vending company, ARAMARK has grown to be a global giant in foodservice, uniform sales and rental, facilities management, child care, and other managed services. Its clients include most of the Fortune 500 companies, top colleges and universities, major hospitals, public school systems, correctional facilities, stadiums and arenas, convention centers, and national parks. If it's a service that's essential but not part of a client organization's core business, ARAMARK will manage it and do it for the client—better and often at a lower cost than the client can do it for itself. ARAMARK has built a multibillion-dollar global powerhouse on this formula. Most of the work it does isn't high-tech, but ARAMARK's 200,000 employees have to do it right, and with the highest level of customer service, day in and day out.

Before a major change was launched, the organization chart divided ARAMARK into autonomous business sectors, and each business unit was, in turn, divided into autonomous regions and business units. Each business unit manager had the authority to run his or her operation with great independence and little collaboration with the rest of the company. The buck stopped there. General Managers (GMs) were accountable for turning a profit ethically, safely, and in a way that would ensure client retention. They took their accountability seriously and instilled that same accountability in their reports. The formula worked. To be a GM, you were expected to know more than anyone else about how your operation worked and what made money—right down to every product, every service, every piece of equipment, and every intimate detail about your key customers. To be a Regional Vice President (RVP), you were expected to take that know-how to an even higher level.

With all this success and pride, why would anyone mess with a winning formula? With such strong leadership in every business unit and in every region, why would anyone want to shift the business paradigm from a collection of independent, autonomous business units and regions to one of high collaboration? Why act like there's something that has to be fixed when nothing is broken?

ARAMARK's shift from autonomy to collaboration started with a business case, not an ideology. Previously, ARAMARK had believed that it could serve its clients best by allowing each operation to function as an independent business, dutifully serving the needs the clients expressed. After closer examination and rethinking, the company decided that the best way to meet the needs of clients, while also maximizing sales and profits, would be to create "unlimited partnerships." That is, ARAMARK would seek to provide additional services to customers who were already using one ARAMARK service and share the benefits of the resulting synergies with their clients.

Why build unlimited partnerships? Despite all the enviable success ARAMARK's existing business units already enjoyed, the numbers showed vast potential waiting to be tapped—*if* GMs could find customer needs that had never been seen before and address them profitably. No longer would it be enough for GMs to maintain the status quo, fulfill the requirements of their service contracts, execute the orders they were given by their higher-ups, and eke out the same level of sales and profit. CEO Joe Neubauer has asked each and every GM to find a way to contribute to what he calls "Mission One," namely, making ARAMARK number one in organic growth, one customer at a time. And, since, as COO Bill Leonard says, "you can't grow your relationship with a customer you don't have," client retention is also a Mission One priority.

As if this weren't enough, Mission One also asks autonomous and entrepreneurial GMs to take a broader as well as a deeper view of their clients' needs. GMs are asked to pool their knowledge and their resources and go to market as what Neubauer calls "One ARAMARK." So, in addition to growing their business from within, GMs are also asked to look for opportunities across business lines and open the door to other divisions of the company.

Mission One is simple. On the surface, it seems so commonsensical that it's almost pedestrian, like King Sejong's new alphabet. Yet, those who truly embraced Mission One and set their sights on unlimited partnerships found that it required a different way of thinking. No one expected Mission One to create a revolution. But, when it came to shifting from talk to action and from promises to reality, GMs and their RVPs found that Mission One required a different way of leading.

According to conventional wisdom, it takes three to five years for a global corporation like ARAMARK to pull off a transformation like this, even if it is Mission One. But that's not how things work in a fast company. Joe Neubauer, Bill Leonard, and the team at the top of ARAMARK knew that Mission One was crucial to creating honest value for shareholders. They also knew that they couldn't shift the prevailing mind-set from virtual autonomy to unlimited partnerships and from filling orders to finding opportunities simply by announcing it to share-holders, customers, GMs, and their RVPs. The tribute to the courage of ARAMARK's GMs isn't just that the change occurred, but that it occurred more than twice as fast as conventional wisdom would pre-dict, and with so many ARAMARK veterans still in key positions of responsibility.

Why did the revolution succeed? In a word, it succeeded because of courage. GMs who had grown up understanding just one line of business suddenly found themselves dependent on others who knew more than they did and had better instincts about what would work, what would appeal to customers and their constituents, and how to leverage the resources and capabilities of other business units to meet their clients' needs. It took courage to ask others, "What do you think?" and "How can we make this work better?" and to be open to new ideas, new perspectives, and different business models.

Now, even within their own lines of business and their own oper-ations, GMs no longer have all the answers themselves. Tastes and technology have changed. So has competition. It takes a lot more to "wow" the constituents who reside within the client organization, i.e., the employees, students, patients, parents, fans of, and visitors to the organization that has contracted with ARAMARK. Heightened cus-tomer expectations require new high-powered marketing expertise. New technology provides better management tools and new ways to communicate internally and externally, and requires new high-powered information technology specialists. New financial and invest-ment models require better and more sophisticated accounting systems—and experts to set up and run the numbers. And, on the human side, the business is also more competitive. The best and brightest performers have other options—and it is becoming harder and harder to find and train replacements if they don't stay with the company. Enter experts on diversity, compensation, organization de-velopment, and other aspects of people management. It takes more courage to lead when you have to meet with thought leaders from other departments and deal with a complex array of committees, ad-visory boards, and regional, cross-line, and cross-functional business councils rather than size things up for yourself and issue a directive to your own management team.

And that's just on the ARAMARK side of the unlimited partnership. Clients, too, have more complex requirements. They have their own task forces and committees, their own thought leaders, and their own special interest groups. Any one of these can have an impact on the short-term profitability of a managed service contract, on client retention, and on the trust required to enlarge the scope of a managed service contract. It takes more courage to partner with a client in a dynamic business environment than it does to rely on a single decision maker.

Before Mission One, each GM got his or her directives from the top down. He or she might not agree with every decision or with every directive. However, a well-defined chain of command gave people a measure of security and predictability. Everyone knew his or her place and understood the limits of his or her authority and discretion. If their needs weren't met or directions weren't clear, people knew where to turn for answers or clarification. If a customer made conflicting or irreconcilable demands, you knew who had the authority to step in and adjudicate the problem.

Now things aren't as clear. GMs get as many directives, programs, and recommendations from the experts in marketing, finance, human resources, purchasing, and technology—as well as from customers—as they do from their own RVPs. Customers expect more and more and they don't always read the fine print on their contracts. It's a paradox. GMs have less latitude but more discretion. They face far more scrutiny and, since this is still ARAMARK, an organization built on accountability, they cannot say, "I didn't understand" or "I was just following orders." GMs are more accountable than ever for results and for building solid and trustworthy partnerships with clients, and yet they are more dependent on others than ever to achieve those results. There are more experts who are only a phone call away, but GMs can't possibly learn it all and know it all. GMs are expected to be more focused than ever on the success of their operations—yet they serve on more task forces and cross-functional teams, take part in more business development activities, participate in more training sessions, planning meetings, and teleconferences, and respond to more requests for information than ever before. GMs still need their RVPs' approval before making major investments or taking liberties with company policy, but now they are expected to lead upward and laterally as well as downward in the organizational hierarchy. They are expected to question things that don't make sense rather than follow blindly.

Mission One now asks GMs to inspire, as well as exhibit, initiative. For Mission One to work, it isn't enough for GMs to be the only thought leaders and innovators. They need to inspire entrepreneurial thinking throughout all ranks of their operations, starting with department and frontline managers. After all, a GM might be too removed from the front lines to see the next service offering, the next place to set up a kiosk, or the next as-yet-unmet customer need. And it isn't enough for GMs to have all the business acumen. Managers at all levels need the courage to kill an idea when the numbers simply don't add up to justify a new offering, even when it's something that would be fun to do. It takes more courage to inspire courage in others than to exhibit it yourself. Yet, that's the magic of Mission One—unleashing the potential of all members of the ARAMARK team.

You might not think of uniforms, foodservice, facility management, child care, or ARAMARK's other myriad managed services as being the stuff that fast companies are made of, but Mission One has asked every manager to raise his or her level of play to that of a whole new major league. There's more opportunity, creativity, and initiative; but there's also a lot more scrutiny and a lot less room for excuses.

If you've got the right stuff, ARAMARK is an exciting and dynamic place to be. But you've got to have the right stuff. Enter a room with a group of ARAMARK managers and you'll know you're in a fast company. Yes, they're talking about uniforms, meals, or facility services rather than the next generation of computer chips, military aircraft, or a cure for cancer. But the buzz is unmistakable. Without a word being said, you know you're dealing with winners. They bring their "A" game. They work hard, think hard, challenge one another, and compete vigorously to win. They're given the best tools possible and take pride in learning quickly and making the most of those tools. They're appreciated for their accomplishments. Because of this, and more, ARAMARK is a place where the best and brightest players want to be.

Mission One didn't make ARAMARK a fast company. For the real players in the organization, ARAMARK has always been a hot place. But Mission One has redefined who "the real players" are—and how they have to work together as a team. At all levels of management, they talk explicitly about

- **Candor**—putting forward ideas that can enhance business results even before you're asked for your two cents, and soliciting input and feedback from a wide array of constituents, on both the customer side and the ARAMARK side of the unlimited partnership

- **Purpose**—being results focused and personally accountable for the success of Mission One and your own contributions to it, and instilling that sense of purpose so managers at all levels take pride in being part of ARAMARK

- **Will**—having the energy, spirit, and optimism to rise to a challenge and make the most of opportunities, before they get away

- **Rigor**—having the discipline to plan, make optimal use of resources, and say what you'll do and do what you say

- **Risk**—not throwing caution to the wind, but showing respect for those you rely on, considering others' needs, valuing diversity, and conducting yourself in a way that earns trust and loyalty when you need the benefit of the doubt

But now the game has changed. Working in a matrix, team-based, flat, agile, expertise-driven unlimited-partnership organization takes even more courage—more candor, purpose, will, rigor, and risk—than it did before Mission One created a revolution. If courage was helpful before Mission One asked GMs to work together, and before so many experts and thought leaders introduced so many innovations, it's mission critical now. If it was always a "given" in the elite inner circles of the company and the lofty ranks of GMs and RVPs, it is now a "must-have" at all levels of management. It isn't enough anymore to follow the chain of command when you're giving or receiving orders, or to take initiative to achieve your own performance objectives without considering the impact on the rest of the system. It isn't enough to check with a single point of contact in a complex client system, if you want to keep taking your unlimited partnerships to a deeper and deeper level. It's more complex, in a world that's faster and more demanding than ever before. That's why ARAMARK invests heavily in its managers, preparing leaders at all levels to foster courage in the teams that actually do the service delivery work for their clients, as well as in the cross-functional teams that build the infrastructure, the branding, the new generation of products and menu offerings, that sell new business and create the work environment that makes it possible for people to do their best thinking and their best work. Like many fast companies, ARAMARK recognizes that courage is a key ingredient that has to be fostered, nurtured, trained, measured, and developed in all key positions, at all levels, wherever someone's decisions and actions have an impact on the "unlimited partnerships" the company is building with its clients.

Conflict-Prone Realities in Conflict-Averse Systems

Since the 1960s, studies have analyzed the relationship between job design, stress, motivation, and performance. The results are as relevant today as they were a half-century ago. What's different, of course, is the degree to which organizations serve up the very realities that take people out of their comfort zones and require courage for them to do their best work and preserve their mental health.

ROLE CONFLICT

In every major corporation, people at all levels get more e-mails than they can possibly answer in the course of a day and specialists in different departments issue directives that can't all be achieved. Saying yes to one constituent or stakeholder means you'll have to say no to someone else and account for your lack of compliance or follow-through. Before the revolution, you could look upward in the chain of command and count on higher-ups to intercede, clarify priorities, tell you where to focus, and insulate you from the wrath you'd incur if someone, somewhere, was upset with your choices. That was then; this is now.

AMBIGUITY

People experience more frustration when they aren't trained or properly informed up front, when they make mistakes that could have been prevented, and when they have to learn and rewrite the standard operating procedures as they go. Conditions like these used to be considered symptoms of careless or incompetent management. But that was before the revolution. Today's monarchs and ministers may not know enough to anticipate what you'll need to make sense of an assignment and execute it effectively. They may not yet have all the relevant information or may not have it all put together when you begin seeking clear direction and definitive answers. Or the terrain could change before the ink is dry on the maps.

If the answers were clear and the data conclusive, it would be easier to decide and act. If everyone had the same values, it would be easier to logically and objectively analyze the facts and figures and get everyone aligned. If you didn't have tight deadlines and here-today-gone-tomorrow windows of opportunity, the world would wait for you. It wouldn't come down to intuition, judgment, reconciling differences in perspective, and having to question and probe to find out what's fact and what's opinion and prejudice. If, if, if, if, . . . but that's not the way it is in the postrevolution new economy.

AUTHORITY-RESPONSIBILITY GAPS

If everything proceeds on time and on budget, without making anyone nervous, it's easy to maintain the illusion that you have all the authority and autonomy that you need. But ambitious and complex projects don't unfold without a few hiccups. When difficulties arise, or when a few key people get nervous about what you're up to, particularly when you're messing around in what used to be "their turf," are you pressured to back off, defer to someone else, or adjust to someone else's preferred way of doing things? If so, you may find yourself with less authority and autonomy than you thought you had. This can be particularly maddening when you're accountable for the final outcome. But influence, not authority and power, is the way business is done in the new economy. No one has as much control or autonomy as they'd like anymore, including those at the very top of the organization.

RESOURCE COMPETITION

What happens when resources are limited and every project has merit, each one has a compelling business case behind it, and every one will open the door to new opportunities that the leaders agree are needed? Project teams (and project team leaders) have to compete for scarce resources, for visibility, for time, and for executive support. You may have to garner support by trading off, collaborating, or looking for synergies with other project teams. Or you may have to make do with a smaller resource allocation than what you need to do your best work, even though the deliverables and the time lines aren't scaled back.

Even in a business environment that is resource rich and full of opportunity, being overcommitted can lead to a perception of scarcity in the trenches, of perpetually playing catch-up and never feeling on top of things. When you're concerned about who's getting ahead and who's getting more than someone else, it's hard to preserve a sense of accomplishment about the things that have been achieved and the commitments that have been kept. It's easy to get tunnel vision and expect decisions to be made on a first come, first served basis or a "but you promised" standard of fairness, rather than constantly reassessing priorities according to triage criteria.

KNOWLEDGE GAPS

In a speech to business leaders after his retirement, General Norman Schwartzkopf described the daily agony he felt being responsible for thousands of lives in the Gulf War. Even though the war was going well, there was little joy to be found. And what was the most frightening aspect of command for this war hero? It was the fact that he knew less about the technology and field conditions than many of the young men and women under his command. Nobody likes to feel inadequate or uneducated, especially when she or he is supposed to be in control. It takes courage to seek help and admit that you don't know what you don't know. And it takes trust when you are flying blind and must depend on someone else's eyesight and perspective to guide your actions and the results you're accountable for achieving.

AGILE, FLAT, TEAM-BASED STRUCTURES

New team-based structures test the mettle of managers and workers like nothing else in the history of modern management. Bureaucracies and chains of command were slow, expensive, stifling, and cumbersome, to be sure, but they also gave people a measure of security and predictability. People knew their place. They understood the limits of their authority and discretion. If their needs weren't met or directions weren't clear, they simply looked higher up in the organization chart.

Teams serve up a very different reality. They reward people for darting in and out and changing lanes quickly on an information highway that's fast and crowded. There are fewer controls, higher speeds, more traffic, less patience, unfamiliar signs, ever-changing rules, and different languages—all this in a relentless race to the finish line, where those who get there last are left in the dust. On any conventional highway, that's a sure recipe for harrowing moments and an occasional collision. In flat, agile, team-based or matrix structures, this is the reality we now face on our organizational highways.

A BACKDROP OF FEAR

Even before September 11, 2001, it was clear to us that a dramatically higher level of courage was needed to cope with new business pressures. Our research and our experience as coaches and advisors, psychologists and confidants, clearly showed that teams with the courage to act were more resilient and more cohesive and were better performers than teams without this inner strength. In the immediate aftermath of September 11, teams at all levels had to improvise, rebuild, and cover for one another like never before in post–World War II America.

We are still on high alert. Our guard is up. Whether the news is from Venezuela, New Jersey, or Jerusalem, it touches us personally. We watch and breathe a sigh of relief when the attacks are far away. Under siege, it takes more effort to stay focused, to put first things first.

We balance concern for family, travel anxieties, and community responsibilities with the demand for business performance. The result is a confusing mix of empathy and no-nonsense accountability, patience and frustration, admiration and outrage when the betterment of the enterprise isn't number one on someone's priority list. It takes more active leadership to keep the team focused and to make sure that the sense of community doesn't deteriorate under pressure.

THE
DILEMMA

....

Demanding Courage in Others

Real leadership is making other people reach beyond what they
thought their capabilities could be and finding the courage within
themselves to accomplish more.
JACK WELCH

Just as King Sejong the Great, from our story in the preface, could not
rise to new challenges unless his followers could also muster the
courage they needed to embrace the Hanguel alphabet, no manager
can make courage a solo act. And just as King Sejong could not demand that his subjects truly embrace the new alphabet, even under the
threat of death, no executive can demand that teammates act with
courage. It has to come from within.

Here we present two very different managers who try very different tactics to create courage within their teams. Donna is a tough-as-
nails, high-powered bank executive, brought in to breathe new life into
a complacent marketing department. Jake is a gentle, kind plant manager who has to gear his team up to produce short runs of complex,
labor-intensive products. Let's see how they do.

Donna: A Get-Tough Policy

Donna's presence—her poise, her voice, her energy, even her physical size—could fill any room she entered. She exuded personal power. Standing six feet tall, with a healthy tan and an athletic frame, Donna could draw you in with her warm, hearty laugh and a hand on your shoulder. Or, in an instant, her cold, critical glance could freeze you in your place. You learned early not to make mistakes—she didn't forget.

Add to this that she was one of the few women who had advanced to the inner circle at Pepsi. She was recruited to join a very different industry, consumer banking, because she was thought to have the right stuff and she knew it. Both in the boardroom and on the golf course, confidence oozed from her every pore. She had earned it during her twenty years at Pepsi. Now she was asked to provide the leadership for preparing this sleepy bank for a new day. She was tough, smart, and focused and knew what she wanted and where she wanted to go. She appeared to be the right person at the right time for a demanding job.

Donna arrived with high praise and even higher expectations. Sales and marketing were hers—the key to taking the half-billion-dollar bank from the backwater of a regulated and predictable business into the competitive, dog-eat-dog world of deregulation. Change was coming, and soon. There was no time for niceties. She swaggered like a gunslinger coming to town to turn things around, throw the bad guys out, and bring out the courage in the good ones.

A POOR BEGINNING

The bank had been asleep for thirty years. Its local monopolies had lulled everyone into the deepest sort of complacency, crippled creativity, and driven out many of the motivated, aggressive players. Donna dove in at a furious pace, cajoling, yelling, sweet talking, demanding, threatening—anything and anybody was fair game.

A year later, Donna was appalled. Her "team" not only had not jelled but was behaving like an abused pet. Instead of being energized, taking risks, and moving forward, people were becoming increasingly passive, fearful, and apathetic. Donna's now-legendary temper and perfectionism could penetrate walls. No one was safe. Meetings were a platform for scolding, coaxing, humiliating, or demanding. But the get-tough tactics weren't working and Donna knew it. Her brash, mercurial ways were a problem. Instead of being motivated, people were intimidated; instead of being challenged, they appeared diminished; instead of being excited, people seemed depressed; and instead of having the courage to act, they stopped participating.

Things had to change. Time was running out. Originally, Donna was given two years to ready the troops for the inevitable consequences of deregulation. Now she had only one year left and little progress to show for her efforts. She was becoming embarrassed. The expectations had been so high; now those at the top were talking and asking questions. The evidence of dysfunction was becoming apparent. Where was the magic Donna had been expected to create?

DRIVING COURAGE FROM HIDING

Donna decided she would take the team on an outdoor adventure, a program that would force her staff to overcome their fears, work together, and be moved to a new level of trust and camaraderie. Perhaps, Donna acknowledged, she had pushed too hard before the team was ready. A rough-and-tumble team-building program would provide a new day, a fresh start. Some high ropes, white-water rafting, and outdoor problem-solving initiatives would be just what the doctor ordered. She had seen it work elsewhere. Why not here?

Donna asked her secretary to hire a luxurious, fully equipped bus for the six-hundred-mile trip to Georgia; wet bar, TV, movies, cards, and other games would be the seedbed for fun and generate the harmony that had not been possible in the stress of the office. After all, Donna was a master schmoozer. She was sure that environmental therapy would work, that trust would increase, that the fear she saw in people's eyes would change, and that she would be able to rebuild her own confidence in everyone. What's more, with her athletic prowess, Donna could easily demonstrate why the team needed her and could rally the troops behind her strong, tough brand of leadership.

WE'RE IN THIS TOGETHER

If the bus ride down and back was to create fun and relaxation, the outdoor experience would crank up the level of courage and motivation. It would push the team to a new level of commitment. The team-building experiences would result in increased trust, in people being more willing to speak the truth, share their ideas, take risks, and be creative in a work environment that demanded it.

Donna knew the Chatooga River was perilous. She remembered it as the river in the movie *Deliverance*. If anything, this would mobilize the courage of the group; the trip down the ferocious Chatooga would help people overcome their fears. Dangerous, physical expeditions like this were nothing new for Donna. Such an exercise had worked to mobilize and bond people in her Junior League chapter and again at a reunion of her sorority sisters. With Donna in command, these groups had learned to work together as a team. Surely the Chatooga trip would put some steel up people's backsides to replace the passivity and dependency that Donna saw in her team every day. She knew you couldn't be complacent on this river.

The twelve members of the team were divided into five groups; each four-person raft held three team members and a guide. The river was up. Heavy spring rains had swollen it beyond its normally hazardous level. This was serious business, certainly not play. One guide took three of Donna's worried managers out into a quiet spot upriver from the first crashing set of rapids. The guide looked at each of them and quietly said, "Now listen up. When I say forward, you paddle like hell forward. When I say back, you paddle like hell in reverse. And when I say draw, you draw as if your life depends on it, because very likely it does. Get it? Your life could depend on it."

The guide had their attention. In that brief moment, he had driven home a point: these people, together, would determine success or failure. In the year they had worked for Donna, the members of the team had always been treated as individuals, isolated to deal with the boss and unable to cultivate the support they needed as they timorously entered the white water of boardroom inquisitions and the competitive marketplace.

The day was powerful. People reached deep inside themselves. They faced their fears and worked together. They laughed in relief after they survived each impossible, foaming, turbulent cataract. They screamed for each other, hugged, pulled each other out of the raging water, gave each other advice, and experienced teamwork for the first time in one long year.

Perhaps Donna was right and the trip down the river would create different relationships within the team and, eventually, with her. This was a new and auspicious beginning. During the long trip home, Donna pulled the team together and talked sincerely about the parallel between the river and the bank. She told them once again of her hopes and expectations, as well as her fears. She opened up. It truly was a new day.

THE LEGACY OF THE CHATOOGA

The new day didn't last. In six months, Donna would be gone—a failure—still blaming her team. She never learned that courage, trust, and the willingness to risk cannot be wished, cajoled, or demanded. Nor can they be delivered from a three-day team-building experience if the other pieces of the leadership puzzle are missing.

The excursion to the Chatooga could not begin to override the fear, domination, dependency, and suspicion that followed in the wake of Donna's leadership. Because the members of her team could see what Donna was attempting to do—obliterate the sins of the past—they felt manipulated, mistrustful, and angry. Hundreds, perhaps thousands, of teams have experienced amazing wilderness team-building initiatives only to realize that the experience was, for many reasons, not transferable to the dysfunctional office. As a bandage, it doesn't work.

Soon after the team's return to the office, the hopes for a new day proved to be an illusion. Donna's critical, and often abusive, behaviors returned. The social environment created on the way to the Chatooga had provided some much-needed fun and play, and the river trip had inspired brief moments of courage. But newfound inspiration evaporated as soon as the old patterns of blame, ridicule, micromanagement, and "the boss knows best" reappeared. Had Donna realized that much of the problem was the result of her own behavior and had she made observable changes with support from her teammates, the courage that the group found within themselves on the Chatooga might have taken root and flourished. But after planting the seedlings, the leader had failed to cultivate her garden, and when she finally realized she had a problem, it was too little too late, and the weeds won out. Courage, like a garden, grows when leaders give it ongoing care and maintenance—not when they put the right material in the ground and walk away, hoping the plants will take root.

The Moral of Donna's Story

It's not sufficient for a leader to be tough minded, skilled, smart, experienced, and creative. Does it help for a leader to be a model of courage? Certainly. But, by itself, being a model of courage isn't enough. It is possible that Donna's marketing team was incapable of thoughtful leadership in a deregulated and more competitive business environment. But we'll never know for sure because Donna failed to mobilize them as a team and empower them as thoughtful leaders. She could talk tough, and she knew her stuff, but she couldn't succeed on her own.

No amount of instant camaraderie or emotional catharsis on the Chatooga could replace what was lacking in Donna's leadership. As the gap widened between her personal courage and the courage she evoked in her team, her lieutenants became less capable of functioning as cross-functional team leaders championing new marketing initiatives for the bank. Donna had learned to "talk the talk" of the five courage factors. She could give an impassioned and eloquent speech about candor, purpose, will, rigor, and risk. But she did not incorporate these qualities into her daily behavior. Her tenure was characterized by several factors.

- Donna ran a one-woman show. Working at the bank wasn't a scene out of a John Wayne movie. Donna's team was not the fast-paced, hard-driving, competitive group that was common at Pepsi. For years, people had been well rewarded for minimal risk and minimal effort. The "demanding great aunt" would only evoke resentment unless the group could be drawn into defining some mutually satisfying goals that would demand new behaviors. Instead of having shared goals, the group perceived Donna's own personal challenge as creating a turnaround so that the victory would be hers, another merit badge on her Girl Scout uniform. While not initially desiring their new boss to fail, the team members were not motivated toward her success.

- Donna's charming, devil-may-care, high-energy, can-do entry never acknowledged the team's reality. Neither did it acknowledge people's sense of inadequacy, lack of experience, and fear of failure as they became witnesses to the revolution that was about to take over their company. First Donna needed to help them buy into the team goals. Then, equally important, she needed to help them believe that they were capable of winning and of developing the skills they would need to meet the new goals. She did neither.

- Donna's unrealistic expectations and tremendous impatience were encountered so often that many people stopped trying. Those who were supposed to be team leaders hunkered down in a state of self-protection; doing nothing was better than trying and failing and incurring Donna's wrath and scathing attacks. On the river, members were learners together; on the trip down there were no judgments. The group was awakened from a troubled sleep, and people, for a brief time, became animated and free. But back at the office, the old behaviors and norms soon kicked in, and out went the short-lived hope and freedom. A climate for learning—one in which failure and experimentation were acceptable—did not evolve.

- Rather than developing the independence and camaraderie she craved from her team, Donna created the opposite. Her legacy was a relentless dependency in which people would demand her input or approval on almost everything rather than risk her displeasure or ridicule.

- As the consummate self-starter, Donna believed that by modeling a go-getter attitude and creating new products and new sales strategies herself, she would soon have others emulating her behavior. But she mistook her need for theirs. Her people needed teaching and coaching; they needed praise and newly minted confidence from early success, whereas Donna's early successes and strong leadership only intimidated them and made them feel inadequate.

- Donna never appreciated the difference between a high-courage team and one in which individuals came together for information, direction, and to be motivated. By the time she saw what could be accomplished on the river through mutual risk, cooperation, and sharing, it was too late. She personally didn't know how to translate it to the office environment. Back home, her micromanaging replaced cooperation, and the team's defensiveness snuffed out the openness and risk taking they had experienced on the river.

Jake's Story

From his gentle, soft-spoken manner and midwestern twang, you would never know that Jake grew up in Boston. After he completed college on the GI bill, the corporation he worked for transferred him to downstate Illinois as a management trainee. Jake and his young bride never looked back. Several years later, Jake was promoted to plant manager. By then he had become a pillar in the small rural community; he was a deacon in the church, a member of the board in the local VFW, a sought-after supporter of local charities, and an articulate spokesperson for the local chamber of commerce. His wife was a respected schoolteacher. Their girls were now grown up and had moved back east—one to Boston and the other to New York—but Jake and his wife had no intention of leaving, even after retirement. This small Illinois town was where they had put down roots and was their comfortable, tranquil haven.

On a cold winter night in early March, the vice president of manufacturing made the three-hour trek from Chicago to visit Jake with a consultant who'd worked with the leadership team in the corporate office. When he got to the end of the exit ramp and turned left toward the motel, he could feel himself entering a different decade. Things moved at a much slower pace here than they did in Chicago. People were more polite and friendlier. Being smart and successful wasn't as important as being nice and down-to-earth.

Over breakfast in the local diner, the vice president politely but frankly expressed his disappointment and frustration. "If you don't get the new equipment installed and get your crews trained on it, we're going to have to get someone in here who will or we'll have to close this place altogether," the vice president told Jake in an earnest but firm tone of voice. He kept his voice down so he wouldn't be overheard, but the waitress still took notice of Jake's discomfort with the conversation. The VP had articulated his concerns in previous meetings with Jake. There was nothing Jake hadn't heard before. But the VP wanted Jake to know that the consultant knew the score before he left the two of them alone.

Jake had records to prove that production was every bit as strong as it had been for the past five years. He began to pull the spreadsheets out of his briefcase. The vice president shook his head and brushed them aside. He wasn't interested in history. Despite what the numbers told Jake, the VP was convinced that the plant was underperforming. "We're straining several other plants to pick up the slack because your operation hasn't raised the bar high enough," the VP told Jake. "I'm sorry, Jake, but I just can't allow that to continue." There was an uncomfortable silence at the breakfast table, which the waitress tried to change by offering a refill on the coffee and a trite joke.

SLOW PROGRESS

A year ago, when the new manufacturing strategy was first announced, Jake had held town meetings on all three shifts. He presented the business realities to the entire crew, with the passion and articulateness of a Sunday morning preacher. He personally invited product engineers, equipment engineers, key customers, and sales representatives to come from Chicago and attend an open house at the downstate Illinois plant. He chartered buses and took the entire crew—from the sweepers to the maintenance chief—to Chicago to visit the company's flagship plant, so they could see the new production methods and the new equipment in use. Over the year, Jake had held a series of workshops, training sessions, and task force meetings about the new technology and what it would take to work together in cross-functional production teams.

Now, a year later, Jake had made some progress. Plant employees could tell you why they were supposed to retool, and why the plant needed to manufacture specialty products with a higher profit margin. They knew that the company needed more manufacturing capacity for their specialty products, since demand was increasing and the flagship plants in Chicago and Dublin, Ireland, could no longer fill all the orders. They knew that the plant in Mexico was ready to make their old products at a much lower cost and that their own plant wouldn't be competitive unless they did work that required a higher level of know-how and that earned a higher profit margin.

A GAP BETWEEN UNDERSTANDING AND ACTION

It was one thing to talk about change—new equipment, computer systems, global supply chains, and radically different working relationships. Talk was easy. But working differently and achieving new productivity and inventory management objectives were not the same as talking about the future.

The new equipment threatened many of the plant workers and made them feel inadequate—not that they would tell you that directly. Jake knew how to decipher the grunts, downcast eyes, and casual laughs in the lunchroom and in his office. He interpreted for those who needed closed-captioning.

The older, experienced maintenance engineers were good, solid wrench mechanics. But they had trouble reading the technical manuals and making sense of computerized systems. Besides, when new equipment was sent to the plant, an engineer had always come from corporate to unpack it and set it up for them. When the vice president asked why nothing had been unpacked and checked against the inventory list, the maintenance supervisor crossed his burly arms and shook his head. Jake explained what the supervisor meant: "Why should we do all this book work and trial-and-error installation, just because the engineers are too lazy to get in their cars and come down here and give us the support we need, instead of flying all over the world?"

The crews didn't like the plant of the future that they saw in Chicago. Jake described the banter that he heard on the bus during the ride home. Using the old presses, operators had to work only fifteen minutes out of every hour; they could read, relax, or socialize while the presses ran themselves. From what they saw in Chicago, the new equipment and the new team structure would require them to work thirty to forty minutes out of every hour. With the old equipment and the old products, operators had to do only one setup per day, and they might be able to go a whole week without doing a changeover. The new specialty products were different for every customer and required far shorter production runs. In a single shift, operators would now have to do multiple setups and one or two changeovers.

The changes meant that everyone would have to work smarter *and* work harder. They'd have to think and problem solve, rather than make a phone call and wait for engineering or logistics to get back to them with directions and answers. They'd have to learn computer routines and use complex mathematical formulas to meet quality standards and manage inventory levels. They'd have to work together and coordinate with other departments, rather than work in whatever style suited them as autonomous individuals or as an autonomous production facility.

One senior operator shook his head and said, "We'll see," when he was asked about the new processes and equipment. Again, Jake interpreted for the dense city folks: "I've worked here ten years to get into a comfortable position. I can't believe you want to take that all away from me and want to make me work as hard as I worked when I first started out in this plant. And I can't believe that you're going to put me back in some high-school math class. Ask anyone here. I wasn't good at math the first time I went through school. Why should this be any different?"

NOBLE INTENTIONS, STEADY PROGRESS

Jake wanted his crews to be comfortable with the change. He wanted the maintenance supervisor to be confident that he could install and maintain the new equipment, and he wanted to wait until more of the operators saw the reasonableness of the team structure and the increased work pace. He wanted to build a consensus. He wanted everyone to be excited about the possibilities—for the plant, the community, and the future of their children. He didn't want to rile the old-timers or give the union agitators something to talk about.

After a year of workshops, plant visits, and bus trips, Jake could see real progress and glimmers of hope. Some of the younger teammates, who had an easier time reading and writing and who were looking for a challenge that would break the boredom, were excited about a faster-paced work routine and an intellectual challenge. Some of the workers who lived in town and didn't have farms to generate a second income were relieved that the company was willing to invest in the plant and ensure its future. A new member of the maintenance crew took the initiative to read the manual and uncrate and install new materials-handling equipment in the plant. He worked only from drawings and written instructions, without assistance from the engineers at corporate headquarters. Despite the razzing and the lack of support he received from the veterans on the maintenance crew, his installation was successful. When the switch was turned on and the equipment actually worked, this maintenance engineer became an instant folk hero.

With the support that Jake was beginning to muster in the plant, he believed the changes could be implemented smoothly and comfortably within four to six months. The VP shook his head when Jake presented his schedule. "I can give you six weeks, Jake, not six months," the vice president declared, in a tone of voice that left no room for negotiation. "That's six weeks to be in production, ready to ship new product. Not six weeks to put together a plan, organize another employee participation group, or conduct another training class. It's been over a year already, and our customers aren't going to give us another six months if we can't ship the product they want."

With that pronouncement, the vice president excused himself. He left the diner and set out on his three-hour drive back to Chicago. He left the consultant there to counsel Jake about leadership, change, mobilizing the team, and courage. It was the last thing Jake wanted to hear.

"How am I supposed to make people comfortable with such a ridiculously fast transition?" Jake asked the consultant, half rhetorically and half resentfully, still shaking his head. Driving back to the plant with a Ph.D. consultant from the big city wasn't Jake's idea of fun; nor was the prospect of ordering a reluctant maintenance crew to uncrate and install the new equipment that was sitting on his loading dock.

Jake was angry and scared. The vice president's ultimatum seemed grossly unfair. Still, Jake kept his composure. He never raised his voice when he explained the injustice to the consultant who'd been sent down to help him shake things up. "Some of the workers in this plant have been here longer than I have," he explained. "They've put more than twenty-five years into this place. I'll be damned if I'm going to tell them, 'Sorry. It's been nice. But the world has changed. Be prepared to work harder, go back to school, and take responsibility for doing work that's supposed to be done by someone else, or you can find yourself another job.' You'll fly back east. The VP will drive back up to Chicago. But I have to see these people every day and sit next to their families in church."

EMPATHY ISN'T ENOUGH

No one could argue with Jake's empathy. His heart was in the right place. But trying to make people comfortable with the change was a losing proposition. Jake couldn't protect his crew from the risks they were being asked to take. He couldn't insulate them from new products, new technology, and new working relationships. He couldn't get the engineers to take responsibility for the installation that was now supposed to be managed locally. Jake couldn't honestly tell his crew that their old skills and routines, their old work pace, and their old knowledge base would be adequate.

Five years of consistent performance was yesterday's news. It was no longer enough to secure the future. It may not have been fair. But the vice president's ultimatum was real. Jake and his crew would have to show a higher level of courage—quickly—or all of them could be replaced. Jake could try to insulate his crew and protect them from these new unfair realities, or he could egg them on, one small step at a time. But comfort, fairness, and not rocking the boat too hard would ultimately result in the plant being shut down altogether.

In the end, Jake rose to the challenge. He called his plant task force together to meet with the consultant. He apologized for "getting radical on them," as he called it, and explained the facts of life to them. Then he appealed to their sense of pride. "Let's show those city boys, including doctor Ph.D. here, what a bunch of Illinois corn farmers can do when they put their minds to it. And, while we're at it, let's show the engineers a thing or two as well."

Raising the bar and keeping it there didn't make Jake a popular leader. But, as a result, the downstate Illinois plant is still open and has added several new production lines. Some of the members of his plant task force who took charge and drove things forward have been promoted for their initiative and creativity. But some of Jake's closest friends had to step aside because they couldn't or wouldn't keep up.

What did Jake learn about courage in the process, and what can we learn vicariously from his success?

- Courageous leaders don't pander. Bob Galvin, former chairman of Motorola, is credited with saying, "Real leaders don't take people where they already want to go. Real leaders take people in a new and different direction." Jake became a leader with courage when he challenged his team to reach for more than they thought they were already capable of achieving, rather than enabling them to stay where they were already comfortable and secure.

- Building courage starts with being an astute diagnostician. Because his group wasn't verbal, Jake had to pay close attention to read their reactions and anticipate their concerns. It is tempting to confuse silence or acquiescence with buy-in, particularly when you ask, "Are you okay with this?" and your teammate answers, "I guess so." Jake knew better. And he knew how to listen, probe, and interpret what wasn't being said as well as what was being said.

- Money alone doesn't build pride and doesn't provide an intellectual challenge. Compensation keeps people in the game, but it doesn't make them play hard or make them inventive when the going gets tough. Jake had to find a better source of inspiration than saying, "You'll get to keep your job," or, "We'll all receive a bonus." He appealed to their esprit de corps ("Let's show them what a bunch of corn farmers can do!"). Some teammates embraced the plant's transformation as an exciting and interesting technical challenge, and Jake encouraged them to rise to the challenge instead of trying to direct the effort himself or assigning it only to his elite inner circle.

- Jake assumed that everyone could understand and appreciate the business realities rather than assuming that technical people or production workers couldn't understand complex global business strategies. He treated them with respect rather than feeding them details and instructions on a need-to-know basis. He wanted to make sure they were in the loop on business decisions that would affect their work lives and their community. He was patient with their questions and was direct and straightforward with his answers, even when the truth was something different from what they wanted to hear.

- He was willing to share leadership and turn to others for support and strength, rather than assuming he had to direct everything or be everyone's cheerleader. Jake saw himself as an orchestrator and mobilizer, rather than someone who had to lead every step of the parade from the front of the line. He encouraged teammates to be there for one another, to teach and learn with one another. He could recognize when people's energy was waning or their frustration level was getting dangerously high, and he had an instinctive knack for knowing which team members were best suited to work together.

- Jake invested time in building the team and strengthening relationships before the crew faced adversity together. Could Jake have spurred his team to act in less than a year? Definitely. But how much sooner isn't totally clear. By the time Jake sounded the call and said, "The time for rehearsal is over," a critical mass within the plant understood the business strategy and bought into the rationale. They had studied, taught, and learned from one another. They knew how other team members dealt with frustration and what they'd need to do to move their colleagues past those mental and operational barriers. This understanding didn't just happen by magic or executive fiat. It happened because Jake had invested the time that the team needed to jell and see that members could, in fact, trust and rely on one another.

Weighing the Cost of Courage

Jake learned the five courage factors (candor, purpose, will, rigor, and risk) and took the template to heart. As he applied it and mobilized teams within the plant, he discovered that building the courage to act is not a passive or by-default effort. The five-factor template is simple.

But just because it's easy to learn doesn't mean it's easy to do, day in and day out. Jake still had to make tough decisions, had to develop a different set of instincts about forming and mobilizing teams, and had to live with a level of chaos and improvisation that ran counter to the world of order, predictability, command, and control that he was most comfortable in.

Jake was glad to see the plant stay open and attract new investments, and he was proud of the members of his team who rose to the challenge. But the victory was bittersweet. Even when the team was doing extraordinary work and corporate engineers were calling his crew for answers, Jake didn't look victorious or beam with pride. He didn't look happy. A few months after Jake took the trophy for "most impressive turnaround" and dedicated it to the men and women in the downstate Illinois plant, he announced his retirement. He knew how to build, nurture, and raise the level of courage. And he'd done it effectively.

At what many would consider to be the pinnacle of his career, Jake stepped aside and turned over his command to someone else. The choice was a conscious one. He knew that he would most likely earn less in a less hectic and demanding job, one that required less personal courage and less of the emotional labor required to imbue courage in others. Jake's ultimate act of courage was coming to grips with the fact that he wanted a slower, easier, and more comfortable life.

Like Jake, we believe that most team leaders and team members can learn to act with courage and build courage in others. We also believe that one doesn't have to become hardened, insensitive, or egotistical to demonstrate and evoke the courage to act. In fact, from what we've seen in practice and in research, the bravado and individualism that aggressive, competitive, take-charge leaders like Donna demonstrate can actually inhibit courage in the team.

But learning to model, inspire, and teach courage isn't the same as wanting to be the constant linchpin in a high-courage team. Ultimately, to remain a player in this league, you have to want to be there. Fortunately, most of us, like Jake, do have choices. There is an alternative if we choose to take it. If you opt out, we wish you a healthy and pleasant retirement (or semiretirement). But if you choose to stay in the game, keep reading and we'll explain more about the five courage factors and the ways you can inspire in others the courage to act.

COURAGE
DEFINED

The Five Factors

*You gain strength, courage, and confidence by every experience
in which you really stop to look fear in the face. You must do
the thing which you think you cannot do.*
ELEANOR ROOSEVELT

Imagine you are standing behind a one-way mirror and have the opportunity to view an assemblage of ten individuals from each of the
following groups for an extended period of time. Your task is to guess
which members from the different groups will overcome adversity and
thrive, given the difficult circumstances they face.

- From a group of ten Holocaust survivors, who will be able to rebuild
  their lives in spite of their tragedy and who will not be able to pick up
  the pieces, start over, and create a new and positive existence?

- From a group of ten victims of childhood abuse and other equally
  egregious traumas, which individuals will have the ability to transcend their experience and which individuals will remain stuck and
  unable to move forward with their lives?

- Ten soldiers are caught in a life-or-death exchange of fire. Who will stay calm, sort out the options, and execute a plan, and who will freeze or act capriciously and fail to contribute positively to the outcome in a dire situation?

- Ten patients are in a rehabilitation hospital, each in extreme pain, coping with life-threatening injuries. Who will persevere and construct a fulfilling new life, and who will give up, even if giving up condemns them to death?

- Ten refugees arrive with nothing and face the challenge of learning a new language, a new culture, and new skills. Which ones will isolate themselves and remain in their own social ghetto, frightened and intimidated by the world outside, and which ones will integrate themselves and make it in the new culture?

- From a group of ten workers who represent ethnic or political minority groups, who will overcome their justifiable anger at being persecuted and discriminated against and will have the presence of mind to work for change, and who will internalize the abuse and act in ways that are self-defeating and confirm the worst of the stereotypes about their minority group?

- Ten teammates face new pressures and organizational demands and don't receive the support, direction, resources, or training that they need to do their very best work. Who will take initiative, be accountable, and make great things happen, and who will sit back, wait, become disheartened, and find ample reason to justify lackluster or mediocre performance?

According to Clare Booth Luce, courage isn't a virtue to add to a list of positive character traits. Instead, she declared, "courage is the ladder on which all other virtues mount." Identify the individuals with courage and you'll know which individuals will come through their plights, transcend difficult or trying circumstances, and ultimately prevail in the face of adversity.

Forty Years of Research

A vast amount of research provides confirmation of what most of us would imagine is the case anyway. Yet it is this very confirmation that provides the impetus for taking new approaches to significant change and for understanding how individuals and organizations face and deal with certain problems and dilemmas.

What is obviously the best course of action and the best choice, in difficult and trying circumstances, is not always what's easiest. After all, it is easier to "spank the little brat" than it is to control one's temper and work constructively with an acting-out child. It is easier to write up and punish recalcitrant employees—or ignore them altogether—than it is to coach them into new approaches or new ways of thinking. And it is far easier to accelerate an argument when we feel that we are being attacked than it is to adopt a more patient and understanding point of view that does not add fuel to the proverbial fire.

What we have learned from forty years of research includes the following about what moves some individuals to act courageously and what makes others withdraw. Together, the data provide a clear avenue toward more effective team development and motivation, particularly when teams face the ambiguity and conflict-prone realities that confront organizations in the new economy. For example, we know that

- **Some people attribute both success and failure to external causes.** They point to powers outside themselves that are often out of their control. When things go wrong, they feel like a victim of fate or of someone else's negligence or malevolence. Contrast this response to that of individuals who believe that, no matter what life throws at them, positive or negative, they are in control and responsible for their own destiny. Research by Julian Rotter and his associates in the 1960s and 1970s (see Rotter, 1982) showed that individuals with an internal locus of control are far better performers than those with an external locus of control, particularly when they face difficult or seemingly impossible conditions.

- **Some people have a passive and fixed view of the world.** They hold tightly to others' expectations of them, abiding by tradition and clinging to habitual ways of doing things, waiting for success to find them and grant them their just rewards. Compare these people to others who are prone to be active, to take risks, and to see life as an ever-changing kaleidoscope of opportunities that demand that they continually reinvent themselves and go after what they desire. Research by Enrita Fried and her associates in the 1970s and 1980s showed that those with an active orientation can take the lessons of the past without being trapped or stuck in it and recover more quickly from setbacks and disappointments (Fried, 1985).

- **Some people have more desire and drive to achieve and to "be the best" than others do.** Achievement-motivated individuals continually challenge themselves to aspire to lofty goals and personal fulfillment, as well as traditional rewards. In adversity, they look at what's possible to achieve and set challenging, though not unreachable, goals. Contrast these individuals with others who go for a sure thing and who tend to lay back and take the path of least resistance. It's no surprise that David McClelland (1976) found that individuals with a high need for achievement consistently outperform those who are content to take whatever measure of success lies easily within their grasp.

If we return to our hypothetical one-way mirror and look at those who have faced adversity, this research allows us to look at the assemblage of individuals through a new lens. Again and again the research points to a positive correlation between those with an active, achievement-oriented, master-of-your-own-fate view of the world and the ability to deal with crises, setbacks, contentious situations, and the unexpected or ambiguous. People with this orientation have a realistic view that life itself is a series of challenges to be overcome. These individuals believe that the future is in their own hands. They tend not to be overwhelmed when fate deals them an unfair and unpredictable blow. Instead, they show the resilience and tenacity necessary to rebuild their dreams (Seligman, 1984).

The Team Versus the Individual

Self-initiators, optimists, risk takers, and individuals who feel personally empowered would be expected to act more courageously than others. They would rise to the occasion, take the lead, and not be daunted by formidable odds or roadblocks in their paths. But since not every individual has these characteristics, it would, theoretically, be the role of a team leader to help instill these attributes in team members, with the assumption that as a group, the team could then expect more courageous actions.

Reuven Bar-On started his seminal work on emotional intelligence (EQ) with fascinating research in the Israeli Defense Force. His studies debunked the myth that leaders with charisma, bravado, and macho toughness—those traditionally held up as role models—are most successful in dangerous and trying circumstances. Instead, Bar-On found that the most successful leaders have other qualities, including compassion and sensitivity to their troops, openness to giving and receiving feedback, and the ability to not be reactive or feel compelled to make quick decisions. The most effective leaders, those able to engender courage in their troops, showed a distinct balance among intellectual, physical, and emotional aspects of leadership. Daniel Goleman (1998) built on Bar-On's early findings on emotional intelligence and put forward a new model of effectiveness for business leaders as well as military leaders.

The Courage to Act:
A Template for Guiding Team Leaders

Our own studies, plus the previous years of research reviewed here, have resulted in the isolation of five factors that, together, help to imbue team members with the courage to act in situations of stress, conflict, or ambiguity. We have termed these factors *candor, purpose, will, rigor,* and *risk* (see Figure 2).

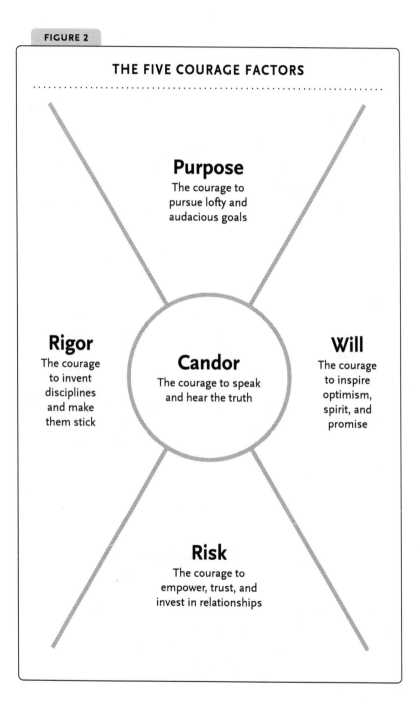

FIGURE 2

THE FIVE COURAGE FACTORS

CANDOR: THE COURAGE TO SPEAK
AND HEAR THE TRUTH

You can't mandate or require candor, yet it stands as the first quality for building courage. It is the one upon which everything else is built. If individuals on a team are inhibited from speaking the truth, or if they fail to take feedback about their current reality to heart, they might fail to act quickly enough or skillfully enough.

In most organizations, the level of candor could be higher. Too often we find ourselves in a meeting in which feelings and ideas are held back. The worst part is that most of those in the room are conscious of what is and what is not being said. If the nonverbal behaviors—the rolling of eyes, the squirming, the flushed faces—were not sufficient to signal the plight of the group, then the knot in the group's collective stomach should tell the story. Leaving meetings that are bereft of candor brings symptoms of pent-up frustration: sarcasm, anger, even guilt.

In our work with teams of all types at all levels, we find that people desperately want to speak their minds and their hearts, but they are unwilling to be humiliated, publicly criticized, or put on the defensive, or to have their futures jeopardized. Threat and intimidation are like land mines in many teams. With experience, we learn where they are and how to avoid them. The price paid for such avoidance is huge. If members of a team cannot risk speaking the truth, then the essence of courage is undermined in a most public way, reinforcing increased complacency and passivity in the future.

However, when we witness individuals putting their ideas and feelings on the table and see that they are accepted without repercussion in the moment or later reprisal, then people are emboldened and courage is imbued in other team members. Who has not taken heart when another has had the courage to speak out, paving the way for their own foray into a high-risk arena of discourse?

PURPOSE: THE COURAGE TO PURSUE LOFTY
AND AUDACIOUS GOALS

Most organizations live and die by the numbers: profit, market share, customer loyalty, employee retention, quality, productivity, performance against time lines and budgets. But pursuit of the numbers is, by itself, insufficient to sustain meaningful effort when the going is tough, fraught with pain or frustration, or the right course of action isn't mapped out clearly.

One aspect of the art of leadership is the ability to tie the numbers to a loftier mission, sense of purpose, and achievement. One company posted business performance prominently, on a huge chart hanging right next to the entrance to their office. Yet, when asked, few employees knew how to read the chart or took an interest in what was posted there. Even more telling was the fact that all employees were paid a handsome bonus, as much as 25 percent of their regular salary, based on the posted performance indicators. So why didn't they take a more active interest in the charts?

The fact is, in this company, few people felt personally connected to the numbers. They didn't see how their own activities made a difference, and they derived little gratification from the performance results, except for the matter of knowing what they would be paid. At the end of the quarter, they knew what was posted. But they treated the performance results like a lottery ticket rather than a set of outcomes that they could influence and control.

We work hardest, research shows, when we feel personally connected to the outcomes we are achieving—when the work is personally meaningful, gratifying, and interesting and when we see a benefit to our daily work. Alfie Kohn (1999) has done an exhaustive review of the literature, showing that we work harder for our own sense of accomplishment, fulfillment, justice, and intellectual satisfaction, and out of loyalty to a cause than we do to achieve praise, recognition, and economic or tangible goals. Five decades ago, Harry Harlow (1971), an experimental psychologist at the University of Wisconsin, showed the same was true of rhesus monkeys. In test situations, the monkeys would forgo food and spend prolonged periods of time attempting to solve a problem if the problem was interesting and provocative enough to capture their attention.

WILL: THE COURAGE TO INSPIRE OPTIMISM, SPIRIT, AND PROMISE

Our research shows that a "can-do" spirit is one of the factors that separates high-courage individuals from those who shrink from responsibility and action. In times of adversity, it takes a special brand of strength to overcome the all-too-natural tendency toward defeatism and complacency. Optimism is a spark. Not only does it help the individual burn brighter, but it also affects others. The ability to inspire, to create a sense of hope and opportunity, can infuse a team and have a multiplier effect on the group.

According to Seligman (1984), those without hope are often more in touch with reality than those who find promise and potential in trying or desperate times. Those who keep hope and promise alive have a healthy defense against reality. They see life on two levels: the level of "what is," which is temporary and changeable, and the level of "what can be," which is a goal or vision that they mobilize themselves and others to reach for. Without leadership, reality overpowers and stifles optimism, promise, and spirit. Inertia sets in. By default, you take whatever fate has in store for you and become a victim of circumstances.

In difficult or trying circumstances, most reasonable people do experience fear, anguish, pain, and worry. Those with the will to persevere and act look fearless, brave, and impervious to pain. But looks can be deceiving. According to research with decorated war heroes conducted by Reuven Gal (1986), former chief psychologist of the Israeli Defense Force, even the bravest soldiers often admit that they were scared, frustrated, and hurt. Their course doesn't hinge on whether they experience these emotions; what matters is whether they let these emotions hold them back from doing what needs to be done.

Another aspect of will is related directly to the cohesion of the team. How often does an apparent agreement go south and energy and optimism wane because unspoken opposition or unresolved conflicts are driven underground and played out in passive resistance? Lack of candor undermines the group's spirit and hope, as fears and doubts are driven underground, out of sight but not at all out of mind. When teammates look to leaders, experts, and executives and see that some lack the will to persevere when the going gets tough, the resulting lack of cohesion can have a powerful negative effect on the group's sense of optimism and self-confidence. "If she doesn't support the plan, what does it say about those of us who do?" some people may start to wonder. A message of shared commitment, solidarity, and cohesiveness generates more hope and spirit than one of ambivalence or divided loyalties.

RIGOR: THE COURAGE TO INVENT DISCIPLINES AND MAKE THEM STICK

With rigor, a team establishes protocols, rules, and agreements that bring consistency and predictability to the way that the team operates. Rigor helps the team commit to new ways of doing business and re-contract to alter old norms, expectations, and interdependencies. It sets new standards to ensure safety, quality, data integrity, and effective communication.

For some, creating and committing to new structures represents giving away freedom, reduces spontaneity, and spawns greater rigidity and control. Our experience is quite different. When rock climbers and teams on a high-ropes course are strapped into their safety harnesses, supported by colleagues on firmer ground, and are securely "on billet," for example, they can take greater risks, improvise, and be more spontaneous than they can if they are worried that every step could be their last. When you can count on colleagues to keep commitments and do as they say they will, you can spend less time following up and double-checking; you can take things on faith rather than require detailed audits. Preventive maintenance is always less expensive than a breakdown and overhaul.

In a world of solo performers and solo heroics, autonomy and spontaneity are the keys to success. But in a world of orchestrated and complex harmonies, where the instruments have to blend and complement one another, there is a time for improvisation and a time for following the score. We have seen courage break down when people feel they have been played out of position and have seen candor deteriorate into noise when feedback is delivered in a way that is self-indulgent and careless rather than respectful and considerate.

In their work on the culture of excellent companies, Peters and Waterman (1982) describe a paradox that they call "simultaneous loose/tight properties." Teams and organizations with courage empower people and give them discretion and autonomy and, at the same time, expect them to operate within a strict code of ethics and honor, in which the spirit of the protocol is even more important than the letter of the regulation. Robert Cooke (1994) differentiated between rule-bound, low-courage, conformist, and power organizations—where people follow rules blindly out of fear of reprisals or lack of creativity—and self-expressive cultures, where people invent, teach, and learn from one another, to achieve as much as they are capable of achieving.

RISK: THE COURAGE TO EMPOWER, TRUST, AND INVEST IN RELATIONSHIPS

Whose agenda should take precedence: yours, mine, or ours? In hierarchical, chain-of-command teams, competitive self-interests are the driving force, mediated and adjudicated by those at the top of the pyramid. Such opportunism is often understandable, since the reward system rarely supports self-sacrifice and commitment to others.

Unfortunately, actions that are understandable or easy to fall into are not always effective or helpful. Risk reflects a dramatic shift in values wherein the key question becomes, What's best for the team or the enterprise as a whole? Risk—the courage to trust the goodwill of other team members and their willingness to share their own limited resources and precious opportunities—creates a greater measure of success.

Risk begets a move from power and turf-based relationships to one that embodies trust. Collaboration is the adhesive that bonds the team and its activity. A true culture of teams and a true matrix cannot occur unless the members of the organization are willing to let go of old entitlements and suspicions and believe that personally taking less can result in more in the long run.

Risk is a vital factor in the process and maintenance of team life. Without taking the risk of doing what's right rather than what's expedient or in one's own narrow self-interest, the remaining four factors—candor, purpose, will, and rigor—will all be undermined. Thus, a primary focus must be how to build and maintain a sense of community and relationships of trust within the team; building community is a business consideration, not just something that's nice to do when you have spare time or resources. The experience of support and affection that results from successful collaboration stimulates the desire of individuals to sacrifice for one another, to risk in the service of others on the team. Extraordinary acts of selflessness, valor, and altruism ultimately are the true tests of courage, and they are essential for a flat, matrix, team-based organization to get the job done, free of bureaucratic controls and second-guessing by the chain of command.

Courage Can Be Cultivated

The five courage factors do not just appear because of good intentions or because we have recruited courageous individuals. Certainly it helps to hire individuals with "the right stuff," but there is no guarantee that a team or organization will act courageously because individuals have the appropriate attributes. Conversely, it is clear that ordinary performers can exhibit extraordinary levels of courage in stressful and even dire circumstances, if that is the group norm.

Collective courage is a lot like collective intelligence. Just because your team is blessed with an inordinate amount of brainpower, there is no guarantee that the unit or organization will think clearly and solve problems effectively under pressure. Such intelligence has to be nurtured and developed, or the team could sink to the lowest common denominator or even end up doing worse than any single individual working alone. The key is the chemistry, synergy, and cohesion among the team members. Cultivating a team norm with respect to candor, purpose, will, rigor, and risk can imbue individuals with a greater level of courage than they would exhibit if they were working alone.

HOW NOT TO DO IT

Imbuing a team with courage is not a simple walk in the park. It demands resolve and dedicated commitment. Let's take an example. The lead project team of one of our clients proved to be a disappointing underachiever. Team members were assessed as having high levels of individual courage, yet, over and over again, they were reluctant to act and seize opportunities. The company is an entrepreneurial biotech firm with a promising new drug delivery system. The founders crafted a compelling and visionary business plan, raised more than three years' worth of working capital, and recruited a high-powered proven brain trust of top scientific talent. However, over time, a malaise had set in that brought down the collective courage level of the entire group. Here's how it played out.

Candor

It is not difficult to imagine the state of open and aboveboard feedback in the organization. The lack of candor began early on, when, in private, individuals bemoaned a business plan that was unrealistic and far too aggressive. Yet publicly they remained mute and told top management what they thought management wanted to hear. The gap between the top brass and the scientists responsible for meeting the deadlines continued to grow. Management lost more points when they would meet the investors and the business press, smile, and assure them that the scientific development process was on time and just slightly over budget. The hypocrisy added fuel to the stress created when the scientists could see failure overtaking them in the rearview mirror.

Purpose

Publicly, because of its high visibility, the project team was cautious and would commit itself only to safe and pedestrian goals. Privately, however, individuals on the leadership team were much more aggressive and would criticize one another for pitifully low ambitions and for the lack of challenge and audacious goal setting they knew would be required to take them to the next level. Comments like "I'd personally like to tell you we can get the job done in less time" made their way to the executive suite and the CEO, followed by "but the rest of the team won't commit to such an ambitious goal." Paradoxically, the group paid close attention to the stock price and to investor and customer confidence, but they failed to see the connection between inflated budgets and time lines and increasingly lackluster business performance.

Will

Most of the scientists had cut their teeth in competitive, high-pressure situations where there were significant scientific hurdles to overcome. To a person, they had a "never-say-die" belief in their own abilities. Hard, energetic work and a can-do spirit—what the CEO called "the killer instinct"—was a key hiring criterion. Yet, over time, a pattern of blame and blame avoidance, cajoling, and resentment had stifled people's spirits. While individuals believed in themselves, they were not optimistic that the rest of the team or, for that matter, the organization as a whole, could deliver the goods. Looks of passive resignation and defeatism were endemic, as were shoulder shrugs and mutterings such as "Whatever." The executive team still had enthusiasm and knew how to get one another fired up and motivated, but down the ranks, to the scientists on the lead project team, the same spirit and energy had been stifled and beaten out of people.

Rigor

The belief in the individual scientists was so great, they were provided the resources to work somewhat independently. They all brought with them to the new project their own protocols and ways of doing their research. Early on it was evident that personal entitlements were more important than team efficiencies. It wasn't long before a deferential "star system" grew, as individuals continued to isolate themselves. In such a competitive environment, with pressure on individuals from the top, there was little reason to adopt the techniques of others. Duplication of effort and poor communication were increasingly common. Even worse was the sight of these high-level individuals sniping and discrediting the work of their own colleagues.

Risk

Everyone talked about the need for teamwork and the kinds of risks necessary to bring the product home. They would even brag about the risks they had taken on other projects, working in previous companies. But when it actually came to sharing equipment, opportunities, resources, visibility, and credit, no one was willing to make the first move. Ostensibly, the team worked with an honor code that encouraged collaboration and honest communication. Yet under the surface, personal agendas prevailed as individuals lobbied for their own resources and showed little concern for the good of the larger team or system.

WHY SOME CULTURES THRIVE

Professor Robert Cooke (1994) spent his career attempting to understand why some work cultures thrived and grew over long periods of time, while others could never reach their true potential. He identified two types of cultures that are associated with lower levels of creativity, quality, safety, and productivity, and, in our terms, with a low level of courage.

Passive-Defensive Cultures

In cultures that Cooke described as being passive-defensive, there is, in our terms, a low level of shared purpose, along with minimal levels of candor, will, rigor, and risk. Instead, authority often goes unquestioned, passive dependency and conformity reign, and people tend to mind their own business and do what's most expedient or pragmatic. Pointing fingers, blaming, and avoiding blame become the routine source of gossip, often just below the politeness of surface conversation.

This was the culture that was alive and well among the various project teams in our ineffective and demoralized biotech firm. By the time we were called in, there were few signs of any of the five courage factors. The scientists continually deferred to the executive team. Rather than taking risks personally or on the work teams, they worked at pleasing the boss. Looking after their own or their team's interests was the logical goal of many staff members. At a time when creative risk taking was required, people hunkered down, protecting their turf and avoiding controversy and conflict. The high degree of individual courage demonstrated within the executive team, instead of motivating members of the organization, tended to lower morale, causing a decline in the acts of overt courage so badly needed to move the organization forward.

Aggressive-Defensive Cultures

Cooke's second type of low courage culture is one in which a high level of individual courage may be demonstrated, yet there is a low level of group or team courage. The organization is built on the premise that success is dependent on hiring ambitious self-starters who are willing to place themselves on the line and be accountable—people who will take charge, drive themselves and others hard, and do whatever it takes to deliver the goods. In theory, such an environment will encourage competition, vigorous debate, tough-minded skepticism, and people who aren't afraid to take a stand and argue a position.

The problem is that, more often than not, such cultures provide short-term success but over time begin to have problems. Teams and individuals can become polarized into winners and losers. Individuals with the most "courage" often rise to the top at the expense of their colleagues. This acts to reinforce individual ambition, opportunism, and self-interest as the drivers of success instead of the cooperation and collaboration required to act with risk. Promising ideas are often discouraged or criticized because of personal agendas rather than the quality of the idea itself. Intellectual fencing among very bright people can become the norm.

The consequence, Cooke's research showed, is that among such aggressive-defensive cultures there tends to be a negative correlation between the valued behavioral styles and such items as quality performance, idea generation, esprit de corps, safety, and staff retention. In addition, it is difficult to recruit people capable of undertaking challenging and difficult goals in a stressful business climate. Again, there is little question that personal ambition, competition, and focused rewards can result in short-term production and high levels of performance. Yet, as we are increasingly experiencing, such a short-term view can corrupt the integrity of the team, eating away at the trust that underlies risk and candor, both so essential to an individual's willingness to act courageously.

In the biotech company, there was a significant difference between the degree of courage shown among the individual members of the executive team and the degree of collective courage they were able to stimulate among the individual work teams. In fact, when these team members were asked to describe the kinds of behaviors the leaders elicited and reinforced, the behaviors they listed were very different from the behaviors executive team members used with one another.

Why the Team?

There are clear differences between an aggressive-defensive, individually oriented work culture and one that is truly team based and courageous. The effort in the team is focused on helping individuals achieve a higher level of performance than they would without the support, trust, discipline, and honesty that is possible in such a team culture. Over time, teammates feel an increasing responsibility toward one another with respect to each of the five factors of courage. They develop the courage to

- Create open lines of communication, including the giving and soliciting of feedback in order to keep unfinished business among individuals or groups from hindering the team's effectiveness

- Challenge one another to raise the bar and stay focused on doing what is mission-critical to make the enterprise thrive, promoting an unselfish, cooperative drive toward team goals, which, theoretically, override individual ambitions

- Renew one another's spirit and optimism and share in providing the lift teammates need in difficult times

- Create the necessary structures, standards, and team discipline to ensure high levels of quality, safety, and overall performance essential to team success

- Build strong relationships among team members, even if doing so demands shifting one's personal priorities to those of the team and sharing resources for the good of the team or organization

Courage Is Not a Halfway Proposition

As a team leader reading this description of the five courage factors that are essential when, as Churchill put it, "your other virtues are stretched to the limit," you might be taking an inventory of strengths and weaknesses. "Well," you might say, "on our team we could use some improvement in candor and perhaps trust. But we're strong in purpose and will. And as for rigor, it's not that important. We can wait to address that until the pressure is off and things ease up."

It's tempting to say, "We're 60 percent or 80 percent there." But nothing could be further from the truth. The five courage factors are not independent. Each feeds and bolsters the other. When you're stretched, pressured, facing ambiguity, conflict, and the other stresses that make it difficult for teams to do their best work, success requires all five factors.

Imagine slipping in behind the wheel of a sleek, new convertible sports coupe. You start the engine, turn on the stereo, and make your way down an open country road. It's a perfect spring day. Suddenly, a red light appears on your dashboard, and the car starts to buck and sputter. You pull into a service station, and the mechanic comes out, wipes his hands, and opens the hood. "Not bad," he says. "You're doing fine on three out of four cylinders, the fourth is working at 75 percent of what it should, and the fifth really isn't that important, is it?" You might not be an expert in auto mechanics, but you would know you're in serious trouble. The analogy applies to the five courage factors. Four out of five isn't enough, particularly when you are making your way uphill and carrying a heavy load.

ASSESSING COURAGE

Diagnosing the Courage to Act

Some people see things and say, "Why?" Others dream things that never were and say, "Why not?"
ROBERT KENNEDY

In this chapter, we will outline the questions you might ask to assess your team's level of courage. The answers your honest appraisal provides will tell you which of the five courage factors need attention if you aim to strengthen courage within your team. The questions are derived from our assessment tool, the Courage Index, which offers a concrete, statistical measure for those who are interested in developing a formal profile of a team's courage factors and for use in diagnosing and developing high-courage teams.

The Myth: Anyone Can Do It

Most team leaders are paid for "doing something"—for technical or operational contributions—rather than leading their teams. Team

53

leadership, it is sad to say, is often not the major responsibility of the typical team leader. Somehow, as if by magic, teams are expected to be naturally evolving entities that, with clearly defined goals and a modicum of goodwill, should evolve into a high-performing work unit.

Nothing could be further from the truth. If we maintained machines in the cavalier, seat-of-the-pants way we maintain teams, most of them would have a short life expectancy. Our computers would crash or would spit out GIGO (garbage in, garbage out) reports. Coping with the performance pressure, pace, and chaos of a matrixed, merged-today-divested-tomorrow organization requires more than good intentions and good people skills. It requires care and attention.

Do you remember the truly high-courage teams of which you have been a member at some point in your career? The teams that put wind under your wings, that lifted you to a level of performance that surpassed what you felt you were capable of achieving? For most of us, high-courage teams are a rarity. We have few models to work from. Yet, with minimal training, we are expected to create something that we desperately need but that few of us have seen or experienced firsthand.

Developing a Diagnostic Mentality

Whether or not you have much training in the secrets of team leadership, you can learn to assess courage. Even if you don't have the time or budget to do much formal team building, you can still imbue your team with candor, purpose, will, rigor, and risk. Building your team's courage starts with an assessment of its strengths and development needs. This will help determine how to intervene in the life of the team to move it forward.

Asking the Tough Questions

Sam Freedman*, retired chairman of Web Clothes, a 150-store retail chain in the United States, was a master at asking tough questions

_____
* fictionalized name of chairman and retail chain.

when he visited the stores in his chain. In less than ten minutes, Sam could ask a few diagnostic questions, listen and watch carefully, and tell, without looking at a single financial report, how the store was performing. It was uncanny.

Sam couldn't have accomplished what he needed to do without asking tough questions. Think about it. A good, tough question—Sam's kind of question—is like a sharp knife that can peel away the surface and allow a penetrating look into the inner world of the team. As Sam said, "It tells more than what's going on. It tells you what people think and how they set their priorities and order their world." Asking a tough question itself takes more than a little courage, since it may uncover information that makes us uncomfortable or vulnerable. However, it often unlocks opportunity in the guise of the choices not available until we have the courage to ask. Armed with a good question, we suddenly have the potential for alternatives based on the information we uncover—if, like Sam, we pay attention to what is said, what isn't said, how things look and smell, and how what we see compares with the words people say.

A good, tough question is a vehicle for discovering truth that adds significance to all five courage factors:

- To **candor,** by seeking the truth and feedback
- To **purpose,** with a train of thought that leads in a particular direction, consistent with what drives the business
- To **will,** by building confidence and optimism, particularly if there are serious gaps to address and serious problems to put right
- To **rigor,** with the discipline to bring order to both our thinking and our actions
- To **risk,** by drawing people together, building trust, and forming a tighter bond and a stronger partnership

Following (see pages 58–68) are thirty tough questions that will enable you to assess the strength of your team regarding each of the five courage factors. As you read each question, think about the behavior you observe in your team. You'll find a scoring template for the thirty questions on the next page. Flag that page now for easy answering.

COURAGE INDEX SCORING

Directions: Place an **X** in the boxes for the questions you can answer with a strong **YES**.

CANDOR	PURPOSE	WILL	RIGOR	RISK
1	7	13	19	25
2	8	14	20	26
3	9	15	21	27
4	10	16	22	28
5	11	17	23	29
6	12	18	24	30

Add the total number of Xs for each of the five factors.

CANDOR	PURPOSE	WILL	RIGOR	RISK

Transfer your total scores to the chart below by placing a dot on the broken vertical line that corresponds to the total score for each factor. Connect the dots to create a graph of your team's current level of courage.

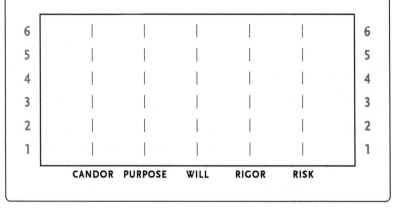

Interpreting Your Courage Index Profile

After you answer the thirty questions and total your scores, you'll be able to identify your team's strengths and weaknesses. If you answered five or six of the questions with a strong *yes*, the chances are good that your team already exhibits that courage factor most of the time. If you answered fewer than five questions with a strong *yes*, the chances are good that your team needs some work on improving that courage factor. Chapters 5 through 9 focus, one at a time, on the five courage factors. After you identify the factors that need the most attention in your team, we suggest you turn to the chapter that tells what you can do to improve that factor.

For example, consider the profile of a team in a biotech company that scored high on all factors except risk. What exactly does a profile like this suggest? It tells you that the team may do good work internally but it isn't as adept as it needs to be at sharing resources, shifting priorities to support teams working on other mission-critical projects, and empowering other disciplines to take the lead and exhibit thought leadership even when another discipline should be given a mandate to lead.

As another example, consider the profile of a retail store that scored high on will, rigor, and risk, moderate on purpose, and low on candor. What does this profile suggest? This team is one that keeps its spirits up, that is willing to pitch in and help other departments, and that makes sure store displays conform to the planograms that were developed in the corporate office. In good times, the store crew did their jobs and the business results took care of themselves. But when the market got tougher, they refused to commit to aggressive goals and got downright resentful when they were given feedback about missing sales opportunities.

Or consider the profile of an internal auditing group whose field investigators scored high on rigor and candor, moderate on will, and low on purpose and risk. When this group set out to become strategic business partners offering a valuable service to business units and engineering laboratories, rather than "after-the-fact" investigators and enforcers, it's easy to see what new skills they needed to develop—skills that would enable them to contribute to enterprise-wide success rather than be pulled in the opposite direction, and to build trust and give their constituents the benefit of the doubt.

Courage Index

....

CANDOR: THE COURAGE TO SPEAK AND HEAR THE TRUTH

Candor is the foundation of the five courage factors. Without it, there is little room for purpose, will, rigor, or risk to take root. When candor is alive and well on a team, the members speak freely and share ideas and insights, feelings and needs. Feedback is not withheld or driven underground but is delivered in a tactful and timely manner. The result is a climate of openness and nondefensiveness in which what needs to be said is said in a manner that can be heard. Members of the team don't just say what needs to be said; they also report that they feel heard and respected by those around them. Tough issues are raised and dealt with straight on, rather than avoided for fear of reprisal or embarrassment.

1. Does someone raise thorny or difficult issues? In some teams, there is so much collusion to maintain silence that you can feel its icy grip around your throat. When difficult issues are raised, people avert their eyes, talk in vague generalities, or change the subject. Or there is a superficial attempt to create harmony and avoid conflict, which stifles creativity and drives dissent underground. This, obviously, is the antithesis of candor. In cultures in which face saving and deference to authority figures are valued and breaking rank is taken as a sign of disloyalty, bluntness and public disagreement may not work. But that doesn't mean a mechanism can't be found to put truth on the table, even if the communication is done offline to save embarrassment.

2. Are disagreements explored openly, without the team getting polarized and locked into adversarial positions? Do teammates hear each other out in face-to-face and telephone conferences and read each other's e-mails and background memos? Are teammates allowed the opportunity to grapple with the issues rather than argue their positions and wait for the most senior person in the room to make an executive decision? Or are people so intent on winning the argument or scoring points that they fail to hear one another, even when they are expressing the same idea in different words? In some teams, people are so poised for a fight that who said what or how someone gestured becomes more important than the idea itself. When people close down and fail to hear and engage one another, candor is restricted.

3. During team meetings, are structures established to equalize the opportunity to receive input so that the natural tendency for the same few people to dominate does not occur? Are the individuals who simply talk more than others allowed to take over and dominate virtually any meeting in which they participate? Or are structures used to equalize participation so that you hear from people who may be less articulate, confident, or quick to speak? It is one thing to listen to what people have to say and quite another to actively solicit others' ideas, attitudes, or feelings. If some people are sitting quietly and taking it all in, are they asked for input or recommendations? Is there genuine interest in what quiet members of the team have to say, or is cultivating their input a gratuitous ploy to have people feel involved? Do team members feel that their ideas are solicited and welcome, even in the midst of strongly held beliefs?

4. Are defensiveness and skepticism acknowledged and addressed? It's easy to feel shot down when you present important data and the receiver bites your head off. But it's naïve to expect someone to say "Thank you for sharing" when he or she is confronted with critical data or when you raise issues that challenge his or her aspirations or deeply held beliefs. Candor doesn't mean that everyone will be open to everything all the time. It doesn't mean that every team member will "let it all hang out." It means that feelings, as well as facts, will be acknowledged and considered. It means that information givers will show empathy when they raise issues that could be threatening or embarrassing. It means that they will watch for signs of closing down on the part of the receiver, and will intervene with comments like "Stay with me" and "We'll get through this." It means that bystanders will not sit passively but will act as peacekeepers and facilitators with comments like "I know this is tough to hear" and "Let's try not to take this too personally." And it means that you may have to take a break and let the receiver stew for a few minutes or a few days before you can get past the sting and get to the heart of the issue.

5. Does humor play a role in diffusing tension and helping the team not take itself too seriously? Hardworking and highly motivated teams can easily fall prey to taking themselves too seriously. Situational humor can keep things in perspective and provide the underpinnings for other activities that help members care for one another. We know that affection is partly spawned by play, celebration, and efforts to recognize good works. What is done in your team meetings and communication exchanges to keep the tone light and to take the edge off tension when discussing contentious or difficult issues?

6. Do people of diverse backgrounds feel welcome and respected as equals? Is there a zero-tolerance policy for put-downs, even if they are meant "only in jest"? Is there a real attempt to understand the unique perspectives that people of different genders, ethnic and national backgrounds, professional disciplines, personalities, and lifestyles bring to a team's deliberations?

PURPOSE: THE COURAGE TO PURSUE LOFTY AND AUDACIOUS GOALS

Teams with purpose have a compelling, clear direction that drives them forward and that all members of the team support. They don't settle for the low-hanging fruit they can scoop up easily but, instead, challenge themselves to reach to the top of the tree. Striving for optimal performance, they benchmark themselves against the "winners" and pay attention to what the data tell them about their performance.

7. Are charts, graphs, and performance metrics posted and visible? Are performance data posted prominently for your team—for example, on real or virtual bulletin boards? Are metrics up-to-date and accurate? Do they give an honest picture about organizational, team, and individual performance? If you ask "How's business?" do the answers tell you that people have read the charts and take the benchmarks, metrics, and goals seriously?

8. Can people articulate their personal contribution to the core of what drives the business? There is a story about an organizational psychologist who visited an IBM plant in a small town in the South. On the third shift (midnight to 8 A.M.), he approached a sweeper in the plant who took particular pride and care in keeping the place clean. He asked, "Why do you work so hard?" The sweeper looked at him incredulously. "You see that sign that says something about our customers," the sweeper explained patiently, as if he were talking to a four-year-old. "When daybreak comes, customers occasionally walk through this plant. Would you buy a million-dollar computer system from a company that couldn't keep its floors clean?" Could your team members answer just as intelligently if they were asked, "What difference does it make if you give your job 110 percent?"

9. Is there a link between strategic, big-picture goals and day-to-day performance? The manager of a large supermarket announced that sales needed to be increased by $500,000 per month. People nodded but did little to make it happen. By doing the math, the manager determined that two more items per shopping cart would enable the store to meet that objective. People on the front lines couldn't relate to a goal of $500,000, but they could act on a goal of two more items per shopping cart. Are your team goals specific, concrete, and timely enough for teammates to know how their efforts add up to create a much larger success?

10. Do teammates have an understanding of business conditions and of the wider business environment? Ask open-ended questions about customer tastes and about the business environment. Do you get fresh insights and ideas "from the bottom up"? Can you get inside the heads of your teammates and find out what they know about the business and the competitive environment? Do the answers you receive tell you that teammates buy into more aggressive performance standards and appreciate the larger business realities?

11. Are people willing to do the jobs that make the greatest contribution to lofty and audacious goals, even if those aren't the jobs that are most comfortable, interesting, or enjoyable? On any team, some jobs are more glamorous and intrinsically interesting than others. When you ask about people's sense of achievement, what do you hear about first? Do teammates talk about the performance of the enterprise and the contributions they've made to enterprise success, or do they focus on pet projects, cool new technology, and artistic successes that, while personally fulfilling, make little contribution to the enterprise or the lives and well-being of those who depend on your organization?

12. Do team goals and individual goals stretch people, challenge them, and evoke a high level of achievement motivation? Is there a challenge tied to a compelling goal that can light a fire under team members, individually and collectively, or are goals set at a low level so that success is assured? A sense of purpose is derived not from the threat of not completing the goal but rather from the excitement generated from pushing through barriers and surpassing normal expectations. Are your teammates passionate about making a solid contribution to the well-being of the people who are counting on their best efforts?

WILL: THE COURAGE TO INSPIRE OPTIMISM, SPIRIT, AND PROMISE

Teams with a strong will believe in themselves. They have a "fire in their belly," a belief that their hard work and good intentions will ultimately pay off. When a team has will, it knows it, and in its best form, will has them believing that they can rise to any challenge and accomplish almost anything.

13. Do team members reflect a sense of eagerness and enthusiasm about their roles and the challenges that face them? Assessing the will of a team doesn't take a special effort or special questions. It does take paying attention to the tone, spirit, and energy that teammates project. Do people smile and exude enthusiasm when they talk about their work? Do they walk with a bounce in their step? Attitudes are contagious; in teams with the will to succeed, people project an upbeat, positive attitude that sweeps others up in their energy.

14. Does the team have a can-do attitude toward its work? What happens when you talk about new possibilities, new projects, or more aggressive performance goals? Do teammates groan, roll their eyes, and tell you why the extra burden isn't fair or reasonable? Or do they tell you what it will take to pull the job off successfully and what help and resources they'll need? With practice, you can tell whether a can-do attitude is mandated and contrived or whether it comes from the heart and from a strength of spirit.

15. Are unexpected setbacks taken in stride based on an overall optimism about the future? If you're paying attention, and you ask a few open-ended questions (e.g., "How are you coping with . . . ?"), you can quickly see how resilient a team is when it encounters setbacks and difficulties. You can also see whether setbacks strike a fatal blow to the team's self-confidence.

16. Is the team in a constant search for creative solutions and approaches to the problems with which they are faced? Strong-willed teams are self-starting and their members believe they have the capacity to solve most problems. Other teams stop in their tracks altogether or wait for the boss to direct them and show continuing signs of passive dependency. Strong-willed teams thrive on the challenge of problem solving. They get on with the task at hand. Any mistakes they make are ones of going too far too fast rather than that of sitting and doing nothing. Does your team take this kind of initiative?

17. Do individual team members have a general sense of optimism toward who the team is as a team and how well individuals work together? In strong-willed teams, individuals don't just exude self-confidence; they also talk in positive terms about their colleagues and their managers. They egg one another on and challenge one another to be the best that they can be. Do team members see each day as a new challenge to help their teammates exceed their personal best rather than settle into a complacent, albeit comfortable, routine?

18. Do teammates take pride in their work? Do they strive for their personal best, rather than being blasé or complacent? When they talk informally, does it look and sound as if they put their heart into the job, rather than just going through the motions?

RIGOR: THE COURAGE TO INVENT
DISCIPLINES AND MAKE THEM STICK

Rigor involves a respect for the methods, routines, and protocols necessary to keep the team and its members on track. It is a step beyond good intentions and represents the institutionalizing of practices that ensure greater discipline in the process of how work is accomplished. In a fast-paced and agile business environment, rigor ensures safety and regulatory compliance and prevents expensive or embarrassing miscommunications and miscalculations.

19. Is there is a built-in expectation among team members that they will help each other learn the best practices essential to perform at the highest level? Not all team members learn at the same rate, particularly when they have to self-train from a manual or diagram. Do those who learn quickly and problem solve more adeptly help those who are struggling? Do people share the best practices they have invented or keep "tricks of the trade" to themselves?

20. Has the team established procedures for planning, including gathering relevant data to make informed and prudent decisions? Quick thinking and problem solving aren't synonymous with acting capriciously. Taking setbacks in stride isn't an excuse for failing to think things through and prevent difficulties. Watch what happens when a team is asked to commit to aggressive new time lines. Do they have to reinvent the wheel or shoot from the hip, or do they have a planning process that will enable them to respond expeditiously and logically when they are asked to do more, faster, with less?

21. Are equipment and supplies well maintained and kept in order? What do you see when you open the closet door, review maintenance records, or scratch the surface? Do things look orderly? Have team members invested in preventive maintenance of the tools they depend on? Have they taken the time needed to put things away and clean up after themselves? If you ask for a report, for inventory, or for a piece of equipment, can it be found and retrieved quickly, with a minimum of hunting and searching?

22. Are rules and guidelines used to ensure the maintenance of the highest possible standards? When teammates believe that disciplines and protocols are arbitrary, compliance is lower than it is when team-mates see the logic and value of those same rigors and take pride in mastering those regimens. So, what do teammates tell you about the protocols that they're expected to learn and follow? Can they explain the logic and rationale for those regimens, or do they roll their eyes, laugh cynically, and look for ways to avoid detection and penalties?

23. Do members of the team follow through and actually do what they say? Do teammates have to be reminded of their commitments, or do individuals demonstrate personal accountability, writing down their commitments, budgets, and time lines—and following up without being prodded, chased, or cajoled? If tomorrow's priorities mean that today's commitments cannot be kept, do teammates let you know early enough to adjust your plans accordingly, or do they wait for you to no-tice that something hasn't been delivered on time?

24. Does the team pay attention to the consequences of problem solv-ing and decision making both within the team and in relation to other parts of the organization? When you listen to members of the team solve problems and discuss what will work best, do they talk about the impact of their actions and decisions on other teammates, on other de-partments within the organization, and on other strategic business partners? Do they know enough about other parts of the operation to anticipate how decisions and actions will affect other groups? Do they demonstrate a desire to do what will work best for the entire organiza-tion, including partners, suppliers, and customers?

RISK: THE COURAGE TO EMPOWER, TRUST, AND INVEST IN RELATIONSHIPS

Traditionally, organizations have been built on competition and self-interest. But that isn't enough in a business environment that requires people to share information and resources, work together, and deploy talent and resources in a way that will optimize enterprise-wide performance, rather than one's own individual or work group performance. Risk revolves around relationships, cooperation, and support; it is reflected in what people do, not just the image they try to put forward. With risk, teammates are willing to make themselves vulnerable to support one another, go the extra mile for one another, and entrust their success to someone else's actions.

25. Do all team members talk about team efforts with reference to "we," or do a few individuals talk in terms of "me" or "us and them"? Consider what it means when members of a technical team talk about business or investment goals with reference to "what *they* decided," rather than "*our* goals for the enterprise," or when someone boasts about "what I accomplished," rather than "what we achieved as a team." Words, including subtleties like the choice of pronouns, offer clues about how people really see the world around them. Do words tell you that teammates see themselves as part of a larger and united group?

26. Do team members celebrate the success of other teammates, sharing in each others' achievements vicariously? Or do they harbor professional rivalries and jealousies, coveting others' honors and accomplishments? To get a true picture, you may need to watch how teammates are congratulated and accomplishments celebrated, and listen to what's not said as well as what is said, off the record as well as in public. You can also ask open-ended questions such as "What makes you proud to be part of this organization?" and "Tell me how your teammate's success has affected people in other parts of the organization."

27. Is work delegated to the best person, with no hoarding of work as a means of control and personal entitlement? How are the most prestigious, interesting, high-visibility assignments meted out? When they are delegated, how much autonomy and empowerment does the delegator grant? Do people receive the counsel and support they need to assume responsibility and make good, independent decisions, or are they left to sink or swim on their own?

28. Is there an atmosphere of benefit of the doubt, trust, and acceptance? Is this a safe environment in which people can be themselves, take initiative, and make themselves vulnerable by giving to others? Do teammates feel enough trust in one another to take setbacks or oversights in stride, rather than respond to them with blame and ridicule? Or do teammates live in fear of blame and feel that their every move and decision is being watched by someone who is waiting in the shadows to pounce on the slightest mistake? Micromanagement, second-guessing, and quickness to point out mistakes can erode trust and make it nearly impossible for teammates to pitch in and help one another.

29. Do individual team members show the ability to shift their priorities based on changing urgencies and the needs of others? Is the team as a whole willing to renegotiate time lines and performance standards so they can support efforts that will, at least temporarily, contribute to the enterprise as a whole? Or is there a twinge of resentment or stoic resignation in people's voices when they talk about putting their own pet projects aside? Are they tuned in enough to recognize when someone else needs help and what the enterprise-wide implications are without receiving instructions from someone at a higher level of the organization?

30. Is time invested in building the kinds of relationships that foster trust and dedication? Or are people thrown together as a face-to-face or virtual team, without adequate time to get to know one another or anticipate one another's needs?

What Does This Tell You About the Courage of Your Team?

. . . .

If you, as a team leader or team member, answer each of these thirty questions about your team, you will have a good idea of your team's particular strengths and weaknesses. You will also have a better understanding of the level of courage you could anticipate from the team.

Record your responses to the questions in the chart on page 56. Identify the columns with the most items checked *yes* and those with the most blank spaces. Those that are heavily laden with Xs are the areas where courage is strongest; those that have the most blanks could use improvement.

The next five chapters focus, one courage factor at a time, on concrete actions that teams and leaders can take to strengthen courage.

How to
BUILD
Courage

CANDOR

....

The Courage to Speak and Hear the Truth

*Our lives begin to end the day we become silent about
things that matter.*
MARTIN LUTHER KING JR.

We have all been there: sitting silently, filled with emotion, biting our tongues, afraid to speak up for fear that we might offend, be criticized, or, heaven forbid, look stupid. In a polite society, we try to avoid conflict whenever we can. In an image-conscious society, we try to manage appearances and politics when we decide how much we are willing to risk. Caution and discretion are almost always the better part of valor.

Candor is so simple. Supposedly, we value people who tell the truth, who deal with us straight. We value people who look at the facts, take feedback, and acknowledge their shortcomings. We want to work in a place where what you see is what you get, where you're encouraged to put forward your ideas and insights, where you're treated with openness and respect.

Yet, despite what we value, candor is a rare commodity. Its absence, whether on our teams or in our boardrooms, adds untold millions to our bottom lines and kills our best efforts to improve morale. Without candor—when truth is withheld—feelings are stifled and unfinished business goes underground. Suspicion, rumors, and disrespect fester and infect other parts of the business with their toxins. In as many as half of our client systems, a lack of candor is a cancer that has eaten away at courage. Unless candor can be restored, there is little hope that any other aspect of courage can become part of the fabric of the team.

The Regional Management Team: Don't Ask, Don't Tell

Prior to the merger, the regional management team had headed the company's flagship region. Before the market became more competitive, this region had been the crown jewel—the most profitable region in the merged company. It's still home to the corporation's most prestigious accounts.

The core members of the regional management team have been around forever and remember when they sat adjacent to the old, now-shuttered corporate headquarters. They are a tight, elite clique. They would do almost anything to cover for one another and for their boss, the regional vice president, who personally picked each of them for promotion after the merger. Newcomers can sense that they'll never fully be accepted into this exclusive club. Over time, they see that their mistakes will be dealt with more harshly and their career potential judged more critically than will those of club members. That's especially true for people of color, women, gays, and those who haven't come up through the ranks—as the vice president and his Boys' Club have.

From the Courage Index, we could see that the group was severely polarized. Half of the regional management team reported that candor was extraordinarily high. The other half reported an abysmal lack of candor. We were called in because a climate of politics and suspicion overlaid every new initiative, marketing program, and new account presentation. As a result, new program implementations were delayed or stalled altogether. Many high-profile departments at the corporate office complained that they couldn't get good information out of the region and that their e-mails and phone calls would go unanswered for weeks. Even the regional vice president was frustrated. When he tried to get to the heart of the matter, he found a tangled maze of rumors and finger-pointing. Off the record, there were bitter accusations and righteously indignant counteraccusations. In public, there was a thin veneer of civility and collegiality.

JUST DO IT

John, the director of finance, was the last member of the management team we interviewed. John was newly hired and had been dispatched to the region by the corporate CFO. "We wouldn't have these problems," he said, "if people just stood up and told the truth. Take me, for example. I don't play this, 'Shhh! Don't say anything!' high school game. I call it like I see it. The worst they can do is fire me, and if they do that, I have no doubt about my ability to land something else. But I learned a long time ago that anyplace you've got to tiptoe around in and walk on eggshells isn't a place worth being."

In his work on groupthink, Irving Janis (1982, 1989) identified a number of ways that peer pressure and the implicit threat of repercussions make people "go along to get along," even when they know that the group is wrong. The cost of groupthink and its presence in high-level government and business decisions has been well documented. But social psychologist Jerry Harvey (1999) reexamined the notion of groupthink. Like John on the regional management team, Professor Harvey concluded that collusion is an individual choice, justified by team members who hide behind the convenient fiction of "peer pressure." The collusion is broken when one or two individuals like John refuse to play the game.

DARE TO ASK

Brian, the regional vice president, is a charismatic, mercurial, and dominant presence. His office features a ten-foot wall entirely covered with plaques, trophies, statuettes, air force memorabilia, and framed photographs that recount his fifteen-year history with the elite inner circle. Brian's large desk and captain's chair dominate the room, in a way that makes it clear why his office is referred to as "the throne room."

When you first meet Brian, he seems so warm and unassuming that you question the stories about his ego and his impatience. He has such a command of the big picture and thinks so strategically that you wonder about his oft-cited penchant for micromanagement and for giving orders that directly countermand his district and location managers' instructions and undermine their authority.

Because most people like and respect Brian for his many strengths as an operator, and because they don't want to get on his bad side, they put up with his idiosyncrasies and try not to get in his way. A deep breath, rolling of the eyes, or a long gaze downward is the only sign of their dismay at some of his less sensitive or ineffective behaviors. To push back will inevitably start an interchange in which they have little hope of winning, let alone feeling heard. So they don't. They let him lecture, uninterrupted, and tell him what he wants to hear, even when they are convinced he's wrong. They assure him that they'll try to take his advice to heart, which Brian hears as buy-in and commitment, rather than permission to give his recommendations a halfhearted effort and then do what they believe to be best.

To raise the level of candor, it was clear that we'd have to work with Brian. He wasn't going to be an easy nut to crack. When others before us had tried to talk with Brian about people not feeling heard or respected, he'd laughed and blown them off. He'd said that was just the price of doing business and you can never satisfy everyone. Such responses, however, are like a parent justifying the fact that his child steals, lies, and cheats by blaming the kids he hangs out with or perhaps our materialistic culture. That may be partly true, but it isn't a valid justification any more than business conditions are a valid justification for leadership that fosters a lack of candor.

The first advice we gave Brian was to change the questions he asked at the end of his monologues. Typically, Brian would ask, "Can I count on your support?" We gave Brian a script with open-ended questions such as the following:

- What concerns you the most about making this plan work?

- What will be the hardest aspects of this for you to sell to your team or to your customers?

- I've told you what I'd recommend. What other ideas do you have that could accomplish the same business objectives?

- What will you need to get started on implementation? What help do you need from other parts of the organization to make this plan work?

- Who else do you need to consult with and get input from before you put your plan together? When can we get back together to talk about how you're going to proceed?

DARE TO LISTEN

When Brian first started to use the new questions, very little actually changed. After years of conditioning and compliance, few members of the team took a different set of questions as an open invitation. When they said, "I don't envision any problems," Brian took them at their word. The pattern was unchanged. Brian heard buy-in, the team members felt coerced and countermanded, and there seemed to be little opportunity to offer an alternative point of view.

Asking the right questions was clearly only the start of reopening closed lines of communication. Brian also needed to learn to probe and to listen for what wasn't said, as well as what was said. He needed to learn to tune in to the signs that adept parents recognize in their teenage children—signs that say, "Talk on, old man, but it's going in one ear and out the other." He needed to know when it was time to stop talking and let others fill the silence, even if the silence got uncomfortable or started to seem like a waste of valuable time.

If you are the leader in a team like Brian's, a team that needs to raise its level of candor, we might invite you to do the same things that we advised him to do. Talk less and listen more; tell and sell less and get into people's heads and hearts more.

- **Shut up.** If you don't fill the room with talk, someone else will feel compelled to break the silence. If you're not the one jumping in to offer ideas and directions, someone else will. Therapists and group facilitators are masters at using silence constructively, giving people time to gather their thoughts and creating an environment in which people feel compelled to speak.

- **Probe.** When once-silent team members begin to offer ideas or insights, rarely do they say everything they need to say. Instead, they're more likely to test the waters by offering a small tidbit or introductory comment and waiting to see how it's received. You can encourage them to elaborate by saying, "Tell us more," or "Please continue," or with probes such as, "So that . . . ," "And therefore . . . ," or, "Which you'd interpret to mean that . . ."

- **Solicit input.** In the first management team meeting we attended, we saw five people dominate team discussions and ten people sit for a full day in total silence, doodling and occasionally taking notes. Some of the silent ten were among the most outspoken in our individual interviews. Yet, unless you asked them, you would never know that they had ideas, insights, relevant experience, and serious reservations about the apparent, but phony, team consensus. Brian had to learn to ask for input rather than assume that silence meant consent.

SHIFT THE BALANCE OF POWER

Even before Brian became aware of his own intimidating and stifling behavior, he realized that a few outspoken and vocal team members dominated any meeting, regardless of subject, and wore the star label at the expense of their peers. At the same time, he believed others needed to step up to the plate and participate more fully in the issues facing the organization. Brian was aware that people held back and that candor was almost totally lacking. He also realized that there were conflicts within the team as a whole and among individual players that required resolution.

While quiet members of the team didn't overtly act fearful, an air of reluctance permeated many of the management team's meetings as individuals withheld ideas, emotions, and feedback. A surreal politeness and superficiality prevailed. Most issues were quickly addressed, and those that invited conflict were avoided or were decided on the basis of rank and authority rather than logic and open discussion.

We were skeptical when Brian said that he wanted to see a higher level of candor in the team. Clearly, candor was impossible unless Brian was willing to change in some significant ways. Our concern was that what Brian would have to give up in personal power and in his own behavioral idiosyncrasies would, in the long run, not be worth the price to him. After all, he had been extraordinarily successful, and he had a loyal following that enjoyed privilege and prestige and had no interest in seeing Brian upset the balance of power in the organization. Brian's elite inner circle—the Boys' Club, as it was called—had just as much, or even more, to lose if Brian created a level playing field for all members of the regional management team.

Unless the team could see that they had more to gain than to lose by staying the course and raising the level of candor, our best efforts were doomed to fail. The work had to be more than an exercise in good manners and social justice. Fortunately, it wasn't that hard to make a compelling case:

- The team's level of turnover was horrendously high compared with that of management positions in other regions. Apparently, it was easier for management talent to move on than to put up with being second-class citizens or try to fight their way into the Boys' Club.

- It was getting harder and harder to fill management positions from within the company because of the reputation that Brian and the Boys' Club had earned. Many up-and-coming, high-potential executives, unlike John, weren't willing to stake their careers on a rotation in Brian's region.

- Corporate programs were not being implemented as quickly in Brian's region as they were in the rest of the company—in marketing, sales, finance, technology, or human resources. Project teams didn't have the same level of courage in Brian's region as they had elsewhere. And the difference was noticeable enough to draw the attention of Brian's boss and other corporate executives outside the operations pyramid.

Both in our work with Brian and in Brian's work with the Boys' Club, we had to be clear about the price that would be paid for holding on to power and privilege. Even so, there was no guarantee that the consequences would be taken seriously, any more than one can be assured that a smoker will heed the health warnings that are printed on cigarette packages.

Still, the attitude that Brian and the other Boys' Club members showed was key to the success of the whole effort. We could advise them what to do and what not to do. We could provide feedback and coach them on new behavior. We could provide structures and designs for meetings, questionnaires, and other honest, healthy exchanges. But we couldn't make them care about whether the management team was inclusive or exclusive, and we couldn't make them want to share or let go of power and control. The courage to let others in had to come from within each individual, starting, of course, with Brian. The rest was a matter of technique.

CREATE SAFETY

Brian, with his quick wit and sarcasm, could put people in their place with as few as two or three well-chosen words. With little more than a glance and a gesture, in a few careless seconds of frustration or impatience, he could "kill the messenger" and undo all the work he'd done to open the lines of communication. The point isn't whether you agree or disagree with a member of your team. It's whether, like Brian, you've built a power base on talking loudly and failing to reflect on what is said; speaking in a dismissive tone; or using nonverbal expressions that suggest you either have not heard someone or don't care. It's whether you insist on having the last word and giving the definitive answer. It's whether you make yourself feel smart by making other people feel wrong and stupid when they're grappling with problems they've never faced before.

GET PERSONAL FEEDBACK

It's one thing to say, "Don't kill the messenger." It's another to disarm an inveterate gunslinger. Off-site workshops and personal coaches offer the great benefit of getting people away from the habits, routines, and demands that have become like second nature. They allow an environment to be created where it is permissible to practice new behaviors that are not yet part of the team's norms or part of the team leader's natural style.

But how would Brian know whether he was, indeed, changing his response, particularly when he was frustrated, impatient, or convinced that he knew the right answer better than anyone else on the team? How would he know whether the rest of the Boys' Club was changing with him, or whether people were simply driving their disrespect underground, where he couldn't see it? The answer is feedback.

Watch it; this could sting. Imagine, like Brian, that you haven't received real feedback for ten years or more. Imagine that you've been praised and rewarded for the courage you've personally exhibited, no matter how it's affected the courage you elicit from others. Would you be open to having others tell you when you're resorting to old habits, and would you embrace that feedback as a means of learning new habits and new skills—maybe as a means of keeping your job? Or would you be protective and rationalize your old reactions? Most people in Brian's position both desire and fear the truth. The fear is increased when they know others are watching, assessing their progress, and making career decisions.

Courage. We admire it in every executive like Brian who has called on us for coaching and who has enlisted other team members to provide ongoing, real-time feedback. New courage-building behavior may be learned in a training or team-building session, but it doesn't get internalized or become a habit there. That happens back on the job. Brain understood that. We breathed a sigh of relief when he picked three members of the management team—none of them from the Boys' Club—and asked them to tell him when his gun was out of the holster and he'd reacted out of habit. In writing, he promised to stop and listen when he received their feedback and that there would be no retribution. Was this a huge risk? You bet it was. When one of the three gave Brian the "Time out!" signal in the middle of a budget review meeting, and Brian said, "Thanks; I guess I needed that," we knew we'd turned the corner.

Practicing Candor

. . . .

Even when people have permission to say what's on their minds, they don't want to look stupid. In workshops, we give participants a number of ways to gather their thoughts, test them out, and refine the delivery before they have to "go public." We've learned that too many people aren't as vocal and uninhibited as John, and they sit silently when put on the spot and asked for a command performance. In meetings, teleconferences, and even on-line chats, you can use the same techniques that we've used successfully for years to promote a high level of candor.

- Form duos or trios; groups of four are too large. Ask a question that requires some thought and allow fifteen to thirty minutes for the small group to work on it before reporting their ideas to the entire forum. Even in teams of as few as ten people, this method provides more input than a free-for-all, round-table discussion.

- Send background material out ahead of time, with specific questions that you'd like to discuss or specific feedback and input you'd like to receive. You'll find this tip in virtually every book on running effective meetings. It's so simple. Yet it's remarkable how infrequently it's actually done.

- Ask participants to respond to a document with new operating procedures or performance data by asking three questions:

  a) What were you **glad** to see?

  b) What were you **concerned** to see?

  c) What **questions** do you have?

  Or, before putting together a new action plan, ask participants:

  a) What do you **hope** we'll accomplish if we're successful?

  b) What concerns or **reservations** do you have about conditions that could keep us from succeeding?

  c) What **questions** do you have about what we need to accomplish?

- Poll the group in a secret ballot process using a scale of 1 to 10. Or post a flip-chart at the front of the room and ask participants to come up, en masse, and post their ratings.

- An alternative to this is a rating technique that a colleague of ours, Professor Robert Atkinson, calls the "fist of five" technique. Frame a "yea" or "nay" vote on an issue. A strong "yea" is indicated by holding up five fingers, a strong "nay" by holding up one finger. Those who are on the fence or who could live with either outcome hold up two or three fingers.

- Take a short break in a meeting and ask individual participants to jot notes in a journal or on a worksheet. When you start the meeting again, go around the room and ask for a report from each participant or ask a recording secretary to recap the individual worksheets. (With meeting management software, available from both Apple and IBM, you can do this electronically to capture the group's collective wisdom.)

SAVING FACE

Candor isn't a one-way process. Sure, it takes courage for image-conscious, command-and-control types like Brian to be open to hearing the truth. But we also have to realize that the way truth is delivered can set people up to take it to heart or dismiss it defensively. Of all the rules for giving feedback, none is more important than giving it at the right time. It's harder to hear the truth when it's publicly embarrassing or humiliating or when people in power feel that their authority or position isn't respected.

Brian's agreement to receive feedback when he reverted to old behaviors did not give his designated coaches carte blanche. Behind closed doors—whether one-to-one or in the context of a regional management team meeting in which everyone had agreed on a change process—Brian's designated coaches could be as frank as they liked. But Brian wasn't likely to continue with a process that undermined his authority or credibility. The same is true when you have difficult or potentially embarrassing feedback to deliver. It's going to be easier for the receiver to take it to heart if you walk into his or her office, close the door, and say, "We have a problem," than it will be if you express your anger or frustration with the other person's behavior in public, no matter how justified or offended you are.

In some cultural contexts, respect for authority figures and saving face are even more important than they are in American and other Anglo cultures. In France, for example, disagreeing with your boss in public isn't an act of courage or candor; it's an act of treason. There is a sharp distinction between what's acceptable off-line and behind the scenes, when you're arming your superiors with the data they need to be prepared and on top of things, and the united front that you're expected to present in public. In Eastern societies, both in Asia and in the Middle East, rank and stature are key to delivering candid feedback. If you do not have the proper professional credentials, organizational position, or prestige to be recognized as a legitimate authority, your candid message will need to be carried by someone who does.

TIMING

"Why didn't you tell me sooner?" How many times have we thought or said this when we receive feedback after a decision has already been made or when it's too late to react or do damage control?

Brian explained the issue of timing this way: "After deliberations are over and a decision has been made and announced to corporate, it makes us look like we don't have our act together if we reverse it a day or a week later. I'd rather know that someone didn't agree with the proposal I was championing before we commit to it publicly or run into problems that we should have been able to foresee and prevent."

Several months before the collapse of Enron, Sherron Watkins, one of the vice presidents, tried to get her concerns about the firm's accounting practices on the CEO's radar screen. In a memo she wrote detailing her observations, Watkins told the CEO that she had grave concerns about the company's future. "Is there a way that our accounting gurus can unwind these deals now?" she asked, fearing that the die had already been cast and that backtracking would be impossible.

By the time Sherron Watkins's warnings were taken seriously, the damage was already done. Other people had tried to bring warnings to the people at the top before the crisis was imminent and had been ignored. It isn't always easy to alert people to a problem before there is an emergency and they see the collision course with disaster or the lost opportunities that you see. It's easy to be dismissed as overcautious, unambitious, and uncommitted—like the character in the children's fable *Chicken Little*, who runs around declaring, "The sky is falling!"

There's no guarantee that your voice will be heard, even if you bring mission-critical information to those who need to hear it. And there are risks. But it isn't impossible to be heard, if you have the following.

- **The facts.** Just the facts can be organized in a way that is compelling and that paints a picture, without editorializing or sensationalizing and without commenting on the character of those who seem to be at the heart of the problem.

- **The right people assembled.** It may take some preselling and some building of consensus about the importance of the issue, possibly in a series of personal invitations and one-to-one, off-the-record discussions, before a formal investigation is launched or a task force convened. It may also take courage to bring the problem to the attention of higher-ups in the organization or to colleagues in other departments.

- **A process to define shared goals and common ground.** Determine whether people are working together toward the same goals rather than at cross-purposes. Brian wouldn't have been likely to stay the course and continue to encourage candor unless he was convinced it would contribute to the success of his business and his career rather than to the indulging of a few disgruntled subordinates at his expense. We'll never know what would have happened if Sherron Watkins's colleagues had been more concerned about the long-term implications of their accounting practices than about chasing the next deal to avoid paying for yesterday's mistakes.

A LIGHT TOUCH

Think about your participation in a group when you walk into the room and feel a heavy, grave, judgmental tone. If you're like most team members, you're going to be more cautious about what you say and more conservative and conventional about the possibilities you put forward. Contrast that with behavior in a team that is upbeat and cheerful, that maintains a light tone and a proper perspective.

We aren't suggesting that you trivialize issues of grave importance. We aren't suggesting that you start a serious meeting with a joke, particularly if you are working in a Korean or Japanese culture, in which joking would mark you as someone who can't be taken seriously. But we are suggesting that you watch the climate and tone that you create when you present data and take part in deliberations. Heavy, judgmental, grave tones can cast a pall over a group and can stifle participation. A lighter and more easygoing touch can bring out the best thinking that everyone can offer.

SEEK HELP

Teams and their leaders can do a lot on their own to raise the level of candor. But in a case like Brian's, where the team had become polarized to the point of being dysfunctional and where Brian himself was part of the problem, it's hard to imagine things getting better without outside help. What can an outside coach and group facilitator do?

- **Validate the business consequences of a continued lack of candor.** Like Brian, key leaders can see what the real stakes are, beyond their own comfort, image, and power needs.

- **Collect data.** Use questionnaires like the Courage Index, which get the issue on the table squarely, without judgments and moral pronouncements, as well as interviews and observations, which reveal the dynamics that inhibit candor and the changes that will create more openness.

- **Get the issues on the table.** For individuals who have lived for years in the stifling reality of being told what to do and rarely being asked for their feedback, putting the issue of candor on the table is bound to release a floodgate of emotions and opinions. Harsh criticism is inevitable. So is some shock at the degree to which some people have felt intimidated or discounted by others. It's almost impossible to participate in this kind of discussion and facilitate it at the same time. It's the facilitator's job to make sure that frankness and honesty are tempered with respect and care, that criticism is not coming from a place of abuse or anger, and that the picture shows a fair balance of strengths and limitations.

- **Show that there are better alternatives.** The purpose of team exercises and activities is twofold. One purpose is to create the upbeat and positive climate that makes it possible to raise sensitive issues and work through them. A second purpose is to provide practice in working with a higher level of candor and to show what's possible when the group really begins to open up and involve everyone in the deliberations. The courage to act should include some new action right there, right then—even if it's on a contrived or simulated team problem. That way, the group can see what can be accomplished when people walk the walk as well as talk the talk of candor.

- **Recontract.** Creating increased candor is a process built on new skills and the understanding of the dysfunction of old behaviors. Such skills can best be practiced away from the rigid norms, bad habits, and expectations of the workplace. But without a clear contract to do things differently, there is no guarantee that the lessons from the off-site meeting will work their way back into the world of work. Off-site work needs to end with more than good intentions and inspiring new insights. It needs to end with specific agreements about how the old collusions will be broken and how new norms will be created in their place. Those agreements need to be recorded and posted so they can't be forgotten or watered down. Contracts need to acknowledge the reality that behavior change rarely happens all at once, without relapses. Dealing with setbacks and with reversion to old behavior has to be part of the new contract between the team and its leaders, and between the teammates themselves.

In Summary

If the questions you've answered about the five courage factors tell you that candor needs to be improved, what steps can you take to create a different reality for your team?

1. Speak the truth as you know it. Like John, you can make a conscious decision to stand up and call it like you see it and to make the best contribution you can possibly make to the team.

2. Ask for feedback. Like Brian, you may need to seek information that you'd really rather not hear, information that comes from questions that go beyond "Are you okay with this?"

3. Dare to listen. Don't accept others' reluctance to speak up as an invitation to increase your participation. Solicit feedback actively, even if it means that you have to go looking for concerns and bad news. Keep quiet to allow others an opportunity to talk. Probe for details so that people feel heard and understood and so that you truly grasp the whole picture.

4. Shift the balance of power. Be humble. Show that you really, honestly, sincerely care about what others think, feel, and believe. Empathize. Muster the courage to make yourself vulnerable by keeping your eye on the prize and remembering that there's far more to success than your own image, ego, or power needs.

5. Make it safe for others to express their data, ideas, and perceptions. Don't "kill the messenger," overtly or subtly. Remember that shy, reluctant groups may be hypersensitive to ridicule or threats and may need encouragement to continue opening up. Be alert for cultural differences, particularly if you are asking teammates who have been treated as subordinates to participate as equals.

6. Solicit personal feedback. Find out what you, personally, are doing to inhibit candor and what you can do differently to create a new reality. Like Brian, you may need to be open to feedback that stings a bit and may need to empower someone to serve as your conscience or coach, lest you fall back into old habits.

7. Provide an opportunity for quieter and more deliberate team members to gather their thoughts before "going public." Design every meeting, phone conference, and exchange of e-mails so that everyone—not just the most outspoken or informed individuals—has an opportunity to participate and be heard. Send background information out ahead of time so people have time to gather their thoughts and so meeting time can be used for dialogue rather than a one-way presentation or lecture. List hopes, concerns, and questions as a framework for deliberation. Use questionnaires and other data-gathering mechanisms to make it safe for people to put the real issues on the table.

8. Provide feedback in a way that saves face. Provide feedback in private. Respect others' authority and dignity. Remember that everyone doesn't take candor the same way, particularly those from cultures with different norms about criticism, feedback, face saving, emotional expressiveness, and respect for authority.

9. Raise problems early. Deal with difficulties and differences before they become a crisis and while there is still time to turn lemons into lemonade. Build a mandate to deal with the real issues while there is still time to address them without a last-minute, embarrassing emergency.

10. Lighten up. Maintain a cheerful, upbeat tone—particularly when you are dealing with serious issues. It's easier to promote candor when people aren't walking on eggshells and weighing the consequences of their every word.

11. Seek help. A lack of candor is the most serious of conditions that contribute to a deficit of courage. If the team has become dysfunctional or if leaders are unwittingly inhibiting courage, you may need outside assistance and an opportunity to deal with the team's dynamics outside the business setting.

PURPOSE

The Courage to Pursue
Lofty and Audacious Goals

Never believe that a few caring people can't change the world.
For indeed, that's all who ever have.
MARGARET MEAD

Think about the last assignment you had when you felt a real sense of purpose. Did you take your responsibilities seriously, no matter how many jokes you told and how light your mood may have been? Did you wait for things to happen, or did you take the initiative to make things happen? When setbacks occurred, as they inevitably do, and others weren't working in alignment, did you settle for whatever meager support you could get, or did you persuade others to work together?

People with a strong sense of purpose look busy, engaged, and determined. They seek out and capitalize on opportunities. They're willing to persevere and to defer personal gratification to create a far bigger "win" later. Like key players in a competitive sport, they are keenly aware of what the score is, how much time is left, and what has to be done to win, even when their mood is lighthearted.

People with a sense of purpose are ambitious. Place a mountain in front of them and they'll look for a way to climb it. Given a choice, they prefer to do things that stretch them professionally and are artistically rewarding, and they eschew tasks that are tedious or routine. They want to feel that they are making progress, and they take pride in being at the top of their game.

When there is a sense of purpose, people feel connected to the organization's vision and understand how they, personally, contribute to bringing that vision to life. They are willing to hold themselves accountable for their own performance and the performance of the people they lead and influence, as well as for their impact on the performance of the enterprise. If everything doesn't turn out as they planned and hoped, they take steps to put things right and to learn from the experience.

Purpose gives people a psychological stake in the success of their team and the larger organization. Even if they are a continent away from the epicenter where the big decisions are made, people with purpose use words like "we" and "our" when talking about new strategies, acquisitions, and product launches. They beam with pride when they talk about the performance of the enterprise, its contributions to society, and its potential for the future.

Alienation at the Steel Mill

When Jerry came home from Vietnam, he considered himself to be one of the lucky ones. He married his high school sweetheart and took a job in the steel mill where his father and grandfather had worked. At the age of thirty-five, he turned down a promotion to shift supervisor, preferring to take on a bigger responsibility. His union brothers and sisters asked him to serve as their shop steward. Life couldn't get much better than this. He was still in love, still had his hunting cottage in the woods of central Pennsylvania, and had a position of leadership and respect.

Jerry had only a high school education, but he didn't need a Ph.D. to see that most of his co-workers didn't share his sense of purpose. They came to work, put in their time, went out hunting and fishing with the guys, and followed the Pirates, the Steelers, and Penn State football. Mostly, they got by. As long as they could make it from one payday to the next and do what they enjoyed doing, life was okay. Work was simply a way of putting bread on the table; it had little purpose or meaning other than that.

If you asked most of Jerry's union brothers and sisters, they'd tell you that they didn't really care whether the mill made a profit or not. That was management's job, and, as far as they could tell, the mill owners did pretty well at looking out for themselves. If the workers showed up on time, did as they were told, and stayed out of trouble, they figured that they were entitled to everything the union could get for them—cost-of-living raises, full benefits, and the occasional opportunity to work a double shift and earn overtime. If you asked them about customer satisfaction or product quality, they'd joke and change the subject. And if you asked about productivity, they'd get downright mad. Productivity meant the same work could be done by fewer people, which, in turn, meant that someone in the mill was going to be out of a job.

As shop steward, Jerry was invited to attend meetings with the mill owners and was invited to eat in the executive dining room. He could see that management was growing more impatient with the petty pranks, the malicious passive-aggressive obedience, and the lack of initiative that some of the union members exhibited. Given everything Jerry was hearing about foreign competition and bank loans, it was clear to him that labor and management couldn't continue to work at cross-purposes. Unless they got together, the business wasn't going to survive for another generation. When Jerry told some of the workers that they were playing a dangerous game, a game that could put all of their jobs in jeopardy, he was brushed off and accused of being a management stooge. Jerry could see that management also wasn't about to own any of the responsibility for a company culture that had alienated most of its workforce.

THE PROFESSOR

In the Sunday newspaper, Jerry read an article about a professor from Philadelphia who was working with other union locals and management teams in the area, helping them find a shared sense of purpose. He read that the professor had been to his steel mill, met with top management, and been sent packing because, management said, the union leadership had no interest in working with them to ensure the prosperity and continued viability of the business. Jerry had heard rumors that the owners might throw in the towel and sell the business, but this news report was the first clear warning of a closure that he'd ever seen. It got him scared and angry enough to do something. He picked up the phone and placed a long-distance call to Philadelphia.

A week later, the professor showed up at the union hall. Jerry made sure that everyone got the word about the special meeting. The turnout was good. Even the troublemakers came. If nothing else, they figured, an evening with the professor from Philadelphia would break the monotony, get them out of their household chores, and be good for some laughs over a few beers.

Over the phone, Jerry had pegged the professor as an ex-Marine. He didn't ask, but when the professor strode up to the podium, Jerry was sure of it. It had been twenty years since Vietnam, and Jerry could still spot a Marine from fifty yards. The professor didn't mince words. "Why on earth would someone want to bet his entire family fortune on this workforce?" he asked, throwing down the gauntlet to the crowd and pausing for an answer, lest they think his question was rhetorical. Jerry smiled. He knew the difference between hotshot Marines who indulged their own egos at the expense of others and those who showed they cared by being blunt and provocative. The professor, he decided, was one of the good guys. His challenge would be tough for some of the rabid antimanagement brothers and sisters to hear, but breaking the cycle of alienation and entitlement was mission critical to secure everyone's future.

"I don't need another project," the professor said, "so if you're not willing to create a new sense of purpose with me and with management, the challenge ends right here and now." The professor asked for a yes-or-no vote and made it clear that he'd say goodnight and never come back if fewer than two-thirds of the union members voted yes. By this time, the professor had worked the crowd masterfully. Despite past indignities and despite the prevailing mood of alienation and cynicism, more than 80 percent of the union members voted to give his experiment a try.

A FLASH OF INSIGHT

When they left the union hall that night, the workers still lacked a sense of shared intention. The cycle of us-versus-them, or entitlement-versus-accountability, was far from being broken. Employees still didn't believe they had the power to persuade management to keep the plant open if the mill owners could find an easy way out. But they'd taken a step to take hold of their futures and create a new sense of purpose. For the first time that any of them could remember, they saw themselves on the same side as the mill owners, against a common competitor, rather than fighting an internal civil war.

Six months after the union hall meeting, Jerry joined the professor on the podium at a national convention of union leaders. Their work wasn't over, but it was clear that they'd turned the corner. When they spoke to other union leaders, they talked about the shared sense of direction they were seeing in the steel mill. You may not be a mill owner or a steelworker. You may be in a different enterprise altogether; you may be a knowledge worker with a Ph.D. Even if you're a lab scientist, an engineer, a sales representative, or a health-care professional, you can apply the lessons learned at the steel mill in Pennsylvania to create a common purpose that will align different parts of your enterprise.

FINDING COMMON GROUND

When you're blinded by alienation and bitterness, it's easy to believe that getting the upper hand over "the other side" is an expression of strength. It's easy to measure your success in terms of narrow, petty victories. When you have a history of working at cross-purposes with other groups whom you don't like and don't understand, it's easy to forget that you're in a lifeboat together and to focus instead on your own parochial objectives. It's easy to forget that there's a significant difference between throwing down the gauntlet to get people's attention (as the professor did in the union hall) and drilling holes in the other side of the lifeboat.

In the steel mill, it wasn't hard to see that management and labor had similar interests and goals. They shared a common destiny. The owners would be better off with a thriving business than they would if they were forced to sell the company, and labor would be better off if the union members were gainfully employed rather than living on the dole or moving away to find new jobs. Without productivity gains and modernization, the company couldn't keep pace with domestic, let alone overseas, competitors. Without loyal, steady customers, nothing else would matter. These weren't "management issues." Resolutions were essential to keeping the lifeboat afloat.

So how do you find common ground? And how do you get others to see it when they are stuck in their narrow perspectives?

- **Step back and look at the big picture**. When you're looking for common ground, it isn't that hard to find. Jerry was smart, but he wasn't brighter than everyone else. He was just asking different questions. That's why he understood the common purpose long before he read about the professor from Philadelphia. And it's why he saw the writing on the wall long before his union brothers and sisters were alarmed at the prospect of the mill closing. Jerry wasn't an owner. He didn't have a college education, let alone an MBA. But he dared to take a broader view than the us-versus-them, who-wins-at-whose-expense view and to ask questions such as "Who are we really competing against?" and "What will it take to keep our lifeboat afloat?"

- **State what should be obvious.** When the professor stood at the front of the hall and dared to ask people if they would be better off with the mill open or closed, thriving or struggling, the union members gasped. It wasn't a tough question. But it was a reality that most of the union members had overlooked or believed they were powerless to influence. When he asked top management if they would be better off with labor cooperating rather than working to "cut them down to size," the right answer again was obvious. If you get the big picture before anyone else does, get others to step back and take a look. Make sure they understand what's really at stake and what "winning" really means.

- **Keep score.** In the low-courage steel mill, only a small, elite group had the scorecard. As long as the union rank and file—including people in positions of leadership, like Jerry—saw new Lincoln Town Cars in the executive parking lot and heard about golf trips to the Caribbean, they assumed that the business was thriving. The picture looked different when they focused on enterprise-wide goals such as profitability, product quality, customer loyalty, productivity, and equity. Management gulped at the recommendation that figures be shared with everyone. How could they be sure that the knowledge of business results wouldn't be used against them when the labor contract came up for renegotiation? They couldn't. Keeping score wasn't just about the dissemination of information; it also was an act of faith and a show of trust—even before they knew that the trust had been earned.

- **Go on a campaign.** In the world of the NCAA basketball championship, everyone knows what it means to have your team advance to the Final Four. Aspiring to that level of success is a daring and lofty goal for any team at the start of the season. In the steel mill, the four mission-critical performance measures came to be called "The Final Four." Getting into the Final Four became a rallying cry for everyone at every level in the company—whether they worked in a office job, in a production job, as management, or as a representative out in the field. Leadership guru John Kotter (1996)warns managers about the danger of undercommunicating the vision, of saying it once and assuming that people get it and don't need to be reminded. There was no danger of that happening in the steel mill. Wherever people went, the Final Four were present. They were written on banners in the lunch hall, on T-shirts and hats, and on the cups that came out of the vending machines. They were mentioned at meetings, whether monthly meetings to present the state of the company or weekly safety meetings, and were stated on a daily memo posted by the time clocks. Management and employees alike talked up the Final Four, lest anyone forget what "winning the game" required.

THINKING LIKE AN OWNER

The workers at the mill believed that if they chose to do so, they could easily ramp up and be at the top of their game. The attitude was: "I'd challenge anyone anywhere to operate this equipment better than we can and get out a better-quality product." Management agreed. In fact, the owners said that was the primary reason they had decided to keep the business where it was, despite the adversarial, even hostile, climate that sometimes had them fearing for the safety of their spouses, children, and pets. The owners knew that they could sell almost anything and, as long as it was made out of steel, the engineers and workers in the plant could figure out how to deliver the goods.

Being technically skilled is a valuable asset, but it doesn't guarantee commercial success. It doesn't even guarantee that the business will stay afloat. The mill workers and engineers understood how to turn out state-of-the-art products and get the best possible output from their machinery, but they knew little about the business of business. And they knew even less about the art of attracting and appeasing skittish investors, bankers, customers, and strategic partners.

Precision steel isn't the only business in which there is more than one component to success. One part resides in the realm of craft and the other in the realm of finance. In the world of craft, according to management expert Art Kleiner (2000), you're on top of your game if you can operate the most sophisticated, state-of-the-art equipment competently, if you learn and improvise quickly, if your safety and quality records are stellar, and if, in the end, you deliver the goods. In the world of hype, success is defined by the deals you cut and the capital you raise. It's defined by telling a story that's compelling enough to keep your customers, investors, bankers, and strategic partners at your side and your coffers full, even before you deliver the goods.

Do Whatever It Takes

Thinking like an owner doesn't mean that you can do the jobs you like and trivialize those you dislike. Like many technical professionals, the steelworkers and engineers at the mill believed that they did the more important and skilled jobs, and they looked at the office workers as a group of overstuffed and overpaid bureaucrats. They resented the turn-on-a-dime requests, interruptions, and tighter than reasonable deadlines that management imposed. "Don't expect us to ask 'How high?' when you tell us to jump!" one of the union engineers told the managers in a weekend workshop conducted by the professor to air conflicts and find a productive way for labor and management to work together. "Deadlines might look arbitrary, and sample orders might seem like they're more trouble than they are worth," one of the senior managers explained, "but without them, it's hard for us to convince anyone that we're credible enough to deserve financing or advance payments. When we request something from you, it isn't because we believe you have time on your hands and aren't working hard already. It's because we need it to convince a reluctant customer, broker, partner, or investor about our capabilities—and about your skills."

Focus on the Market

"You expect us to act like responsible and informed adults," Jerry said when it was his group's turn to report on what would make it possible for the workers to think and act like owners. "But you treat us like stepchildren who can't be trusted with any information about the state of the business or our standing in the marketplace. If you want us to act like partners, then treat us like partners!" The most profound change that came out of the weekend workshop was a commitment to ease into open-book management. Fortunately, the chief financial officer of the steel mill had long been an advocate of opening the books to the workers and had studied the practice, hoping he would someday get the green light to bring it to this company. For management, the lesson is clear: Share the information. You can't keep partners and investors in the dark about the health of the business and about competitive realities in the marketplace. The lesson for the inner circle is just as clear: Be as responsible as any other owner or lien holder would be with proprietary information. If you use the information against those who share it voluntarily, don't be surprised when they shut you out and say "No" without feeling that they owe you a second thought or a reasonable explanation.

Promote Business Literacy

Don't expect workers to think and act like owners if they can't make sense of the financial picture and don't see a connection between their daily activities and the success of the enterprise. That's particularly true if you're going to defer expenses or investments that people have been counting on. If workers can't see how they're going to profit in the long run, you can't expect them to hang in for long-term gains rather than insist on immediate gratification. "You don't talk straight," one of the workers blurted out in the midst of a particularly tense conversation about where the money was going. The CFO meant well. He wasn't holding anything back when he presented the whole financial picture. But he might as well have been speaking in Dutch. Even though he had studied open-book management and had read numerous books on treating workers like partners, he fell into the same trap that most overly enthusiastic executives fall into. He overestimated the financial acumen and sophistication of the workforce and underestimated what they would need to be able to make sense of the figures and reach the same business decisions that management had reached.

Share the Pie

In normal times, the new gain-sharing plan would have given a real windfall to the workers in the mill. Gain sharing was the only way management could offer the pay increases that the union demanded, and it was the only way that labor leaders like Jerry could sell cross-training, robotics, and increased machine speeds to his constituents. On paper, it looked great. The workers agreed to learn the new production methods and agreed to work in teams, rather than according to strict job classifications. Management agreed to split the productivity gains with the pros who were making it happen.

Then the second tier of performance measures kicked in. The bar was raised, and in the fourth month of the program, the plant didn't make the expected numbers and the bonus wasn't paid. A significant number of workers demanded that management pay up, despite the gloomy performance data. "It isn't our fault that you didn't make your numbers," one of the more outspoken workers shrieked during a month-end financial review meeting. When the CFO said, "It isn't our fault either," he was greeted with boos and catcalls. It was an explosive situation that threatened to undo all the good work they'd done with the professor over the past six months.

The real heroes were the workers who understood the meaning of contingent compensation and pleaded with their colleagues to try harder and to shoot for a bonus payment during the next quarter. If leaders like Jerry and a handful of others hadn't been willing to stay the course, instead of reverting to us-versus-them performance measurement and reward systems, and risk being called a "management stooge," it's hard to believe the sense of purpose would have endured.

Maintaining the Vision

As we travel through Israel, it's hard to believe it is the same country that was so hopeful and electric after the famous handshake (between Arafat and Rabin in 1993) on the White House lawn. Now people grimace before turning on the television or picking up a newspaper. The streets are deserted, the restaurants and movie theaters empty. No one talks about coming to visit. Every car bomb brings a fresh wave of grief and outrage, chips away at the rhythm of life, and puts another burden on the back of an already precarious national economy.

Banners hang from bridges and overpasses on the main highway from Tel Aviv to Haifa. They say, simply, "We continue to live the dream." What is "the dream"? To Israelis, the reference is clear. In the 1800s, when Jews took control of their destiny and escaped the persecution in Eastern Europe and Northern Africa to reclaim and rebuild their historical homeland, the Zionist slogan proclaimed, "If you have the desire, rebuilding this homeland doesn't have to be a dream." That was the call to action—from prayer to purpose, and from legend to activism, fund-raising to buy back the country dunam by dunam, and hiring boats to bring the refugees home. The national anthem of Israel refers to a dream come true and to hopes that are being realized after 1800 years of living in exile, subject to wave after wave of persecution and slaughter.

Yes, the dream endures. But so do the hardships. Ask anyone. If there's one thing that most Israelis can agree on, it's the fact that Zion isn't an easy place to live. There are the constant security alerts, the military roadblocks, and the middle-of-the-night call to report for military reserve duty. Then there's the pushing and shoving, the coarse talk, and the driving that makes Rome look timid and lethargic. Add to that the "buyer beware" business ethics, the low wages and high prices, the outrageous tax rates, and the currency that responds to every act of terror with a 5 to 10 percent devaluation.

THE REFUGEE

Uzekiel works hard and follows the rules but has very little to show for it after twenty years of "living the dream." In Tehran, he was the son of a wealthy business owner, and his family was a pillar of the community. In Tel Aviv, he drives a taxi and doesn't see how he'll ever pay off the overdraft on his bank account. He scoffs at the mention of anti-Semitism in Iran and dismisses Israel as a safe haven for Jews with a wave of his hand. "In Tehran," he says, "we were totally insulated from the rabble in the streets. When I compare my life with that of my cousins and nephews who stayed in Iran, I can't believe how much we gave up to live the Zionist dream." He shakes his head when he talks about the price of freedom and wonders whether it's worth it.

It's one thing to find a sense of purpose when you are gainfully employed in a Pennsylvania steel mill and have a newfound opportunity to share in the prosperity of a flourishing enterprise. But how do you maintain a sense of purpose when times are tough? How do you keep "the dream" in mind when so many of the people you respect and admire are also asking whether it's worth the price? How do you maintain your resolve when you can reassess your options and flee for higher ground?

THE CHALLENGE OF THE DREAM

On one level, the challenges facing Israeli citizens are very different from the pressures facing American workers in a corporation that's struggling to turn things around after a serious business downturn. After all, even in the most challenging of business settings, most American workers aren't putting their college-age children in mortal danger. And even after the terrorist attacks of 9/11, most Americans don't feel their country is being shaken to its roots or that its very existence is in jeopardy.

At the same time, the parallels are worth noting. Whenever "living the dream" is risky or difficult, unless individuals see the purpose of sticking it out, those with viable choices will weigh their options. Some will bail out. If maintaining a sense of purpose requires you to take a significant financial risk or to sacrifice the quality of your life in the short term, you have to know that it's for more than just a job. You have to find a way to turn everyday challenges into a higher calling and to create compelling reasons to continue on, despite the challenges, the workload, and the risks. What do you say to the Uzekiels on your team when they see how green the grass is on the other side of the fence? What answers do you give yourself when you are having Uzekiel's doubts?

Talk Up the Vision

On one level, banners, flags, T-shirts, and "feel-good" public interest articles do little to change the realities on the ground. A catchy and clever slogan isn't enough to persuade an embittered cynic. But banners can get people talking, and talking can be persuasive. By the time we arrived at our destination and got out of Uzekiel's taxi, he told us that we'd touched him and had shaken him out of his despair. We hadn't done much, but it had been a long time since he'd met someone who was still passionate about the dream and could articulate it clearly.

In corporate lunchrooms and meeting rooms, it's easy to see when people have lost sight of the vision and are going through the motions rather than focusing on the turnaround or how they can contribute to the organization's mission. You can say nothing and take the taxi ride in silence, or you can raise your voice and reaffirm your commitment, restate your purpose, and rekindle the light in the tower. When the going gets tough, people need to be reminded what the long hours, the nights away from home, and the hours of painful deliberation are for. Otherwise they will focus only on the hardships and the possibility of finding "the good life" somewhere else.

Focus on the Future

"Let's assume we can get through the current hardships and come out on the other side. What's there?" Unless you can answer that question in a compelling and attractive way, you won't convince those with options to stay in the game. For Michael, unlike Uzekiel, the future looks bright. He too came to Israel as an immigrant. Every time Michael hears his young daughters speaking Hebrew and sees the sunset from his hilltop home in the Galilee, his heart swells with contentment.

Andy is a junior executive in a biotech company who's as uncertain as Uzekiel about whether he should stay the course or move on. His gruff manner and glib sense of humor have offended some of his co-workers, and, as a result, he's being denied a much-coveted promotion. He has some hard work to do to mend fences and to prove that he's worthy of being back on the fast track. Unless Andy can see the prospects of a future promotion, and can see that the tough work of making amends and controlling his quick tongue will eventually pay off, being passed up for promotion will make him a "flight risk" to the company. Management wants Andy to do the tough work that's required to be promotion ready. So do the very same co-workers who don't yet want to see him promoted. They value his scientific contributions and need him to keep performing at the top of his game. The leading cause of defections in scientific companies like Andy's isn't poor compensation or working conditions. It's uncertain future prospects. When people don't see a promising future, they start to look elsewhere for opportunities that beckon.

Make Heroes of Those Who Do the Job

When people are gripped by posttraumatic stress syndrome, even the most mundane acts of daily life require effort. Real heroes don't need a lot of fawning or adulation, but they do need respect, and they feel good when they're given a pat on the back. Is Uzekiel a hero because he continues to drive his taxi through Tel Aviv? Is Andy a hero if he persists at his job and mends fences with his co-workers? Are you a hero when you choose to do what needs to be done instead of choosing a way out or around? We suggest that the answer is yes and that you deserve a toast when you've endured under fire and have accomplished even the simplest missions that tested your mettle and were the right and honorable thing to do. If you know that others are relying on you and that they appreciate your contributions—no matter how modest they may be—you'll be more likely to stay the course and to challenge yourself to be at the top of your game than you will if you feel that your persistence doesn't make a difference. Recognition doesn't require an award or public accolades. It does require someone noticing and saying thanks.

Taking Personal Responsibility

If anything positive has come out of the Enron collapse, it is that we are redefining professional responsibility and personal accountability; what's right isn't always what's politically expedient. We'll never know whether the collapse could have been prevented if someone close to the top had stood up sooner and said, "We can't go on like this, or we will sow the seeds of our own destruction." If truth tellers at Enron had been more adamant and more vocal, earlier on, what would have happened? Presumably, they would have been pushed aside, silenced, or fired, even if they had the best interests of the shareholders and the enterprise at heart. But we'll never actually know.

SPEAKING UP

When we first met Bruce, the battle lines were already drawn. He was on one side of the standoff, like the marshall in an old western movie, looking out at an angry mob with a rifle in his hand, knowing he was outnumbered but had justice and the law on his side. Bruce wasn't an imposing figure. He was shy, slightly overweight, soft-spoken, and beginning to bald, and he wore think eyeglasses that slid down his nose. He was a physician by training, but he had found that a career in biotech research was better suited to his temperament than clinical practice was.

The leader of the angry mob was far more eloquent and strong willed than Bruce. She was the project director and had devoted half her career to the diagnostic regimen that Bruce was supposed to take into the clinic and test with cancer patients. She was trusted by the Ph.D. chemists and engineers, some of whom had devoted their entire careers to proving the efficacy and safety of the diagnostic tests with laboratory and animal studies. The preclinical project team had put together a compelling dossier and received fast-track approval from the FDA to begin clinical testing with human patients. If the program worked, the new technology could save thousands, perhaps millions, of lives and could save countless women from needless exploratory surgery.

When Bruce expressed his concerns about the safety of the new product, the project director and her colleagues dismissed him as another naysayer, out to protect the vested interests of the medical establishment. The project team leader became impatient with Bruce's plodding manner. It was a vicious circle. As she pushed harder, he became more stoic, more cautious, and less communicative. After enduring months of questions and concerns while pushing for an aggressive patient enrollment in clinical tests, the project leader decided to get a second opinion. She hired her own clinical research expert, who wrote protocols that would enroll far more patients than Bruce's would. Bruce refused to sign off on the liberal protocols. And that brought the conflict to a head.

The project team leader demanded Bruce's immediate dismissal for putting the future of the project at risk and raising safety concerns that had never been raised by the FDA. She lobbied for support right up to the CEO's office, presented a compelling case, and put together an impressive list of allies, including company officials, medical authorities, and patient advocates. Bruce stood alone on the other side of the issue, red faced, defensive, and righteously indignant.

THE LONG VIEW

What gave Bruce the courage to take a tough stand? He wasn't a daredevil. He didn't have a huge ego. Bruce didn't know whether the CEO would side with him if it came to a showdown against the project director and the lynch mob she'd put together. He wasn't independently wealthy, and he didn't have another job offer in his hip pocket. But he did have these perspectives:

- **Promote enterprise success over project success.** Sure, Bruce argued, you could set safety concerns aside and push the project forward with a devil-may-care attitude. You could side with the chemists and animal researchers who argued that no dramatic medical breakthrough is totally without risk. And you might even win FDA approval. But, Bruce claimed, there were basic questions that the project director and her followers weren't asking. What would it do to the long-term health of the enterprise if safety concerns that were overlooked later came to light? Could the company defend itself if

Bruce were asked whether he could have foreseen concerns that the project team chose to overlook? Could Bruce himself avoid personal liability for such an oversight? Did it make sense to invest millions of dollars in an aggressive clinical research program to prove that the diagnostic procedure worked, if safety issues would make it too risky for clinicians to adopt the procedure? Courage, Bruce claimed, isn't about short-term gains and this quarter's stock price. It's about preserving the integrity of the franchise and doing what's ethically right, rather than compromising your reputation with the FDA or the physicians and health insurance consultants who want to know whether they can trust the conclusions you present.

- **Decide what you stand for.** The Hippocratic oath gives physicians like Bruce a clear definition of what their job is about and what choices they are expected to make. Bruce knew that it wasn't his job to be popular. Instead, he believed, it was his job to be a professional physician and ask the same tough questions that any clinician would ask before recommending a new diagnostic and treatment regimen. Bruce didn't like being shunned in the dining room and joked about in meetings. But he knew that other physicians would respect his judgment. That professional respect, Bruce decided, would sustain him if the company decided to let him go in order to push the project forward without addressing the safety issues that he found so compelling. Most of us don't have a canon of professional ethics that's as sacrosanct as the Hippocratic oath, which makes it tougher for us to decide what to do when our judgment and ethics contradict the group consensus or the company's policy. In an era when very few people can count on employment for life, it's easy to accept the group consensus, follow the path of least resistance, and not put our jobs in jeopardy. It's easy to rationalize costly mistakes when we are just following orders. "If you don't stand for something," a popular anti-drug slogan says, "you'll fall for anything." So, like Bruce, you may have to decide what you really stand for and trust that another employer will respect you for that, even if your current one doesn't.

- **Accept personal accountability.** Bruce explained why he wasn't afraid of the CEO's ruling when it came down to his word against the outside medical expert that the project director had enlisted. "If I were in the CEO's role," Bruce explained, "I'd want to know that I could trust my key people to hold themselves accountable for more than project time lines, personal glory, and incentive bonuses. I'd want to know that they put enterprise success ahead of all that." Even with the most careful planning and innovative design, most reward systems can be outsmarted. Most managers have to choose how far they'll go to hit their own numbers and maximize their bonuses, when doing so can jeopardize the long-term health of the enterprise. Just because you're told that you're empowered to make particular choices doesn't mean that you won't have to defend your judgment—or ask for special dispensation if you sacrifice your own performance statistics to help the enterprise achieve a bigger win. Bruce saw the connection between his own professional objectives and enterprise success. He saw how the long-term interests of the enterprise would also be served if he did his job and held himself accountable for the highest of professional ethics. He believed that the CEO had to see the same connection and had to respect him for accepting personal accountability for the reputation of the company with the FDA, the medical establishment, and the health insurance community. If the CEO couldn't see that, Bruce reasoned, the company was as doomed as a sinking ship, and he'd better start looking for a lifeboat rather than try to secure a posh stateroom.

Raising the Bar

"You don't understand the business," Bob Harris was told when he started asking veteran managers some tough questions about productivity in their respective operations. "We can explain how things work and why your benchmarks aren't valid."

REVIEWING THE FACTS

Bob was convinced that the division wasn't performing adequately, even though people were working hard and putting in long hours. As he drilled down and asked questions, more and more of the performance data gave him cause for concern. In other divisions, it took twelve weeks to get a new engineer up to speed; in this division, it took twenty weeks. Other divisions could write up the technical specs on a new product within six weeks; this division required forty weeks. On the average, it cost this division $64,750 in custom-design expense to accomplish what other divisions could achieve with $17,200. The division was spending $2.2 million more on outside contractors for beta testing than other divisions who were doing the same work. What's worse, whenever Bob presented the data, the management team always responded that his comparisons weren't valid and that they were already doing their very best.

Bob was brought in to breathe new life into the underperforming division. He was promoted to division vice president from a different line of business. The executive committee expected him to turn things around and knew that he'd have to shake things up to do it. The committee was out of patience and fed up with excuses. They wanted results—now.

A TIGHTROPE

Bob couldn't afford to alienate his veteran managers, who knew far more about the technical realities of the business than he would ever know and had deeper relationships with the customers and strategic partners than he might ever develop. But neither could he accept their definitions of what was and wasn't reasonable. The managers had to believe what the entire executive committee believed—that a higher standard of performance was possible and that achieving it was everyone's fiduciary responsibility.

Every meeting repeated the same tense and difficult discussion. Bob presented performance comparisons, and the managers justified their present results. The managers expected Bob to "educate" members of the executive committee—to explain why they should be satisfied with the performance they were getting out of the division. "For every case you bring that shows someone performing better," one of the managers said, "we can bring you three or four that are performing worse than we are." It was clear to Bob that these debates weren't getting anywhere and were only strengthening the team's resolve to justify less-than-acceptable performance. It was a vicious circle that had to be broken.

Choose a Starting Point

Bob could see that focusing on top-line or bottom-line performance was too broad a starting point. To break the deadlock, he had to start somewhere—with a concrete performance improvement. If he simply imposed a ceiling on outside contractor expenses or a 20 percent cut in staff, he'd give the management team a new justification for poor performance. Instead, he issued a challenge: Without spending any more money, you have to get your specifications issued within six weeks after the testing is completed, just as other divisions do. Some of the more adamant managers gasped. Bob insisted that failure was not an option. He gave the group one month to come up with a list of changes that would enable them to achieve the six-week standard and announced an off-site retreat, which was convened to hammer out an improvement plan.

Make the Goal SMART

The acronym SMART stands for what goals should be: specific, measurable, aggressive yet achievable, rational and relevant to the success of the enterprise, and time bound. The challenge that Bob issued could be stated in a way that satisfied all of these criteria: Within one month, submit a plan that will reduce the time required to issue new specifications from forty weeks to the industry standard of six weeks (i.e., a 667 percent acceleration) and that can be implemented within the next four months. This gave the team a focus for improvement and drew a line in the sand that was clearer than the statement "Work hard and do the best you can."

Assume the Benchmarks Are Valid

"I know that we're asking for a real leap of faith," Bob said to his dumbfounded managers, "but I'm going to ask you to start with a fresh assumption. Let's assume that the benchmarks are valid. Assume that you could do what other divisions and other companies like ours already do. What would have to change about the way we do things here, about the way we manage our customers and development partners, about our systems and procedures?" Some people call this approach "starting with the end in mind." It's the kind of problem solving that enabled NASA to send humans to the moon. Assume that every constraint can be managed and orchestrated. Assume that it all works out according to plan. What would it take to make it happen?

Don't Let Failure Be an Option

Of course, when Bob walked out of the room, the managers first turned their attention to how unreasonable and unsympathetic he was. A few of them came to him privately, lobbying him to back down on his challenge and make the goals more "reasonable." It was clear, however, that Bob wasn't going to back down. He refused to hear reasons why the goal couldn't be achieved. He acknowledged that 667 percent was an aggressive improvement. He acknowledged that "working harder" or "putting in longer hours" wasn't the answer. But, he said, there is a lot of wheel spinning and wasted effort that we simply have to streamline.

In Summary

. . . .

If the questions you've answered about the five courage factors tell you that purpose needs to be improved, what steps can you take to create a different reality for your team?

1. Step back and look at the big picture. If everyone could win, what could be accomplished if different constituents worked together instead of at cross-purposes or instead of defending their parochial interests?

2. State what should be obvious. Don't assume that people already see the big picture and are focused on it. Restate your mission and a vision of what success should look like in terms that all the stakeholders you want to enlist will understand and resonate with.

3. Keep score. If you aren't measuring and posting the factors that really matter, different constituencies will develop their own narrow performance metrics. If there are a few metrics that everyone should be pulling together to achieve, make sure those are well understood and posted conspicuously.

4. Go on a campaign. Make sure the score is not only posted but also announced. Create excitement and interest. Ask about it. Talk it up, lest anyone get distracted and forget what "winning the game" requires.

5. Do whatever it takes. Ask what you can do to contribute to the results, even if those aren't the things that you most want to do or that are the most comfortable and stress-free routines. If you get a request that seems irrelevant, ask how it contributes to the result that everyone should be pulling together to achieve.

6. Focus on the market. Make sure people understand the market and competitive realities, particularly if you are asking for a standard of performance that seems overly aggressive. Provide information so people understand where the business stands in comparison to competitors or valid benchmarks.

7. Promote business literacy. If you are on the creative side of the organization, learn what drives the business. If you are on the business side, understand the technology and help the artists understand what drives the commercial success of the enterprise, as well as what will fuel new investments and new funding. And fix times to review performance metrics so your teammates know where they stand.

8. Share the pie. If you are asking people to give extra effort or creativity or to take a broader perspective to make improvements, be willing to share the wealth.

9. Talk up the vision. Don't just talk up the score. Talk up the vision. Remind stakeholders what "the dream" means and why they are part of a worthwhile endeavor, particularly if they are doing tough or dangerous duty.

10. Focus on the future. If you are asking stakeholders to be patient, delay gratification, and "hang in there," show them the benefits—for them personally, as well as for the enterprise and the community.

11. Make heroes of those who do the job. No contribution is trivial. A chain is only as strong as its weakest link. Inspire pride and striving for your personal best. Make sure that everyone who makes a contribution feels like he or she is valued and part of the celebration when victory finally occurs.

12. Promote enterprise success over project success. It's easy to get wrapped up in the pursuits you are closest to, especially if they are your artistic and professional passion. Look instead at what they are supposed to contribute to the enterprise as a whole.

13. Decide what you stand for. Have a code of honor as a professional and lines that you aren't willing to cross. Understand how your personal code of honor and professionalism contribute to the long-term success of the enterprise, and be able to articulate those contributions before you are put on the defensive.

14. Accept personal accountability. Don't make long-term enterprise success someone else's job. Hold yourself accountable not just for your own objectives but also for understanding how your objectives make the entire enterprise successful.

15. Choose a starting point. Enterprise-wide performance improvement may be too big to tackle all at once or from where you sit in the enterprise. Choose the starting point that will advance things furthest and that you can control.

16. Make the goal SMART. Make goals specific, measurable, aggressive yet achievable, rational and relevant, and time bound. Frame your objectives in this way.

17. Assume the benchmarks are valid. Ask, "What can be done to reach parity or set a new benchmark?" rather than justify why you should be exempt or a special case. Calibrate your performance against that of industry leaders, lest you give yourself a false sense of security. Ask what can be done to make progress, rather than why making progress is unreasonable or impossible.

18. Don't let failure be an option. If the purpose is compelling and mission critical, be unreasonable. Don't empathize in a way that lets people off the hook and compromises the results that have to be achieved.

WILL

·····································

The Courage to Inspire
Optimism, Spirit, and Promise

Pessimists (who lack courage) are more in touch with reality than optimists (who have courage). Optimists have a healthy defense against reality, which enables them to create new possibilities that don't already exist.
MARTIN SELIGMAN

If you have passion, energy, and enthusiasm, adversity feels like an adventure, an opportunity to test your mettle and experiment with new possibilities. Challenges are fun. A tough assignment gets your adrenaline flowing and makes you feel alive. It reminds you how good you really are.

Sure, there is a chance of failure, but that's not what preoccupies you. It's the prospect of success that propels you forward and lifts your spirits. "Hit me with your best stuff" is what your body language conveys to partners and colleagues. "I'm ready, willing, and able to handle whatever I encounter, with perseverance, determination, and optimism."

Going Through the Motions

Most of us also know what it's like to go to work without optimism, spirit, and promise; to go through the motions; and to feel that the wind has been taken out of our sails. As Sara sat waiting for the line of traffic to start moving so she could make the turn into the parking lot, she sighed. She could remember a time, not so long ago, when she actually couldn't wait to get to the office. It wasn't clear when, exactly, the job stopped being fun and started to be a grueling routine, but the change was undeniable.

Sara never actually talked about her change of heart with any of her colleagues. Nonetheless, she could tell that she wasn't the only scientist who wasn't having fun anymore. Recent project team meetings had a different flavor. There was less banter and less laughter. There were fewer congratulatory comments and more willingness to settle for what was easy or convenient rather than to strive for what would jump the technical hurdles and achieve a breakthrough. People talked more about what they couldn't do or shouldn't be expected to do than about what else they could try. There was tension and palpable frustration.

It couldn't be the technical challenges. After all, Sara had thrived on tough technical problems in every job she'd ever held. She knew what it was to work long hours, to live and breathe a project, to stay online exchanging e-mails and searching Web sites until she found the right resource material or the right people with the right expertise. When she had first joined this team of scientists, she could tell that everyone on the team worked just as long and hard as she did and was just as excited about being part of this new enterprise. There was a buzz in the conference rooms and the cafeteria. Now she wondered whether she could count on anyone. Her self-confidence was waning and so was her confidence in the rest of the team.

Though she put up a brave front, and though she could justify all the work she'd done, Sara often felt she was in over her head. Lately, she wondered if she'd lost her touch or if she wasn't really as good as she had thought she was. One day last week, she even found herself on the verge of tears.

In previous jobs, Sara hadn't needed a guarantee of success to jump through hoops and do whatever it took. She understood that scientific breakthroughs don't always happen, no matter how hard you work and how clever you are. But the ever-present risks never stopped her from giving a project her all or being optimistic about the possibilities. She used to welcome a healthy, vigorous exchange of ideas and perspectives, which never made her lose her sense of humor or her scientific perspective. Now she cringed and wanted to hide when a tough question was raised or when an experiment didn't work out as she'd hoped it would.

HOW COULD THIS HAPPEN?

This was one of the hottest biotech companies in Europe. The company's stock was a runaway success, even though the company was still two to three years away from having an approved, saleable product in the marketplace. From the press releases and annual report, you'd never know the lead projects were facing technical hurdles. Success looked like a sure thing. Yes, there had been a couple of delays. But a few setbacks didn't change the fact that the project teams were working full speed ahead, and it didn't change the high hopes that the research partners and investors still had.

On paper, leaving academia and joining this company was the best move Sara ever made. Her stock options made her a very wealthy woman, as long as she hung in and the bubble didn't burst. She sometimes thought about moving on, but she dismissed that option quickly when she did the math. If she left now, she'd have something to tide her over until she landed another position, but she would have little real wealth to show for all her hard work and sacrifices. She wasn't happy staying, but throwing in the towel prematurely seemed to be the worst of her alternatives.

THE CTO'S FURY

When Peter, the chief technology officer, received our assessment about the scientists' low level of will, he was furious. "After all we've done for them," Peter declared, clearly outraged, "how can they turn around and say this is how they feel about working here!? These scientists and engineers were nothings when we found them," he shouted. "Now, thanks to us, they're millionaires!" He stood up, threw our survey reports across the room onto the coffee table, and paced like a caged lion looking for prey to pounce on. We'd been warned about his temper; a few of our survey respondents had commented on Peter's impatience and his angry outbursts accusing the scientists of laziness and of a plodding, overly methodical work pace. Now we were seeing one of his tirades firsthand.

Peter asked us to rerun the survey results and conduct interviews with every member of the group who reported a low level of will. If we didn't find a mistake in our statistics, Peter demanded to know who felt disenfranchised and why. He suspected a few key malcontents (like Sara) of stirring up trouble, and he wanted us to help him identify the culprits so he could read them the riot act and remind them about all they had to be thankful and grateful about. "If I can't get a fire lit under them," he said, "no one here is irreplaceable."

The fact is, of course, that Peter's outrage and fury didn't help to improve the situation. The more he gave voice to his frustration and disappointment, the less Sara and her colleagues felt confident, valued, and appreciated. Feeling that she could be replaced at any minute, on the slightest whim, for problems she hadn't created and had done her very best to resolve, didn't light a fire under Sara. It made her angry and resentful, discouraged and despondent. Every angry e-mail, every mind-numbing project review meeting, and every pep talk elicited a flurry of righteous and cynical indignation, followed by a noticeable drop in the team's energy level.

At the last project review meeting, the team presented a fresh approach to overcoming the technical problems. Sara was proud of the work they'd done. Peter saw it differently. "Why couldn't you have thought of this months ago?" he asked, exasperated. The team was stunned and didn't know if the question was rhetorical or if he actually expected an answer. When they didn't answer, Peter pressed on. He demanded to know how the team was going to make up the lost time and whether they'd considered asking a few of the people in the review meeting to cancel their family vacations. "If this is how hard work and initiative get rewarded," one of the engineers told Sara, "I'm done with giving this job 110 percent." Sara sighed and knew she'd have to work hard to undo the damage that Peter's critical outburst had done.

Appreciative Inquiry

Most people in Peter's position approach performance improvement by looking for the factors that inhibit or slow the progress of the team so that they can focus on and fix the problems. They set out to improve employee morale by finding out what makes workers unhappy or frustrated so they know where to focus their attention. Or they look for the people who are causing problems and single them out for remedial attention. A chain, we've been told, is only as strong as its weakest link; identify, then strengthen or cut out, the weakest links, and the chain will be sturdier. In part, this also is how we've suggested that you use the results of the Courage Index: by identifying which of the five courage factors most urgently need remedial attention, you can fix the problems that inhibit courage in your team.

But the logic of this approach to performance improvement has a flaw. Watch a group articulate the things that bother or frustrate them, and see what happens to their energy and optimism, their enthusiasm, and their will to persevere. Invariably, it wanes. In contrast, watch what happens to the energy of a team that talks about their hopes and aspirations, their accomplishments and successes, their strengths and passions. Their passion and enthusiasm rise.

In a systematic study, Martin Seligman (1998) observed two approaches that psychotherapists can use when they meet with patients for the first time. One approach is problem centered, focusing on painful childhood memories, the details of relationships that aren't working, personal failings, and the places where patients feel stuck. The other approach is goal directed, focusing on aspirations and hopes and on the successes, however small, that give patients confidence that they can create the future they want for themselves. The problem-centered approach is cathartic but, for many patients, reinforces feelings of despair, worthlessness, and passive resignation. After this kind of cleansing, far too many patients lack the will to return for a second therapy session. In contrast, the goal-directed approach evokes a far higher level of enthusiasm and hope, as well as greater will to come back for a second session.

It takes will to persevere in any program of performance improvement, whether in psychotherapy or in a scientific laboratory like Sara's. The key to mobilizing and renewing this will, Seligman concluded, isn't a thorough and painstaking diagnosis of what hurts and what's wrong, but the vision, promise, and hope that the future can be better.

David Cooperrider and his colleagues (Cooperrider, Sorensen, Whitney, and Yaeger, 1998) made the same observation about teams and organizations. Instead of focusing on the dysfunctions of a team or the factors that sapped morale, Cooperrider advocated focusing on the hopes, strengths, and successes that build goodwill. He called this approach "appreciative inquiry" since, he observed, will is strengthened when people feel valued, affirmed, and appreciated for their efforts and abilities rather than put on the spot because of their shortcomings.

Appreciative inquiry isn't about eliminating problems and stresses. Instead, it's about kindling vitality, optimism, and a sense of fulfillment about the present and the future. It doesn't make people feel like failures or "problem children" when their teams get stuck. Instead, it renews their joy and enthusiasm, so they invest more of themselves in the team's success. Peter, the CTO, did a very effective job of presenting the scientific challenges in this way when he recruited new employees, new research partners, and new investors. He did a very effective job of making them feel valued and appreciated. But he assumed that that energy, once evoked, would be self-sustaining and that people would need little besides an occasional pep talk. Nothing could be further from the truth.

Appreciative inquiry doesn't end in a sales or recruiting pitch. It doesn't end in the workshop or management pep talk in which strengths, aspirations, and hopes are articulated. If, like Peter, you need people on your team to invest the same passion and energy that came naturally when they first started their projects, you might have to switch from a problem-centered to an appreciative approach. Specifically, this means you must do the following.

- **See the glass as half full.** If you're as frustrated as Peter and have as much on the line, it may not be easy to switch from a "glass-half-empty" to a "glass-half-full" assessment of the talent on your team. You may be painfully aware of what they could do better. You may need to remind yourself why you wanted individuals like Sara on your team in the first place and get beyond your own frustration and panic to identify the things they do well.

- **Make it personal.** If you don't know the individual members of the team well enough to articulate their personal strengths and contributions—as individuals, rather than en masse—find a way to get to know them better. Carve out time for observation, or ask people who work alongside them to describe their accomplishments and talents.

- **Make it relevant.** Praising people for things that they don't value or that they take for granted in themselves doesn't have as much impact as recognizing the strengths that give them pride and a sense of professional accomplishment. Sara might be an attractive woman, but praising her for her good looks and fashion sense isn't going to affirm her accomplishments as a scientist. What, specifically, do you see in each of your team members that makes you believe they are up to the challenge that lies ahead?

- **Make it explicit.** We could comfortably retire if we had a dollar for every team member who's said, "I never knew anyone noticed," after a session in which appreciations are shared. Openly comment on the successes, virtues, and skills that give you confidence that teammates can succeed in achieving the lofty and audacious goals that are expected of the team. Let them know why you have confidence in them, even if, when the going gets tough, you see their self-confidence start to wane.

- **Make it for real.** Most teammates are perceptive enough to know when praise isn't sincere. It isn't always easy to focus on strengths when someone's lack of will is the weak link on the team and when your own career is on the line. If you can't think of a single reason why you're glad to have a particular individual on your team, or why you have confidence that she can make a solid contribution when facing challenges that require courage, lying to yourself and to that person isn't going to help. If you truly can't see an individual from a glass-half-full perspective, it's time to counsel her off the team.

- **Keep score.** When you ask hard-driving, hypercritical executives like Peter about the balance between the amount of praise and the amount of criticism they provide, they frequently see their behavior very differently than do colleagues like Sara. To change the balance, we suggest using a five-for-one rule; we sometimes insist that executives give five pieces of praise and thank-yous for every one piece of criticism. We also suggest "no-criticism" afternoons. The object is to make the Peters of the world more conscious of the "glass-half-full" (or "glass-half-empty") perspective that they convey.

YOUR "GO-TO" PLAYERS

When Sara looked back on Peter's decision to hire an expensive consulting firm to collaborate on major portions of her project, she sighed and shrugged. At first, she applauded his decision. She'd never met the consultants, but she knew the firm by reputation. She was excited about working with such an elite team of scientists, welcomed their help, and looked forward to the intellectual challenge.

Within a few months, the presence of the consultants had had the opposite impact. They were an elite group, but it was a closed shop. They pushed aside company people like Sara, upstaged them, and left them feeling undervalued. "I don't understand why our people are complaining," Peter said, when we spoke about the consultants' role and their negative impact on the will of Sara and her colleagues. "No one has been demoted or displaced. No one's salary has been cut," he said, "even though people are being asked to take on less pressure, less travel, and less accountability."

Truly, Peter didn't understand. Achievement-motivated players want to feel that they're being stretched and challenged and that others have confidence in them to do what it takes to make great things happen. Sports psychologists Kreigel and Kreigel (1984) presented a graph like the one in Figure 3 to show the relationship between pressure and sustainable levels of performance. The graph clearly shows

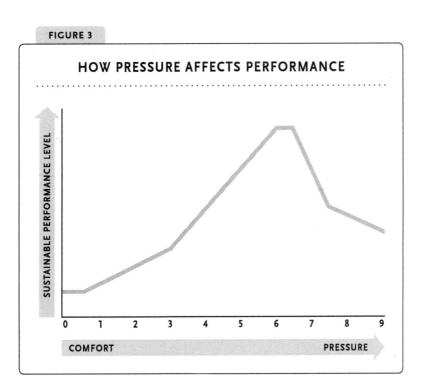

FIGURE 3

HOW PRESSURE AFFECTS PERFORMANCE

SUSTAINABLE PERFORMANCE LEVEL

0 1 2 3 4 5 6 7 8 9

COMFORT   PRESSURE

that optimum performance occurs when people feel a certain level of arousal, fear, anxiety, and pressure, not when they're feeling safe and insulated.

What are the lessons of the graph above for executives like Peter and team members like Sara? For Peter, it's recognizing the fine line between arousal, fear, and challenge—which can be positive—and feeling set up to fail no matter how hard you try, which is debilitating. For Sara, it's learning to filter Peter's comments and decide which to take to heart and which to let roll off her back, with or without a humorous quip. Sure, it would be better for everyone if Peter learned to moderate his challenging comments. But Sara can't control Peter. She can only control her own emotional reactions to Peter. Following are some more specific things you can do and say.

• **Set and keep the bar high.** "Play me or trade me," a prominent ballplayer demanded of his manager after he was relegated to sitting on the bench. He didn't want an easy or free ride any more than Sara did. High achievers want to be challenged. They want to get into the action. They want to make a contribution and feel that their talents are valued and made use of. Sara would never have hired on with the company if Peter had promised a low-pressure, low-visibility, do-as-you're-told, sit-at-home job. She expected to work hard and learn a lot. She was excited by deadlines and technical requirements that would require her to breathe, eat, drink, sleep, and live almost every waking moment with her project.

- **Show and build confidence.** Statements such as "You'll get through this" and "I know it's a challenge and I'm confident that you're up to it" may seem gratuitous. After all, you wouldn't be giving a mission-critical assignment to someone who might not be up to the task. Sure, a more inclusive and respectful brand of consultant would have been better for Sara and the other members of her project team. But what if Peter had pulled Sara aside when the consultants first started and said something like, "Listen, Sara, working with these consultants will be like working for four months with a mean professor who really knows his stuff and can teach you a lot. These consultants will ridicule you to see if you're tough enough to play in their league. Don't shy away. Push back. Hang in there, and let me know if you need support."

- **Remind teammates that failure is not an option.** Hook their egos, pride, and professionalism. Throw down the gauntlet. Let them know they have a reputation to live up to or one to reverse and set right. Remind them, "This is your opportunity to show how good you really are." When it's necessary, remind them again.

- **Watch for signs of panic.** The leader who says, "I treat everyone the same and put the same level of pressure on every one of my teammates," is a leader who's in trouble. Why? Because no two people respond to pressure in the same way. For one person, anything short of a shout won't register on the radar screen. But challenging another person may put him on tilt. You may have to send people into a brief panic to get their attention and get them excited and aroused. But you can't stop there unless you want your team to be more concerned about avoiding your wrath than about being fired up to achieve success.

- **Empower teammates to say "When."** There are lots of Peters in lots of organizations. They're blessed (and cursed) with a strong will that won't quit, no matter what adversities they encounter or how many extra hours they have to put in. They push others just as hard as they push themselves. Part of the problem, of course, is that their insensitivity actually stifles the confidence and will of teammates rather than encouraging them to keep going when the going gets tough. But the real problem is that the Peters of the world don't get feedback and don't realize that the Saras of the world are losing their edge until it's too late.

ARE WE HAVING FUN YET?

Remember how Mark Twain described the method that Tom Sawyer used to persuade his friends to take over his chores and paint the fence? Tom didn't talk about the boredom, the hot weather, the smell of the paint, or the marks it left on his skin and his clothes. Instead, he made painting the fence sound like the most fun he'd had in years. "Too bad you don't have the privilege of doing this job," he teased his friends into believing. "I get to have all the fun myself!"

We aren't advocating that you stoop to Tom's level of trickery and lies. But most challenges do have an element of fun and accomplishment, which you can play up, honestly, if you remember the following points.

- **Project an upbeat tone.** Talking about challenges in a serious, tense tone and reminding people about the risks and consequences of failure does little to raise their will. In a study of elementary school teachers, Robert Rosenthal and Lenore Jacobson (1996) clearly demonstrated that teachers who believed in their students' abilities corrected them in a positive, enthusiastic tone of voice, and teachers who didn't believe in their students' abilities conveyed less patience, lightheartedness, and encouragement. Voice tone alone had a dramatic impact on the students' willingness to persevere, even when they were no longer in the physical presence of the teacher.

- **Acknowledge small successes.** When Peter accomplished something, he took little time to pat himself on the back. Instead, he moved on to the next hurdle. When someone remarked how far the young biotech company had come in a very short time, he squirmed and changed the subject, focusing instead on where the company was going and what would have to be done to reach the next stage. He rarely took time to acknowledge others' accomplishments either, leaving them feeling that they were taken for granted, even when scientists like Sara had worked particularly hard and creatively to achieve a measure of success.

- **Celebrate.** There are lots of ways to celebrate and make the job fun. Pizza parties, Christmas celebrations, picnics, Friday morning breakfasts—all of these build camaraderie and enjoyment. Marking holidays, birthdays, anniversary dates, and project milestones in an upbeat way gives people something to look forward to, even if they are doing difficult or routine work. Even hokey motivational gimmicks, such as T-shirts, medals of honor, cartoons, and skits, can lift people's spirits and make the job fun, as long as they don't embarrass anyone.

- **Provide perspective.** When we first heard a salesperson talk about "going through the 'No's,'" we wondered what he'd been sniffing. Then he explained a unique perspective he'd developed to handle the rejection of hearing "No" about twenty times before he finds someone who is interested in and willing to talk about the products he sells. Instead of hearing every no as a negative event, he marks it as bringing him one step closer to the one prospect in twenty who will say, "Let's talk." This doesn't change the rejection he experiences or the objections he encounters. But approaching the job with the expectation that he will eventually succeed gives him the strength and perspective to transcend rejection and keep going. Viewing every foot of fence as one step closer to a hot meal and a rest or a more pleasant endeavor makes the job of painting less onerous. Surely Peter can reassure Sara that the tough times and pressure will eventually pass and build her confidence by saying, "Don't worry. We've weathered storms like this before, and we'll get through this one as well." And there might be more you could do to provide perspective for your employees as well.

- **Create a warm, inviting work environment.** Music, artwork, posters, and other ways of making the physical setting pleasant and inviting can also create a more positive mood, particularly when teammates are doing difficult or routine work. When Sara looked at her drab laboratory, she found little joy in her surroundings, particularly when she compared the drabness of her lab with the warm colors, etched glass sculptures, and photographs found in the company's business offices.

The Few, the Proud

In an extensive compilation of research data, Alfie Kohn (1999) demonstrated that many well-intentioned reward systems can demotivate high performers by trading intrinsic rewards for bribes and bonuses. When scientists like Sara are "in it for the money," their motivation changes. No longer are they inspired to strive for personal excellence, think creatively, and transcend obstacles. The work becomes a means to an end rather than a source of gratification in itself.

Kohn's research with grade school and graduate students, computer programmers, salespeople, scientists, and performing artists doesn't give executives like Peter an excuse to pay people less or withhold rewards, but it does send a clear warning: If people already take pride in their professional accomplishments and find the work intrinsically rewarding, build on their pride. Don't take the joy out of the jobs they enjoy doing. Winning awards and rewards isn't a substitute for making people feel like winners. In practical terms, here's what Kohn's research means for executives, project leaders, and department heads who oversee artistic, technical, performing, and care-giving professionals.

- **Give them credit.** Give them bylines, artistic credits, and acknowledgments, and list them on patent applications. It doesn't change who owns the intellectual propert, but it does show that you value their contributions and builds their professional portfolio in the process.

- **Replay their personal highlights.** Before a big game or the debut of a new show, the old film clippings come out—a taste of good things to come. Before you send a team in to make an important presentation, handle a delicate negotiation, or find a technical breakthrough, show why you have confidence in members' judgment, talent, and energy. Show why you believe in them, even if they don't yet fully believe in themselves.

- **Appeal to pride and professionalism.** The whole point of Alfie Kohn's work is to confirm that people work hard for a lot more than money or career advancement. If you can, frame the challenge in terms of the legacy someone can leave behind, the contribution he or she can make to a worthy cause, or the sense of fulfillment that goes along with turning out a high-quality product, finding an elegant solution to a problem, or achieving a world-class standard of performance. Connect "doing the job" with a higher purpose that makes performance its own reward.

- **Create an All-Stars Forum and a Hall of Fame.** When Sara reflected on her current lack of energy and compared the biotech company to the world of academia, she thought about how often her achievements were showcased. In her last academic institution, she had opportunities to present papers at professional conferences, to trade insights and ideas with the best and brightest in the field, and to serve on an advisory panel for graduate students regarding state-of-the-art work in her field. Now she had little time for pursuits that fell outside the scope of the narrowly defined project deadlines. It wasn't that she missed being in the spotlight; she missed having her work appreciated by colleagues who knew what it really took to deliver a high-quality product. Even if your employees can't present papers to professional associations or affinity groups—or if doing so would compromise your trade secrets—you might find a way to create an in-company Hall of Fame so that people can show their work to appreciative and admiring colleagues.

- **Provide opportunities to grow.** In a confidential internal study, one global biotech company reported that the vast majority of employee turnover doesn't occur because people feel underpaid or because they don't like what they're doing. Instead, they found, most turnover occurs because talented individuals don't see where their careers are going. They feel they're stuck where they are rather than growing in the job; they're "making do" and producing pedestrian outcomes instead of being given the opportunity to produce something world class. This was confirmed by David Dell and Jack Hickey (2002) in an executive report issued by the Conference Board. If people don't see how their latest assignments are going to take them forward, and if they feel utilized only for what they already know how to do and not for what they can learn to do, you might find that they have as little excitement about coming to work as Sara. They may be just going through the motions. Have you provided your top talent opportunities to learn and develop, rather than just produce, lately? What have you done to give them a chance to stretch, learn, and grow?

- **Create bragging circles.** What have you done lately to build esprit de corps, to make your teammates feel they've been selected to be part of an elite, special squad? What have you done to give them an opportunity to show off their best practices and get credit for their best creative work? What makes them feel like heroes and medal winners for the courage you ask them to demonstrate—and the challenges and risks you expect them to take? What have you done to let success build momentum and breed more success?

Building Confidence

In the play *Man of La Mancha*, Don Quixote charges through the countryside on horseback, determined to do his best to create a better world. In fact, he's a madman who confuses windmills for dragons and has totally lost touch with reality. The play expresses the fine line between a vision and a hallucination. Passion and strong will are positive traits, but if you're charging off like Don Quixote, they aren't enough to guarantee your success. If the technology that Sara and her team are developing has fundamental flaws—or if a competitor gets a comparable product to market first—will alone can't make the enterprise successful.

Some team members look at a plan intuitively and get excited about possibilities and potentials. Other team members are skeptics.

They need facts and plans, and they won't commit unless they're convinced that they won't be charging off like Don Quixote. How can Peter and Sara raise the confidence of scientists, engineers, and operators who need to be convinced that a plan has legs?

- **Raise the level of candor.** The five courage factors have to work together. If both will and candor need attention, you won't be able to raise the level of one without also paying attention to the other. If people feel that their input is not solicited, is second-guessed, or is arbitrarily overruled, and they don't believe you're listening to reason about what can and can't be done, don't be surprised when they don't get fired up about the latest project or the newest revision of the action plan.

- **Allow time to take it in.** As a student, Sara learned that skeptical, fact-based scientists don't often jump out of their chairs and yell, "Eureka!" That's doubly true if they come from an emotionally reserved culture. She used to feel discouraged when someone would look over her work, furrow his brow, and say, "Not bad." Now she's learned to recognize that as a sign of approval. If you want skeptics to be committed, give them a chance to ask their own questions, play with other possibilities, and take stock of the risk factors.

Acknowledge Social Realities

If every member of the team started out on an equal footing, it would still be difficult to maintain your confidence, composure, and enthusiasm in the presence of a hard-driving, demanding, no-nonsense CTO like Peter. In most organizations, people don't start out on an equal footing. That makes it even more important for leaders to know how their actions and reactions are perceived and how they affect others' energy and spirits.

In a U.S. presidential election, candidate Ross Perot was astonished to find out that a comment he made had offended a large block of voters. Many African Americans were incensed at Perot's reference to "you people," which was an all-too-familiar reminder that African

Americans are often lumped together as one homogeneous group. Perot thought his African American constituents were being hypersensitive and balked at the idea of making a public apology. Peter had the same problem. He thought the scientists were far too sensitive and ignored Sara when she tried to tell him how his derogatory references were perceived. He thought he was being funny, irreverent, and frank. What's the answer?

- **Perception is reality.** Ross Perot didn't have the power to tell anyone how they should vote when they step into the election booth. And executives like Peter can't tell people how to feel about coming to work. If you don't understand what the perceptions are, you can't have the impact you might like to have on teammates' confidence and emotional investment.

- **Some people are more sensitive than others.** That's a fact of life in a "one-down" social status—which, unfortunately, is still a reality for women, like Sara, in technical positions, for people of color, for people who are doing business in a nonnative language, and for those with an alternative lifestyle or religion or a physical disability. The answer is not to be patronizing, paternalistic, or charitable; it's recognizing that some people may be less resilient than others when they're insulted, excluded, or publicly embarrassed.

Compression

....

When we interviewed Dave Tapolczay, chief technology officer of Millennium Pharmaceuticals UK, he spoke of the workings of an internal combustion engine as a metaphor for a project team's energy. For an engine to work, he explained, it isn't enough to have fuel; you also have to breathe air into it. If the pressure is on and no fresh air can enter the team, the best you can hope for is a wasteful fuel leak. At worst, you may get an explosion rather than ignition. But the right mixture of air and fuel won't provide an efficient, high-energy burn unless you also add compression. If you put the right amount of pressure on the air-fuel mixture, you dramatically boost the engine's output.

In our own simulation exercises, we see how compression affects the will of a team. When there is little pressure lots of time and success looks likely, the team heaves a sigh of relief and the energy level drops. When the pressure is on, it feels like there's a lot on the line, and the team is confident it can overcome adversity, the energy level increases sharply.

Peter was trying to add compression by lighting a fire under Sara and her teammates. There is much, of course, that Peter could learn to do better. He needs to breathe air into the combustion chambers and imbue teammates like Sara with the confidence, energy, and lift that they need to reach for the stars and persevere. But, in the spirit of appreciative inquiry, we should also recognize the things that Peter does well to get people excited about being part of the team and to add compression to the mixture.

- **Don't let pessimism take root.** The major difference between optimists and pessimists, according to psychologist Martin Seligman (1998), is that pessimists are usually far more in touch with reality. The major advantage that optimists have is a healthy defense against reality, which enables them to see possibilities rather than simply accepting things as they are. It wasn't that Peter didn't see the technical hurdles and difficulties that were confronting Sara and her colleagues. It's just that he refused to be put off by them.

- **Let people blow off steam.** Peter wasn't put off by conflict or by people who expressed strong opinions. Candor was something he valued and worked hard to cultivate both in himself and in others. He probed and listened carefully to find out what fears and concerns gave rise to pessimism and frustration and reframed the difficulties to reveal the light at the end of the tunnel. Expressions of frustration didn't bother him, nor did conflict about what deadlines and customer commitments could be met and what was pushing the envelope too far.

- **Make it possible for everyone to win.** From his background in running a sales organization, Peter knew what a competitive, one-winner-takes-all reward system can do to morale within a team. He set the bar high, but he expected it to be achieved by everyone. There was no forced normal-distribution in his assessment of performance, no requirement that managers make tough choices to identify and ferret out the bottom 20 percent. He wanted to build a team in which everyone knew they could win together.

- **Don't treat others as you are treated.** Peter was the consummate salesperson. He could take a brutal pounding from the investors and the board, regain his composure, and give a rousing, positive pep talk to the staff or to a group of prospective customers. Lethargy and complacency pushed his buttons, but he made a conscious and deliberate effort not to pass on the way he was treated to anyone else around him. Because he was so good at compartmentalizing, he assumed that everyone else could do the same as well—particularly if, like Sara, they held a management or team leadership position. That may have been his biggest downfall, namely, expecting others to be imbued with as much passion, enthusiasm, and quickly renewable energy as he was, whether or not someone else provided the lift beneath their wings.

In Summary

If the questions you've answered about the five courage factors tell you that will needs to be improved, what steps can you take to infuse your team with a different level of energy and enthusiasm?

1. Be appreciative. Don't buy into pessimism and worst-case scenarios. Like Peter, you can make a conscious decision to see possibilities rather than insurmountable obstacles. You can look past the dilemmas and difficulties that are in front of you—without underestimating what it will take to overcome them—because you see light at the end of the tunnel. You can challenge people to do more without negating or trivializing how hard they are already working.

2. Don't discourage or demoralize teammates. Avoid derailing them with public humiliation or a review that focuses on past mistakes without looking at corrective action or at what's already been done to make improvements. Protect and mobilize the team's ego.

3. Treat everyone you rely on like a "go-to" player. Build confidence. Recognize the successes, skills, and virtues of your team members. Share your confidence in them—visibly, explicitly, publicly—and don't buy into their self-doubt or lack of confidence.

4. Make it fun. Remember how Tom Sawyer talked others into painting the fence? Make a game out of it. Lighten up the mood. Provide pleasant surroundings.

5. Build pride. Make people feel like winners and world-class professionals, whether they are doing scientific work or cleaning the sinks and test tubes. Appeal to their sense of professionalism and honor, and acknowledge the importance of the contribution they are making. In the world of teams, some jobs may be more visible than others, but no job worth doing is a small job.

6. Remember that everyone doesn't build confidence in the same way. Some people get enthusiastic immediately upon seeing the intuitive appeal of a great idea or a promising new project. Others need time to digest the information and reassure themselves that they aren't undertaking an impossible quest.

7. Acknowledge social realities. Some people find insults and disenfranchisement easier to shake off than others. Some are more resilient than others. What feels like a positive shot in the arm to one teammate can be a fatal blow to another's confidence. Start where teammates are, not where you would like them to be.

8. Add compression and pressure. High achievers don't expect or want an easy or free ride. They want to be challenged. But when you increase pressure, make sure there is a pressure release valve and a way to dissipate heat. Breathe air into the compression chambers when you add fuel or the engine will stall out.

9. Convey positive self-fulfilling prophecies. Be conscious of transmitting positive expectations in the energy you transmit through your tone of voice, lightness, and the degree to which you take others into your confidence and make them part of your franchise.

10. Recognize that will isn't a luxury. In an era when jobs were routine and people essentially did as they were told, workers didn't necessarily need a strong will. But the requirements are different in an environment like Sara's, where people need to think, solve problems, and be "on." Leading a team of thorobreds is different from leading a team of quarter horses; it requires a brand of leadership that's more agile and perceptive, has a lighter yet firmer touch, and is more tolerant of exuberance and idiosyncrasies.

RIGOR

....

The Courage to Invent Disciplines and Make Them Stick

There are no shortcuts to any place worth going.
BEVERLY SILLS

We want take-charge, get-it-done team members to be empowered and to take initiative. We don't want them to let a promising opportunity slip away while they wait for permission to act. We want them to use common sense, without worrying about whether they'll be reprimanded or have to justify themselves. We want them to think creatively about ways to improve efficiency.

At the same time, there are some lines that we don't want people to cross, some regulations and protocols that have to be respected, even if doing so slows things down. Rigor is a matter of judgment and discretion, consideration and self-discipline. It's a matter of recognizing

- When shortcuts are worth taking and when they'll create problems that, in the long run, will be expensive to put right

- How your actions affect others in the system

- How your success affects the performance of the enterprise as a whole

- The difference between what's ethical and unethical, and whether your values are based on internalized standards of proper conduct or on the fear of getting caught and having to answer for an act of impropriety

With automated systems, you can impose rigor by building it into your default options and security codes. But artificial intelligence isn't idiot proof. Effectively operating sophisticated systems requires a high level of ingenuity and persistence. Rigor is a matter of proficiency, as well as judgment and discretion. It's a matter of

- Learning how things work, whether you're given formal training or a manual or you figure it out through trial and error

- Staying organized and focused to prevent costly mistakes and preventable accidents

- Keeping your equipment, your information, and yourself in top operating condition

- Recognizing what's aesthetic and what's functional to the customers and users who have to live with the products or services you deliver

- Understanding systems and procedures so you can find workarounds when the default options don't make sense or aren't fair

Get It Done, Whatever It Takes

In a large government agency, Jackie was a bit of an anomaly. She ran her operation like a businessperson, not a bureaucrat or a politician. She was a pragmatic, resourceful field manager. She didn't have a lot of time or patience for fiefdoms, mindless obedience, "not-my-job" small-mindedness, or filling out in triplicate forms that no one would look at.

When she was promoted to head of enforcement in the state capital, Jackie was grateful that she'd inherited a team of people who shared her spunk and ingenuity. They were willing to look the other way on small infractions if they could solve major problems that really endangered public safety. They worked with violators to bring them back into companies rather than opening investigations and getting caught in expensive, no-win prosecutions.

At first, Jackie rolled her eyes when she heard complaints about the shortcuts that her lieutenants took. "It's about time someone shook things up in this stodgy institution," she said, congratulating her teammates on their initiative and take-charge attitude. With charm and tact, she appeased complainers and winked at the members of her staff who had been accused of stepping over the line. She viewed it as a sign of success that her team had the courage to make people uncomfortable and take actions that went a step beyond the rules.

But Jackie couldn't dismiss the audit results by rolling her eyes and reassuring her staff. The audit showed that Jackie's lieutenants had crossed some uncrossable lines, albeit with the best of intentions. Jackie didn't react well to that news. She had promised to stand by her team, no matter how hot it got. She assumed the audit was flawed— not her directions or her staff's discretion. Off the record, she speculated about whether some of her less adventurous and entrepreneurial colleagues were using the audit as an opportunity to reassert control or get even or to voice their displeasure about a woman being in such a visible and important position.

As Jackie and her people prepared to face off against the auditors, turf and power were becoming more important than benchmark data or cost/benefit analyses. There were accusations and counteraccusations, some of which spilled out into the press and stirred up controversy in the governor's office. In such a politically charged environment, scoring points was becoming more important than making rational and informed decisions about best practices or about what teammates could and should be empowered to do without a higher level of approval.

The choice was Jackie's. On the surface, it looked like facing off and preparing for a bitter fight against the auditors was the tack that required the most courage. But that wasn't true. It actually took more courage for Jackie to admit that the auditors might have some wisdom to share and that their scrutiny, while embarrassing, might help her team members improve the way they ran field investigations and avoid the appearance of impropriety or favoritism.

Jackie admitted that rising above the cycle of accusation and self-justification was the hardest thing she had ever done in her career. She challenged her people to put ego and defensiveness aside and to engage in a problem-solving process guided by the following principles.

LET LOGIC PREVAIL

Jackie convened a management meeting to review the audit results with her staff and plan her department's official response. She started the deliberations with a pronouncement. "We are going to use this critique as an opportunity to reassess what we are doing and make sure that we are doing the right things in the best way possible. We have nothing to be ashamed of, but that doesn't mean we have no room for improvement either."

Before the meeting, Jackie had read in the morning paper about a group of pilots from outside the English-speaking world who were indignant about being denied permission to work international flights in U.S. airspace. Some of the pilots viewed the English proficiency exam as xenophobia or blatant protectionism. Others had overestimated their English proficiency and were shocked to learn that they hadn't passed the qualifying exam. Fewer than 30 percent of the pilots who were denied permission to fly embraced the reasonableness of the standard.

Jackie used this example to set the tone for the deliberations about the audit results and tougher standards regarding her agency's enforcement and inspection practices. "If I were a capable pilot," she said, "I might not like being told that I have to enroll in remedial English classes. If I employed pilots, I might not be happy about the expense and loss of productivity. But, since passenger safety depends on pilots and air traffic controllers who can understand one another and must rely on split-second timing, I would hope we could look at what's really at stake, rather than at our own embarrassment, inconvenience, or budget constraints."

Jackie acknowledged that some of the auditors' standards might seem convoluted or unnecessary. She knew that her staff would hear some things that they might not like from the auditors. She announced that she would take help from anyone who had suggestions for improving the enforcement and compliance operation, whether those suggestions came from inside the department, from other government agencies, or from the auditors—and that she expected her people to do the same. She refused to allow the debate over good investigatory and enforcement practices to deteriorate into a political or turf issue.

Before rejecting any recommendation, Jackie encouraged her people to ask why the auditors were flagging a problem or potential problem. She expected her staff to listen to the rationale, run an objective cost/benefit analysis, and assess the severity of safety risks, ethical breaches, or the appearance of impropriety.

PUT PERSONAL CONVENIENCE IN PERSPECTIVE

We all have our routines and rituals, the ways we like to aproach an assignment and get things organized. If you have to use a colleague's computer or access files in someone else's desk drawer, you may first have to get oriented to that person's system of logic and organization in order to retrieve the file you need or complete a task in his or her absence.

Conforming to someone else's system of logic and organization can go against your grain. It may not feel natural or comfortable. It may be tempting for Jackie and her lieutenants to write off the auditors' way of doing things as being wrong or more trouble than it's worth. When you are already overworked, it is natural to resent the loss of your personal productivity if you're asked to reinvent your own systems so they conform to someone else's image of best practices.

In pioneering work on change management in the 1940s, Kurt Lewin (1975) talked about a cycle of adjusting to change that involved three phases: unfreezing, learning, and refreezing. During the unfreezing period, the level of discomfort is high. As a quick demonstration of unfreezing, fold your arms across your chest in a way that feels natural and comfortable, and then refold your arms, reversing the arm that you place on top. For most people, even a simple change like this feels unnatural and uncomfortable and requires some unlearning of old habits. Unless you see a clear rationale for practicing and perfecting a new way of folding your arms, you'll automatically revert to the old way of doing it.

Jackie understood this. She understood that her team would view discomfort as a sign that something was wrong, rather than a sign that something was different. She insisted that the team look at costs and benefits, as well as the regulatory requirements that her agency was obliged to fulfill, before considering whether a change in practice would make the team uncomfortable or would take some unfreezing and learning.

A Design Mentality

"Nice guy" was the first comment most people offered when they were asked about Bruce. As head of medical affairs for a large biotech company, Bruce respected the professionalism of his staff. After all, many of them were also physicians, and those without medical credentials had years of experience in research, in academia, in health care, or working for the regulatory agencies that reviewed competitors' dossiers.

Bruce knew how to stand behind his teammates. When another department voiced a concern, he checked into the situation in a way that gave his people every benefit of the doubt. He listened carefully as his people articulated their rationale for doing what they did and challenged their thinking in a way that respected their judgment and kept the lines of communication open. He offered suggestions and perspectives rather than direct orders. Trusting the professionalism of his staff, Bruce figured, meant that you could give them the facts and rely on them to make good, informed professional decisions—even if they weren't the same decisions you would make.

The new director of research and development, however, was alarmed at the lack of concern for time lines and budgetary constraints that he saw in Bruce's department. Individually, people were not dragging their feet or using poor judgment. But work that should take six weeks required five or six months to get through Bruce's shop, and it required a budget that was twice the industry average.

We've all been there. You're operating with the best of intentions, doing what you were asked to do with a high level of skill and ingenuity. Out of nowhere, you are blindsided by a problem—a sudden change in the specifications, a key piece of information that someone forgot to share, or an equipment malfunction or accident caused by someone else's negligence, oversight, or blatant incompetence. It isn't your fault. But it *is* something that can compromise your success and damage your reputation, even though you, personally, did everything you were supposed to do.

A design mentality, applied to products, challenges engineers to anticipate how users will interact with the equipment they take into their homes, offices, or factories. The engineer's job is to foresee accidents that are waiting to happen and to install safety guards and shutoffs to reduce the risk of operator error. There are numerous precedents to suggest that if product designers fail to anticipate problems and someone is hurt as a result, the engineers may be held liable, even if the user did something stupid or careless.

When something goes wrong, it's tempting to blame "the other guy," just as it's tempting for design engineers to blame an accident or malfunction on the poor judgment of the user. Blaming might make you feel better, but it doesn't fix the damage or reduce the cost, and it may not restore your reputation. It takes more courage to think ahead, anticipate consequences, and design your project assignments with the same design mentality that a product engineer is expected to use before turning medical equipment or computer software loose on users.

Following are some of the tough questions that Bruce needed to ask, rather than let teammates off the hook when they said, "It isn't our fault."

ANTICIPATE TOUCH POINTS AND CONSEQUENCES

Product designers have to stand back from their prototypes and look at protrusions or openings that a careless user could grab and use as handles. If the user could get burned or cut, savvy engineers install guards and/or safer handles. Where are the touch points that your stakeholders—your suppliers and users—might grab on the assignment you are working on? Where are the mistakes or accidents that are waiting to happen unless you design a way for people to take hold safely and efficiently? Do you fully understand how others will use what you provide? Or how others provide what you will use?

Bruce could see that his teammates knew their own jobs well but didn't have the background or understanding to anticipate the touch points with colleagues in the department or in other parts of the business. He convened a set of workshops and a job-rotation exchange so teammates doing one job could learn firsthand how their stakeholders would pick up and use the work they completed.

APPLY CONSTRUCTIVE INTOLERANCE

Bruce could muster constructive intolerance if someone violated a canon of professional ethics. There was no room for harassment and discriminatory practices on his watch. These were lines that people knew they couldn't cross and still maintain a position of responsibility and influence on Bruce's team.

But miscommunication, poor hand-offs that created extra work, and blatant refusal to conform to standard operating procedures didn't meet with the same attitude of constructive intolerance. If people could show that they were operating with noble intentions or under extraordinary stress, they were told, "Please pay more attention and try harder next time." If someone boldly said, "The new standard of procedure doesn't work for me," he was given a reprieve until he proposed a suitable alternative.

Bruce remembered his army reserve unit's first practice exercises, advancing into the territory of a virtual enemy. Everyone in his squad charged forward, running and diving for cover as fast as they could. In retrospect, the squad's performance was comical. The swiftest runners were far ahead of the rest of the pack, and the slower ones were struggling to keep the rest of the pack in sight, lurching forward, gasping for breath. Individually, there were some heroes and star performers. The price of victory, though, was the squad's virtual casualty rate, which was far higher than it needed to be, because the individual soldiers were more concerned about showing their prowess than about pulling together and looking out for one another.

The squad commander berated them severely after the exercise. He was especially hard on the fastest and supposedly most heroic members of the squad for putting their comrades at risk. He demanded that the squad analyze each casualty, without excuses or self-justification, and ask, "What could be done to prevent this from happening again?" As the squad commander of the medical affairs group, Bruce had hoped he wouldn't have to resort to the same tough style of communication that his army squad commander used. He could see now, though, that his gentle and understanding style was being misinterpreted as consent by teammates who were running as fast as possible without looking at their impact on the rest of the team.

DON'T BLAME AND SHAME

Conventional wisdom says that people learn best in an atmosphere that is free of blame and preserves self-esteem. Bruce bought into this wisdom. He didn't want his teammates second-guessing themselves. He didn't want them to be so preoccupied with avoiding incurring his disapproval that they would lose sight of good medical judgment, of expeditious opportunities to move their project forward, or of ways to satisfy the customers who had agreed to host their studies.

In a blame-free environment, it's assumed that teammates will recognize when they have made mistakes and will analyze and learn from those mistakes. If you encourage them to keep trying, it's assumed that they will keep learning and, with experience, will improve their execution. But what happens if teammates don't have the judgment to recognize when a mistake is a mistake? What happens if they are getting better at execution but are executing the wrong things at the wrong times? What happens if their egos or sense of self-importance results in a belief that they should be empowered to work in whatever way suits them, without concern for their impact on the rest of the team?

According to a former major league baseball pitcher who now works as a corporate executive, there is an analogy to draw between learning to pitch more effectively and learning to execute business strategies in project teams like Bruce's. Blame doesn't help when a pitcher is already aware that he's made a mistake or when he's open to trying new techniques and is practicing to incorporate them into his repertoire. But pitchers don't always see when a curve would have worked better than a fastball, and they may overestimate their ability to throw something the batter can't hit, particularly when they are fatigued.

At such times, baseball games are won and lost on the ability of the catcher and manager to say no to a highly paid and revered pitcher, even if the pitcher doesn't agree with the decision or feels insulted because his judgment is overruled. The time lines and budgets of research projects are also won and lost by saying no when an error in judgment is committed—or is in danger of being committed.

Saying no to a prestigious physician is embarrassing. The physician isn't likely to react by saying, "Thanks. I needed that." Tempers will flare and egos will be bruised. Before he developed a new course of action, Bruce used to back away from these conflicts. He didn't want members of his team to be angry or threatened. He hoped that with a team of well-intentioned professionals he could count on good judgment and on a healthy suppression of ego and self-importance. Much of the time, he could. But on some decisions that jeopardized time lines and budgets or that created clumsy hand-offs, preventable mistakes, and miscommunication, Bruce didn't see good judgment. He didn't see teammates owning the problems they had created, accepting accountability, or trying to make improvements.

BE AN ACTIVE BYSTANDER

Constructive intolerance and the selective and appropriate use of discipline couldn't fall on Bruce's shoulders alone. If the rest of Bruce's teammates rolled their eyes, refused to take new disciplines seriously, and marginalized Bruce for taking a tougher stand on time lines and budgets, improvements would fail to materialize. If, on the other hand, members of the medical affairs staff closed ranks behind Bruce, insisted on a high level of rigor from one another, and let colleagues know "This is how we do things here," compliance would be far greater.

Bystanders create an environment in which those who break the rules can (or cannot) operate with impunity. As head of loss prevention for several national retail chains, Greg Ireton warned store managers that thieves can't operate in isolation. To steal thousands of dollars of merchandise or cash receipts, Ireton explained, thieves require tacit if not active cooperation from co-workers in the store. If co-workers don't look the other way, thieves can't get away with stealing.

The key to preventing inside theft, Ireton suggested, is a culture within the store in which co-workers do not tolerate thieves in their midst and a code of honor governs the behavior of every member of the crew.

Similarly, airline security cannot be the responsibility solely of airline crews or government inspectors. The effectiveness of El Al security is legendary, but it doesn't happen in a vacuum. El Al security is effective because the traveling public takes the security risks seriously and because peer pressure prevents travelers from trying to trick, take shortcuts with, or act impertinent with security personnel. Those who try to beat the system quickly find out that they will be brought into line by fellow travelers, with more scorn and less patience than the flight crew or security staff themselves would show toward paying customers.

Confusing Rigor with Rigidity

By the time we met Anthony, a senior executive who prided himself on "managing by walking around," he had used up most of his relationship capital by encouraging frontline employees to "think out of the box" and breathe life into the rule book and standard operating procedures. In an instant, Anthony could give an impassioned speech that showed he knew all about finding a way to say yes to customers and finding solutions that would build incremental sales. He could talk for hours about the success of companies like Nordstrom's, Federal Express, British Airways, Disney, and Kinko's, all of whom pride themselves on encouraging employees to improvise, to use complex rules and procedures as tools, rather than obstacles, to delight customers.

Poor Anthony. His credibility had hit rock bottom. It wasn't because he didn't know his stuff. He did. He could see, before most branch managers, how sales opportunities were missed and customers were lost as a result of petty bureaucracy and intransigence that simply didn't make sense. He was outraged when he heard a reasonable but idiosyncratic customer request answered with, "No, I'm sorry, I can't do that. I'd get into trouble. And our systems don't work that way."

Despite Anthony's insight, people dove for cover when they heard his footsteps and saw "that look" in his eyes. The poor souls who couldn't get their heads down or their office doors closed fast enough would hear an opening comment that sounded innocent enough. "Do you have a minute? I just saw something in your area that I thought you should know about." But after a few seconds, when Anthony got wound up, his diatribe would begin. He sounded like a pedantic business school professor. He was right, but he didn't create the courage to think creatively and to act.

What more could Anthony do to shake people out of the comfort and security of hiding behind rules and procedure manuals? What more could he do to get people to improvise, use common sense, experiment, and breathe life into their interactions with customers?

DETERMINE WHETHER RIGOR IS THE ISSUE

Anthony did little to create a foundation of candor, purpose, and will before putting the focus on rigor. He assumed that his followers were already with him. He forgot rule number one about rigor: If you want more than mindless, petty compliance, rigor can't be rule number one. Blind compliance isn't necessarily a symptom of a lack of rigor. When you see it, as Anthony did, you need to pause and find out if the issue really is rigor. Or is that you need to build candor, purpose, and will before you can ask teammates to improvise, teach, and learn?

Without a sense of purpose, other than staying out of trouble or avoiding an insulting diatribe, Anthony's co-workers could not be inspired to think creatively or take initiative. They didn't get it. If frontline workers don't care about enterprise success and don't embrace the objectives that you hope they'll help achieve, stop right there. Talk about success and objectives before you go any further—and make sure your teammates buy in.

If frontline workers don't have the will to do more than follow the rules and go through the motions, they won't muster creative energy when the path of least resistance doesn't work. You can't hold a gun to someone's head and make him think, improvise, or learn. People have to want to do those things. Even though Anthony was technically correct, he made people feel stupid, rather than confident and talented, and he made the top performers look like stooges rather than models to be learned from and emulated. Catching people doing things right and building on successes would have provided a better balance.

If frontline workers don't feel free to to ask candid questions, offer ideas, and let someone coach them when they make clumsy attempts to try something new, they'll seek the comfort of what they know and what the rule book tells them. The more Anthony got wound up and lectured, the less opportunity he gave people to think, improvise, and put their own style and individuality into the job—the very antithesis of what he wanted to create. The more he scolded, the more people froze. It would have been more effective for Anthony to ask open-ended questions and wait for someone to answer, even if that meant enduring a few minutes of uncomfortable silence.

ASSESS SKILL AND APTITUDE

Anthony acted as if he could read people the riot act, and they would slap themselves on the forehead, shake themselves out of their stupor, and get with the program. He assumed they could learn what to do by analyzing mistakes, reading a book on sales techniques, watching a video, or listening to a lecture. A few did. But most members of the customer service team had no idea where to begin. The more Anthony droned on about what to do, the more inadequate and unprepared they felt.

If Anthony was serious about the rigor that he wanted to see when customers presented service reps with a sales opportunity, he had to accept the fact that it wasn't going to happen by magic. The innovative companies he cited as examples make a substantial investment in training before they have people work with customers. They have on-going mentoring and learning programs, so the best and brightest know that they're responsible for teaching what they do, as well as doing what they do. Instead of lecturing, Anthony could have met with the most creative workers, praised them for their successes, and empowered them to be peer coaches to the rest of the team. Instead of returning to the corporate office with indignation and scorn for the field operations, he could have become a sponsor of the teaching, learning, and training methodologies that help people perform better.

Let's say Anthony had done all of that, both in the way he ran his meetings with the service reps in the field and in the projects he championed from his lofty perch in the corporate office. Is it reasonable to expect that 100 percent of the service reps would have "the right stuff" to master the rigor he wanted to see? Or to expect that every single service rep would get up to speed quickly enough to make the investment in their salaries pay off? Probably not.

Whether you are training new hires or retraining experienced teammates to meet new business requirements, you can't avoid the fact that training is an expensive investment. Not everyone will "get it" quickly enough to make that investment worthwhile. Deselection isn't a task that any team leader relishes, especially if the candidate for deselection demonstrates candor, purpose, and will. You can avoid deselection, of course, by hiring highly capable people in the first place, even people who can do the job better than you can. But you may not be able to avoid it if you inherit a team that was hired when less skill and aptitude were adequate to do the job. Carrying teammates who simply aren't capable of learning to perform with rigor, without more attention and supervision than you can afford to provide, is an expensive indulgence. That was one of the unpopular messages that Anthony put forward to the branch managers, and everyone in the field knew he was right. A system of training isn't a cure-all. It needs to include a system of assessment—and consequences if learners aren't making the grade.

CREATE A LEARNING ORGANIZATION

Before the age of courage, there was a demarcation between learning and performing. If you paid enough, you could hire workers who already had the skills you needed. If you invested enough in training, you could prepare new recruits to do the job before you turned them loose and said, "Go for it." But today what teammates already know is less important than how quickly they learn. Mastering today's product mix would not give Anthony's people everything they needed to know to sell tomorrow's offerings. Today's systems will be obsolete tomorrow. Policies change. So do customer tastes and needs.

In Hebrew, there is a word for the kind of turn-on-a-dime flexibility and resourcefulness that Anthony hoped to see when a customer or a new policy threw an unexpected curve. The term is *tushiya*. Ask an American pilot why Israeli pilots get so much more out of the same aircraft, and they'll tell you about *tushiya*—pushing the limits of what the equipment can do, being mentally alert, mastering what is written in the manual and, by inference, what isn't written in the manual and can be invented as you go along.

In the World War II era, there was an English equivalent for what Hebrew speakers call *tushiya*. It was *Yankee ingenuity*—which meant having the resourcefulness and improvisational skills to do what it took to accomplish the mission, even if you had to piece together a contraption out of spare parts or bend the rules, as long as you didn't cause a friendly fire accident. The 1960s' TV situation comedy *Hogan's Heroes*, which showed Allied soldiers running an underground spy operation in the midst of a German POW camp, was totally fictitious, but the Yankee ingenuity that the soldiers demonstrated was not uncommon. It contributed to the Allied victory in World War II, just as *tushiya* has made the Israeli army look like the superior force even when it is the underdog.

Ingenuity, improvisation, and resourcefulness don't just "happen." After the norms are established and people are used to working in a more creative way, whether in army field units or in Nordstrom's sales meetings, improvisation and problem solving seem to happen like magic. But ingenuity is carefully cultivated, with lots of short practice drills, direct feedback, good-natured ridicule, and exhortations to keep trying.

In a resource-constrained, time-pressed environment, forums to share best practices and work-arounds are often sacrificed. When teammates huddle to help one another, it's tempting for visiting executives to see it as time wasting and to tell people to get back to work. When costs have to be reduced, travel and conferences are often cut. So are special projects, even though they provide people with opportunities to push the limits of technology, develop new and better techniques, and share what's working in one part of the business with teammates who are struggling to reinvent the same wheel in another part of the business. Anthony didn't get it. He assumed that he could snap his fingers and demand *tushiya,* without investing in it beforehand. But you can't arm a new unit and send it into battle without taking the time to learn, practice, and perfect. You might win the battle, but you'll suffer a lot more casualties than you need to.

ESTABLISH AS FEW RULES AS POSSIBLE

In highly technical and regulated jobs, of course you need standard operating procedures and technical manuals. But all of the rules that Anthony created, telling service representatives to "do this and say that" and having audits to ensure compliance, actually worked against the spirit of entrepreneurship and service that he had hoped to script for them.

The more complex and technical the job becomes—as was the case with the assortment of products and services that Anthony's field crews offered to their customers—the more discretion and judgment are required. You can't avoid or script these qualities. If you could, you would simply program a computer and automate the function—and be done with human error and the cost of payroll altogether.

The Action Threshold

One of our business simulations, designed to develop the courage to think and act strategically, overwhelms participants with a wealth of information about potential customers and investors, regulatory requirements, and changing dynamics in the marketplace. The clock starts ticking as soon as the briefing ends, and decisions have to be made quickly. There are clear benefits to being the first in the market. Risks are present as well but are harder to assess.

Within less than a minute, most groups in the simulation become polarized. At one extreme are the teammates who believe they have enough information to make a bold move forward and don't want to be left behind. At the other extreme are those who want to wait and gather more facts, lest they make a costly or fatal mistake.

The simulation, of course, is only a game. But in team after team, we see the same tension develop as real options are weighed and real careers and fortunes are laid on the line. Some decision makers are comfortable relying on limited data. They fill in the gaps with intuition and gut instinct to avoid missing a narrow window of opportunity. Others want to map the terrain that lies ahead, interpolate mathematically, and know they are set up to succeed.

Dr. Paul Sherwin, head of Amersham Health's Medical Advisory Group in the United States, shared the "action threshold" concept with us while debriefing our strategic thinking simulation. For physicians, Sherwin explained, the threshold is reached when the risk of not acting outweighs the risk of making a mistake. If the patient might die if you misdiagnose and prescribe the wrong treatment, you want to take the time to ask more questions and get it right. If the probability of a fatal misdiagnosis is small and the patient could die if you wait, you've crossed the threshold and should act rather than wait for another test, a second opinion, or a more detailed medical history.

For Dale, the CIO in a large investment institution, crossing the action threshold wasn't a life-or-death matter, as it can be in a hospital emergency or operating room. But knowing that didn't reduce Dale's stress as head of a team that was set up to cull through a confusing array of options and recommend the next generation of computer technology for the organization. Given the present rate of growth, every day that a decision was delayed increased the cost of the new system, the risk of significant downtime, and the complexity of the implementation. How could Dale be sure that the team was making informed decisions rather than deferring to the loudest or most eloquent voice or being swayed by politics or a majority-rule decision?

CREATE SOLUTION SPACE

If you've ever driven a car that's skidded out of control or piloted a plane through an evasive maneuver—and you're still here to tell the tale—you may know firsthand what it's like to keep yourself calm and rational. Pilots, emergency response teams, and race-car drivers practice reining in their emotions in the face of an adrenaline rush and the need for split-second timing. They know how to put the world in slow motion and run through options until they find a course of action that looks as if it will work. They develop a set of mantras, inviolate decision rules, and rehearsed reactions that are based on rules of physics rather than what "feels right" by instinct.

When Dale first met his steering team for the IT project, he could tell that the assemblage of key executives, traders, and IT professionals was a volatile mix of egos and special interests. The anxiety over an impending disaster, if something wasn't done soon to alleviate the burden on an obsolete computer system, was a lit fuse. When Dale called the group together, he used his best hypnotic voice. He talked in understated, matter-of-fact terms about the inadequacies of the present system and the constraints that the board of directors had imposed. "If we're calm, rational, and objective," he told them, "we can find good solutions and avert a crisis."

One of the key executives pounded his fist on the table and accused Dale of not understanding the severity of the situation. Dale admitted later that he saw his career flash before his eyes. Still, he kept his wits about him. Dale used the same hypnotic voice to assure the executive that he had things under control, as long as the team didn't lose time on personal attacks that wouldn't lead to a solution. It worked. When the most mercurial member of the team settled down, everyone else took a breath and an air of calm filled the room.

SET CRITERIA TO EVALUATE PROPOSALS OBJECTIVELY

After a number of alternatives are presented and people start to line up behind their personal favorites, it can be hard to reach consensus. Reassessing the options starts to feel like switching sides. Political interests weigh in alongside objective considerations as "who's supporting whom" is noted.

When impatient, pragmatic problem solvers get together, the first question they usually ask is "What should we do?" rather than "How will we recognize the best course of action when we see it?" But if the criteria aren't spelled out in advance, there is little common ground to return to when tough decisions have to be made or when the best course of action is the least popular or counterintuitive one.

For this reason, Dale devoted the first steering team meeting to brainstorming a list of criteria for success. After the list was compiled, he insisted that the team reach consensus about which items on the list should be five-point, three-point, and one-point criteria. Later, when the deliberations became tense, the group used the criteria as a decision grid.

Dale knew the process had worked when he heard a vociferous critic justify the team's recommendation to the board of directors. "I didn't want to support this alternative at first either," his nemesis said. "But the objective criteria led us to this decision, even though it's not the one we would have liked to have taken."

START AT THE END AND WORK BACKWARD

Dale knew that there would be serious problems with downtime and system availability within twenty-two months. He had a twenty-month window. Starting at the end meant figuring out where things should be in twenty months, eighteen months, and sixteen months before the team worked its way back to the present to figure out what to do this month and this week.

Starting at the end is not a new idea. It's something that every project management textbook teaches. Yet, over and over again, we see teams start where they are, without a finish line in sight, and wonder why they end up somewhere they hadn't planned to be. We see it in our simulation with groups who get to the market early but fail to reap all the rewards. And we see it in real life, with project teams that miss deadlines and budgets, seduced into overpromising and, by default, underdelivering.

Being a project manager doesn't just mean that you guide the discussion and follow the collective will of the committee you've assembled. Dale had learned this lesson the hard way, by following the lead of the most senior members of the project team instead of taking the lead and guiding them through the planning process. Taking the lead meant he'd have to sell and resell the methodology to an impatient and reluctant assemblage of egos and special interests and sell realistic time lines and budgets to investors and entrepreneurs, who are always trying to do more with less.

Playing Teammates out of Position

Soon after Olivia was hired, she was asked if she would take charge of resource allocation, budgeting, and planning for the product development function. When she agreed to assume that responsibility, the last thing she wanted was a turf war with her predecessor, whose promotion had created the vacancy Olivia was invited to fill.

Six months later, in the middle of a difficult budgeting cycle, Olivia was ready to give up and ask for a new assignment. If you didn't listen carefully, you might not know how exasperated she'd become. Olivia wasn't a chronic complainer. She spoke calmly and rationally. "This isn't an emotional issue," she explained. ""I just want to be in a role where I'm adding value, not being second-guessed and doing work that someone else is going to redo later."

There were a number of reasons that people still went to Olivia's predecessor when they were asked tough questions about the budgets they'd submitted or when they were afraid resources might be allocated differently. Her predecessor, who was Asian, was well connected at corporate headquarters; Olivia was American—a culture, a continent, and ten time zones removed from the company's epicenter. Gender, no doubt, was also a factor. And besides, the old guy was known to be a soft touch. He couldn't say no when someone asked for more resources, and he wouldn't confront people about missed time lines or budget overruns as long as they had a good explanation.

Olivia's predecessor was astonished to learn that there was a problem. He was trying to support Olivia in any way he could, not usurp or undermine her authority. If he answered someone directly, it was only because it was more expedient than waiting until the U.S. office was open for business. Because of old ties and old relationships, he acknowledged that some people were more comfortable hearing tough questions or unpopular decisions from him than from Olivia. Besides, he explained, he now had a broader perspective since he was now responsible for budgeting and resource allocation for all products, including the ones in development, which were in Olivia's purview.

When you encounter a situation like the one Olivia and her predecessor found themselves in, you can take a number of steps to avoid misunderstandings.

MAP YOUR STAKEHOLDERS
AND DEFINE THEIR ROLES

If we still operated in organizational silos, hierarchies, and chains of command, defining our jobs would be an easier exercise. When Olivia was put in charge of resource allocation, this clear definition was what she expected, as did her immediate supervisor, the U.S.–based head of product development. From this perspective, she had been given the assignment but not granted the authority or support to discharge her new responsibilities. She was supposed to be the person in charge, but when she told her underlings what to do, all too often they sought and found a way to work around her.

But if you map the interdependencies and the resource allocation team as a molecular organization, the web of stakeholders and roles looks very different (see Figure 4). Using project team, rather than chain-of-command, role definitions, a map of Olivia's stakeholders included the following:

- **Sponsors.** Olivia thought the director of product development, who had the office next to hers and had nominated her for this role, was her only sponsor. She wasn't thinking of the finance director, product portfolio director, and marketing director as her sponsors, even though her work on the budget and on resource allocation had a major impact that reverberated beyond product development.

- **Expert advisors.** There were others besides the consultants Olivia had assembled in the Unites States to automate the project management, performance tracking, budgeting, and spending processes—and give the company a better understanding of how much it really had to invest to bring a new product through development and make better decisions about the product development portfolio.

- **Executors.** Olivia needed to include more than the development managers working in R&D laboratories and field-testing locations in Asia, Europe, the Middle East, and North America. She didn't think of the managing director of the Israeli subsidiary as a member of her team, for example, even though the Israeli MD's operation would be affected by resource allocation decisions and would be expected to provide input to shape those decisions and, ultimately, to execute whatever decisions were made.

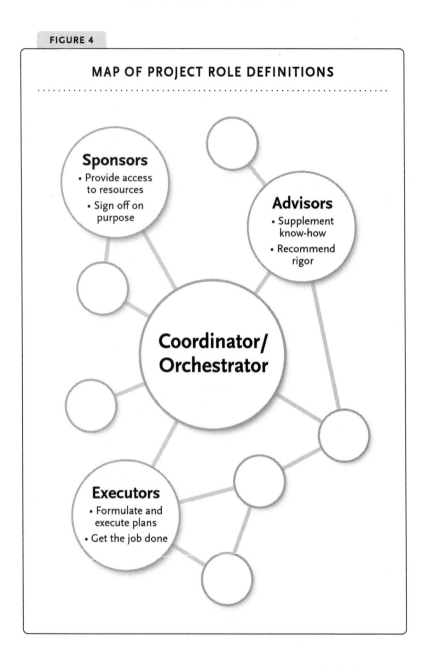

FIGURE 4

MAP OF PROJECT ROLE DEFINITIONS

Sponsors
- Provide access to resources
- Sign off on purpose

Advisors
- Supplement know-how
- Recommend rigor

Coordinator/ Orchestrator

Executors
- Formulate and execute plans
- Get the job done

- **Project directors.** Other project directors were working on parallel processes and parallel technologies that ultimately would need to work together and support each other. Very few projects can be done with total autonomy, without considering the knock-on effect on sister projects and sister divisions and business units. Resource allocation in the development group was Olivia's baby, but it wasn't the only baby in the nursery. Her predecessor was responsible for resource allocation across the entire enterprise, development included, and other managers in the system were equally concerned with squeezing more profit out of the company's product portfolio in a tougher economic environment than any they had seen before.

DEFINE CHANNELS OF COMMUNICATION AND COORDINATION

Olivia and her boss, the director of development, were newcomers in a team whose members already knew one another well and had learned to function as a well-oiled machine. Any one of her predecessor's cronies could put an issue in play as smoothly as a basketball player puts a ball in play from the sidelines and then runs to get into position while the ball is dribbled down the court and passed from one player to another. With the court awareness that enables players to anticipate one another's moves and go where the ball will be, messages were passed with lightning speed from one teammate to another by e-mail and voice mail, inference, rumor mill, and innuendo. The old guard could work as a team and make informed, crisp business decisions without ever having to confer with one another face-to-face, and often without a single telephone contact.

Olivia hadn't yet learned the plays and thus found herself dropping the ball and missing passes every time she came in off the bench. When she threw an issue into play from the sidelines, she would find herself out of the action while others motioned and passed effortlessly to one another. As a result, decisions were often made without her input, and Olivia found herself being treated like just another executor rather than the project director responsible for driving resource allocation in the division that spent 60 percent of the corporation's investment capital.

As the rookie in an existing network of stakeholders who worked together well, Olivia was walking a fine line. She didn't want to show disrespect or look like she didn't know what she was doing. Yet she needed someone to explain the channels of communication and coordination to her, and she needed a way to get others to change those protocols, which worked effectively for people who were on the same continent and had the same knowledge of what was happening at the corporate epicenter but left out stakeholders who were on other continents and on other wavelengths.

It took courage and a lot of effort for Olivia to say, "I'm getting on a plane to cross the ocean and take a few weeks to learn how you guys work together." It took even more courage, during and after that visit, for her to say, "Time out! This doesn't work for me or for the other stakeholders on our side of the ocean. We've got to get together and rewrite the playbook, or we're going to leave out too many of the key players we want to enlist."

DEFINE SHARED AUTHORITY

Consensus decisions, on the whole, tend to be better than decisions that are made without key parts of the brain trust. But achieving consensus also can be slow and expensive. In a fast, complex, resource-constrained global operation, not everyone can be in on every decision.

Olivia had to accept the fact that, even though she was the project director, decisions could and would be made in her absence. And she had to be equally clear about the decisions she would refuse to support unless she had a seat at the table.

In a hierarchy, the rules of decision making are simple and clear. The boss gets the final say, unless he delegates that authority to someone else and chooses not to exercise veto power after the fact. But in a molecular team, it's hard to tell where the buck stops unless you explicitly define who has the following powers.

- **Input power.** Good decisions cannot be made without adequate information. Stakeholders who can provide relevant data, therefore, should have input, which should be taken seriously by others. If the right channels of communication are open and the right data are gathered and warehoused up front, this part of the process doesn't have to slow or block a good decision. If the input of those with input power is ignored or overruled, these people are, by definition, entitled to a cogent and rational explanation.

- **Deliberation power.** Good decisions cannot be made without an adequate understanding of how others will be affected. If there is no impact on anyone else, one person might be able to make the decision alone. But when there are interdependencies, what's good on one continent might create difficulties somewhere else. That, ultimately, is why Olivia needed to be consulted and involved rather than informed after the fact. Of course, not everyone who is affected by a decision can be involved in every deliberation. Even the most democratic parliaments, therefore, work in subcommittees and representative councils. For this system to work, the members of the committee need to have enough intimate knowledge to consider what's best for the federation as a whole, not just for their own constituents.

- **Veto power.** Good decisions are effective only if they stick. If they aren't executed, they're only a fantasy. Some sponsors, experts, and executors have the power to block decisions that they don't buy into. And some make threats and blow loud and hard but, like it or not, have to bow to those who have a mandate to decide. It isn't always easy to tell the difference between these two, and it isn't always pleasant to remind others that you have veto power. As the protocols were defined, Olivia found that she had a far stronger mandate to decide than she at first thought, and she had veto power that she could have exercised but chose not to.

SIGNAL BEFORE CHANGING LANES

In a chain-of-command organization, the player and the position are one and the same. As a technical expert, the boss may not be right—but she is the boss. If she has a definite opinion about how the job should be done, anything less than compliance is insubordination. And if execution fails, others can claim that they were "just following orders."

In a molecular structure, the ground rules and accountabilities are different. If a sponsor steps over the line and acts like a technical expert without having the technical expertise, someone on the team is expected to say, "You've crossed the line." Of course, egotistic or overly controlling sponsors may persist and ignore the warnings. But even that doesn't absolve the real experts of accountability for failures; they need to be able to influence others to accept their advice and counsel.

For efficient coordination in a molecular team, the players have to be conscious of which roles they are assuming at any time, just as dancers in a musical always need to be aware of their stage positions and lines of sight with the audience. Teammates need a way of cueing one another and signaling if someone is out of position. And if the rhythm of the music or the audience reaction suddenly changes, teammates need a way to say, "Give me a little more (or less) room. I'd like to improvise on the written choreography and assume a more (or less) visible or expansive role, at least temporarily."

Some dancers are highly protective of their parts, their trademark steps, and their visibility. For those on the way up, each performance isn't just a recital; it's also an audition for the next role that's up for grabs. The more trust there is within the network of stakeholders, and the less defensiveness and turf protection there is regarding who got the bigger and better part, the more open players can be about their needs and intentions, and the easier it will be to play off one another's strengths and cover for one another's limitations.

In Summary

If the questions you've answered about the five courage factors tell you that rigor needs to be improved, what steps can you take to create a different reality for your team?

1. Let logic prevail. What the solution, system, or procedure contributes should be more important than who came up with it or who will score points if it is adopted. In a heated discussion, this isn't always the case; set it as a ground rule and stick to it.

2. Put personal convenience in perspective. Just because you aren't comfortable doing business in a particular way doesn't make that way wrong. Sometimes the "no pain, no gain" rule applies; your inconvenience or discomfort may not be a bad sign.

3. Anticipate touch points and consequences. And if you don't know what they are, ask other stakeholders, and watch how they use what you produce and how they produce what you use.

4. Apply constructive intolerance. When people say, "This is how we'll do things," make sure they keep their commitments. Mistakes are okay as long as people learn from experience.

5. Don't blame and shame. If people have used good judgment and are still learning to execute, blame won't help. But if their judgment is flawed and they are justifying a lack of rigor, you've got to get their attention.

6. Be an active bystander. If you see a lack of rigor, don't enable it by saying nothing. Be part of the solution.

7. Determine whether rigor is the issue. Mindless performance can be a symptom of a lack of candor, purpose, or will. Make sure there is really an issue of rigor before you start applying solutions.

8. Assess skill and aptitude. Hire large, by bringing in teammates who have more talent than you do. Train. And deselect people who don't have the ability to learn.

9. Create a learning organization. Make it clear that you are hiring people not for what they know but rather for their capacity to keep learning and trying new things. Invest in the time and practice opportunities that people need to learn.

10. Establish as few rules as possible. Don't use rules as a substitute for judgment when judgment and discretion really are required.

11. Create solution space. Don't push people over the action threshold prematurely.

12. Set criteria to evaluate proposals objectively. So that political considerations do not outweigh objectivity, set criteria before you consider the proposals themselves.

13. Start at the end of a project and work backward. Keep your objectives and resources in mind to avoid overcommitting.

14. Map and define roles. Be clear on who is playing what role in the project, and know when the roles shift. Be clear on where the overlaps and pressure points are.

15. Define channels of communication and coordination. Make sure information exchanges work smoothly, that everyone who needs to know is in the loop. When in doubt, overcommunicate.

16. Define shared authority. Figure out who has the 51 percent or tie-breaking vote on which issues and how decisions will be made—by consensus and by mandate.

17. Signal before changing lanes. When you switch hats and play a different role, make sure others know what you are doing—and make sure you have a mandate. Avoid collisions.

RISK

....

The Courage to Empower, Trust,
and Invest in Relationships

*It often requires more courage to dare to do right
than to fear to do wrong.*
ABRAHAM LINCOLN

"I could really use your support on this," a colleague says. Her logic is
sound. The business case is compelling. But there's a good reason that
she's come to you personally and appealed to your sense of fairness
and your dedication to the profession and to the enterprise.

"Your support," as she puts it, would require a real sacrifice. If you
reallocated resources as she proposes, your quarterly performance objectives would be unachievable. You might have to forgo a bonus. Sure,
you'd get a heartfelt "thank-you" from the folks in the executive suite,
but who knows how this hit could affect your visibility and your career
prospects. Despite all this, what she's proposing is the right thing to do.

Risk, the last of the five courage factors, is the courage to empower,
trust, and invest in relationships. If your risk quotient is high, there's
no doubt that you'll do the right thing. You might try to recoup some
of your endangered bonus and get the visibility and respect you deserve for contributing to the greater good, but the point is that your
colleagues know they can count on you to put enterprisewide success
ahead of your own needs. They can count on you to relinquish power

and control when someone else is better equipped to take charge, make the big play, and get the hero's welcome. When someone asks to move to the head of the line, as your colleague did when she asked for your support, you are willing to hear her out and give her the benefit of the doubt rather than question her motives and try to outmaneuver her politically.

Without the need for risk, there would be no real need for courage. Of the five factors, this is the one that makes your palms sweat the most. It's the one that makes you most vulnerable. It involves a leap of faith that can make you a "best supporting actor" or that can leave you upstaged. It involves your willingness to sign off based on someone else's word and someone else's counsel, knowing that you'll be left holding the bag if it doesn't work out. Risk tests your faith when you've empowered someone else to make important decisions and he chooses a course that's different from the one you would have chosen. It tests your trust in those around you, your loyalty to your colleagues, and your support for the organization and the cause that you're dedicated to achieving.

Making Triage Decisions

In a hospital emergency room, or ER, it takes a special brand of courage to trust the system and empower others. This is true of the patients receiving care as well as of the physicians and support staff. But no one needs more courage than the patients and families who sit in the waiting room, not knowing when they'll get help.

Intellectually, we understand that ERs can't afford a large enough staff so that everyone who needs care can get it immediately. We understand that our family members may not be taken on a first come, first served basis. But understanding the economics doesn't ease the pain and discomfort when you're the one who's waiting. It doesn't make the time go faster when someone who arrived later is ushered in and you're still sitting with a child, spouse, or parent who's in pain.

The ER staff take stock of the cases that present for treatment and make ongoing triage assessments. Those that are most serious and life threatening receive care first. Other patients are expected to trust the system, empower the caregivers, and have the strength and compassion to wait and endure their discomfort.

More and more organizations are facing similar resource constraints. There aren't enough designers, programmers, and office support staff to do everything. There isn't enough lab equipment to allow everyone access to what they need exactly when they need it. Budgets are tight, and there are many worthwhile opportunities and projects. Senior management doesn't have enough time to give everything visibility and support. Constant triage assessments are required. The projects that are most mission-critical get care and resources first. People with less urgent requests are told to wait.

If your project is assigned a lower priority, you're going to be more vulnerable. It's going to be harder to achieve your performance objectives. It's tempting to muster all the *chutzpah* you can to champion your cause and push your way to the front of the line. It's more of a risk to trust the system and empower others when you're expected to

- **Step aside** so another project (and another project manager) can get the resources that were originally allocated to your project

- **Admit** that someone else's work deserves more time and visibility on senior management's agenda

- **Delegate** to others and rely on their judgment and skill, even when they may not make the same decisions you would

- **Make do** with a meager allocation of resources or second-rate accommodations

- **Stay silent** while others are hashing out their differences and settling on an acceptable course of action—or let the meeting go on and the decisions stick, even if you aren't able to attend the deliberations

- **Pitch in** to help and give another department (or a rival co-worker) the benefit of the doubt, even when others haven't taken the time to be polite or explain why they usurped your resources or visibility

- **Rely** on trust and empowerment rather than inspection and control when you can't be everywhere, answer every question, or personally oversee every detail

Ultimately, a work group or organization won't be able to sustain candor, purpose, will, or rigor unless its members are willing to act selflessly. In a business culture that rewards competitive behavior and has fewer and fewer opportunities for advancement as people move into positions of influence and responsibility, success requires teammates to give up the possibility of personal gain in favor of working toward the good of the team. Imbuing a team with the desire to act altruistically is not a risk that can be mandated from the leader. You can't order it, demand it, or compel it. When you need it the most, it's too late to begin building the trust, dedication, and loyalty that will be put to the test. Rather, the willingness to risk must be cultivated over time among the members of the team, who must volunteer to make their own egos and ambitions subservient to the collective interests of the group.

What does it take for patients in a busy, stretched-to-capacity ER to wait their turn while others are given a higher priority?

- **Empathy.** Being attuned to someone else's needs and emotions is a special kind of intelligence. Some have more of it than others. Fortunately, research on emotional intelligence has shown that people who lack empathy can develop more compassion, sensitivity, and understanding of others' needs. We've also seen that ER staffs can raise the level of empathy by telling waiting patients and their families what's going on. Hearing "I'm sorry you still have to wait; we just got a heart attack victim" may not take away the throbbing in your arm or stop your child's nausea and dizziness, but it frames the sudden frantic rush of caregivers and the worried cries of family members. In our complex organizations, we need the capacity to understand the needs of other departments, professional disciplines, and markets, and we need a shorthand that evokes empathy when our group is asked to give ground and endure discomfort so others can get the care and attention they need.

- **Belief that others are doing their best.** When others say, "I need your support," it's going to be hard to keep saying yes if you believe their needs were caused by carelessness, lack of planning, or ineptitude. If you see the ER staff socializing or being lazy, it's going to be hard for you to wait your turn and cope with the discomfort. Benefit of the doubt has to be granted for a triage system to work. It also has to be earned. If others get the impression that you're oblivious to their needs or that you're goofing off and expecting them to take up the slack, they aren't likely to be very forgiving or accommodating. Study after study on altruism has shown that people are often willing to help those who seem to have legitimate needs or who are caught in unfortunate circumstances and are likely to turn a deaf ear to the pleas of people who create their own misfortune and fail to learn from experience.

- **Objective criteria.** Triage hurts when you are passed up for promotion or when the budget for your project is cut more than others. It's hard not to take it as a personal attack. The sting will be easier to justify and the embarrassment will be easier to recover from if you believe that objective criteria, rather than favoritism or outright discrimination, were used to make the decision. Do you owe an explanation to those who are sitting in the waiting room, wondering if they will ever get care? Without explanations, people may feel "the cards are stacked against us" or "no one appreciates how hard we are working and how much we really produce." Even when people are given explanations, they may challenge the criteria or try to negotiate. So be prepared to offer an explanation, and be ready to justify it if it is challenged.

- **Someone to talk to if triage conditions change.** We've all seen it happen, either in real life or on television. Someone is sitting in the ER, patiently waiting for care, and suddenly his condition worsens. The family members call for help. With precious seconds ticking away, they have to convince the caregivers that the situation has changed. If they aren't taken seriously, the patient may die or suffer tragic, preventable complications. The same is true with respect to a portfolio of projects or accounts. What was not so urgent yesterday may be more critical tomorrow. If people know that they can ask for the same support and indulgence that they are willing to give as conditions change, it's going to be easier to inspire trust and dedication.

The Bank: Harnessing the Killer Instinct

Being selfish, competing, and working at the expense of others is, in fact, how many of us were raised. We have been conditioned not just to achieve but to win. We may have a veneer of social grace, but that doesn't stop us from recognizing another party's weaknesses and moving in for the kill. If I am able to accumulate measurably more than you—more "toys," more money, more recognition—then it is more than likely that I will succeed in the eyes of the company, my family, and myself.

Nowhere is this more true than in the competitive, dog-eat-dog world of investment banking and securities trading, where thoroughbreds are rewarded for getting to the finish line first and winners are expected to have a "take no hostages, show no mercy" killer instinct. It's a fast-moving world, where being a minute or two late may mean that you've missed the window of opportunity, and where you don't leave money on the table.

In this get-as-much-as-you-can world of deal making, buyers make constant triage decisions, such as which phone calls to take and whom to leave on hold. If you have the best track record and are putting together the hottest deals—now—yours will be the calls that are taken. When you're on the line with the buyer, you know that the clock is ticking. You get right down to business. During trading hours, there's no time to waste on social pleasantries and idle chatter.

AN UNTAPPED GOLD MINE

Through acquisitions and aggressive hiring, an investment bank had assembled a stable of top-notch securities traders, each with a unique market focus. At this bank, one small team specialized in Southeast Asian securities, another in Latin American commodities, and a third in emerging Israeli technology companies. There were ten teams in all. Each had its own source of market intelligence and its own list of institutional buyers, representing some of the most respected pension funds, mutual funds, insurance companies, and trusts in North America.

The bank's diversity was a real asset. When one market was down, another was hot. The brokers representing Latin American growth companies might not be able to get anyone to talk with them or do a deal during a period of instability and currency devaluations, but the Southeast Asian team took up the slack and more than made up for the opportunities that their colleagues in the next bull pen were unable to create.

The new executive vice president saw an untapped gold mine in the white space on the organizational chart. If traders from one area could open the door for traders in another area, the potential for additional profit could be enormous. The bank might be managing 90 percent of an investor's holdings in Israeli high-tech corporations, for example, but the same investor might be working with another investment bank to manage its holdings in eastern Europe or the United Kingdom. The VP was convinced that lead sharing and opportunity sharing could increase the bank's securities business threefold within twelve to sixteen months. This would give brokers a way to add value to the enterprise at a time when their narrow specialties were down. All it would take from the brokers was a willingness to work together.

When the idea was presented to the traders, they were skeptical. They didn't see their colleagues as outright competitors, but few of them had much interest in blurring the boundaries either, even though they understood that it would pay off handsomely for the bank. We heard a wide range of reasons why lead sharing and opportunity sharing wouldn't work: I don't have time. I don't share my client list with anyone, ever. I don't know the trader working in the office across the hall; how am I supposed to trust him with an account I've worked for years to cultivate? I'd rather get new leads from a buyer than I would from another trader. What if a client asks me about an investment I don't know about, and I have to admit that I'm out of my league? What if I leave or my area is sold, and I've handed my client list to another broker in the bank?

The bottom line question was, Why should I take the risk? Why should I put my success and my reputation in someone else's hands? Why should I hand over proprietary information—the result of a life's work—to a bank that bought my portfolio a few months ago and could sell me to another institution tomorrow? Why should I relinquish power, control, or prestige before I can see that others will do the same for me?

We'd love to tell you that the VP had a magical solution that was immediately successful in overcoming the fear and reluctance that kept these brokers from working together. We'd love to tell you that our team-building simulations produced a change in behavior and not just insights about the virtues of leveraging opportunities for one another. But it didn't happen that way. It wasn't that the VP's vision for the brokerage was wrong. It wasn't that the brokers disliked or harbored any ill will toward one another. In theory, they could see that cooperation was the right thing to do, and the simulations demonstrated that clearly. But working together was a risk that made these aggressive, tough-minded brokers very nervous. And it was a risk that most of them weren't prepared to take. Why?

- **Vulnerability could be exploited as weakness.** If one of the brokers found himself in a soft market, he knew that his client relationships were at risk. Would he give his contacts to someone who was on a hot streak? Only if he knew it wouldn't weaken his position and compromise his reputation and following. But those who were dealing from a position of strength knew that they had the upper hand, and they used that leverage to extract concessions from colleagues in need. "Sure," one broker said, "I'll be willing to call your client and let him in on the deal that I'm putting together. But don't expect me to sit on your nest, protect your interests, and then hand the account back to you in a few months without a price." The brokers negotiated side deals with one another and expected special favors and referral fees. This was a far cry from the spirit of "You scratch my back and I'll scratch yours" that the executive vice president envisioned. And it made many brokers wonder whether they'd be better off weathering the storm of a soft market by themselves than making a pact with the devil.

- **They still viewed themselves as a collection of individuals.** Just because the brokers all reported to the same VP didn't make them a cohesive business unit. They had little desire to put the interests of the brokerage as a whole over their individual interests. In fact, as one broker said, "If the bank as a whole does well, then I'll lose my leverage to cut a better deal or go my own separate way." The small teams were more interested in maintaining their independence and autonomy than in creating opportunities for one another and expanding the business together. Work schedules didn't make things any easier. The VP had a hard time calling the group together for meetings because there were very few hours when everyone felt comfortable being off the trading floor at the same time. Off hours in one part of the globe were prime time for deal making somewhere else.

- **There was little reason to give one another the benefit of the doubt.** A buyer has a finite portfolio to invest. Every dollar that is invested in one property is unavailable for investment in something else. Could another broker be trusted to talk up his or her security and talk down competitive products from other brokerage houses rather than talk down an offering from a colleague? Could a broker in the next bull pen be trusted to build confidence rather than fertilize the seeds of doubt if a client made disparaging remarks about another trader from the same bank? No one knew for sure, and people didn't want to learn from bitter experience that they shouldn't let down their guard. There was a lot of banter, and it wasn't clear where a trader would draw the line and keep the teasing "behind closed doors."

AFTER A YEAR OF FALSE STARTS, WHAT NEXT?

If business had continued as usual, the VP would have abandoned his "one brokerage" experiment as an unworkable plan. But the next year was anything but business as usual. The market was too volatile for any single team to go its own way successfully without collaborating with other teams. There was too much consolidation in the industry. Clients were stretched thinner. They wanted to deal with one representative from a single brokerage house rather than receive three or four calls in a single day from brokers representing the same house.

What encouraged the brokers to take risks in the second year, after they had avoided those risks when the VP first asked them to pool information and work together? It wasn't the new business realities. Sure, in theory, it made even more sense for the specialists to work together. But the risks didn't go away; nor did the rationalizations for avoiding them. So, what changed?

- **Risk taking became a requirement.** After a year of pleading, cajoling, and presenting a business case, the VP began to sing a different tune. "If you don't open the door for your colleagues," he announced in private conversations with some of his top-performing brokers, "there's no room for you in this organization." The top performers were shocked. With all the business they were bringing in, they assumed risk taking was an extra-credit assignment that wouldn't affect their career prospects. Suddenly, they found out they were wrong.

It took courage for the VP to make risk taking a requirement. But values don't mean anything if the best and brightest performers are exempt from them. When GE revitalized the company by instilling a new code of conduct, Robert Slater (1998) reported that there were four groups of employees: those who achieved performance objectives and lived the values, those who fell short of performance objectives and lived the values, those who achieved objectives and didn't live the values, and those who neither achieved objectives nor lived the values. It was easy to decide that poor performers who didn't live the values should not be retained. And it was easy to decide that top performers who did live the values should be rewarded. After some discussion, it was decided that those who lived the values but didn't perform should be given a second chance. But the most troublesome group was those who delivered good business results but didn't live the values. Could the company afford to walk away from the profits they generated simply because they didn't follow the honor code? GE concluded that the values would mean nothing if top performers were exempt. If people didn't pull together and conduct themselves as part of the team, they could not be allowed to stay in the company—even if they were making a solid contribution to the bottom line.

The executive vice president at the investment bank came to the same difficult conclusion and had to speak frankly with aggressive, solid performers who weren't willing to take the risk of sharing information, sharing opportunities, and opening the door to colleagues. Taking risks to support colleagues no longer would be an extra-credit assignment for those with a well-developed killer instinct. From this point forward, it would be a ticket for entry as well as a requirement for continued employment.

- **Risk taking was measured and rewarded.** Each broker was given a two-for-two-in-two requirement. Within each quarter, they were expected to open the door for two colleagues, with two existing clients, leading to two new deals. Brokers who met the goal became eligible for special recognition and a special bonus; brokers who didn't were placed "on warning" for not living the values. This requirement made the values concrete and visible rather than subjective and "soft." The requirement created moments of truth in which brokers had to take risks and go out of their way for one another rather than avoid the risk and rationalize their avoidance.

- **Risk takers were honored and risk taking was celebrated.** Office parties, medals, honor rolls, and celebrations made heroes and role models of the brokers who first took the risk and lived the new values by creating opportunities for their colleagues. The celebrations also broke down the barriers among the specialized brokerages and created a sense of community in the bank. You wouldn't think that brokers earning more than $250,000 per year would care whether they'd earned crystal nameplates for their office doors or would care whether they got to keep those nameplates. You wouldn't think they would care whether they got to take the microphone and serenade their co-workers in a karaoke bar. But the symbols of taking the risk to support other colleagues did become important badges of honor.

The Project: Serving the Right Interest

It cost £200,000 per month—£2.4 million per year—to keep Kathleen's project going. The executive committee fixed a review date to see whether the investment still made sense. Kathleen told the project team that the next four months would be critical. They had to show that they were using the R&D budget responsibly and were making good progress. This was the time to set aside parochial interests and pull together as a cross-functional team. It was time to pull out all the stops. They had to build a solid business case and recover the ground they'd lost to setbacks that no one could have foreseen or controlled. Otherwise, three years of hard work would all be for naught.

A month after the review date had been fixed, Kathleen was summoned to the managing director's office. She thought she was expected to give an interim report and was prepared to show how much the team had accomplished in only one month. She was optimistic. But before she could give her report, Kathleen was informed that the budget would be cut. She had two weeks to bring the project to a close, get the records prepared for the archives, and settle accounts with her contractors and suppliers.

When Kathleen left the director's office, she was dumbstruck and furious. "If we had the additional three months we were promised," she ranted, "we could build a compelling case. This isn't fair and it isn't honest. How could they go back on their word like this? If this is the way decisions are going to be made here, how can we trust anything that the management team tells us?!"

It didn't matter to Kathleen that the cancellation of the project would have little impact on her career prospects with the company. "After you close out the project," she was told, "you can kick back for a month or so, and we'll then have another, more promising, project to assign to you." She was embarrassed about giving her word to her teammates and rallying the troops, only to go back to them with disappointing news. She felt that her credibility as a project director had been compromised. In her heart of hearts, she still believed that the project was worth doing and had the potential to enhance people's lives and produce wealth for the company.

When Kathleen called the members of the project team together and sat down with them in the conference room, she burst into tears. Her teammates rallied around her. "How can we fight this injustice?"they demanded. They emerged from the meeting with a more compelling case for the continuation of the project rather than a plan to close it down.

When the case landed on the director's desk, he was sympathetic but disappointed. He was unwilling to take the report to heart. "We simply can't justify another £600,000 in expenditures to tell us what we already know," he explained to Kathleen again, hoping that she would hear his message the second time it was delivered. "This project has to be closed down—now—so we can allocate our resources to projects that are far more promising."

How do you recover from a blow like this? How do you throw yourself into another project, knowing that it too may be canceled, no matter how hard you work, how well the team "clicks," and how much you believe in what you are doing? How do you inspire dedication and loyalty to the organization when it has not shown the same loyalty to you and those who looked to you for leadership?

- **Acknowledge the hurt and rise above it.** It wouldn't be honest to say, "This doesn't hurt," or, "We're not disappointed." If you couldn't get excited about the endeavor and put your heart and your professional ego into it, the project wouldn't be worthwhile. Of course you're going to take news like this as a personal rejection. If you've put your own reputation on the line and asked for a show of support from others, you're going to feel some embarrassment when you have to renege on your commitments. Just because you take a tough stand and do what the company requires doesn't mean you have to be heartless. It doesn't mean you have to hide your feelings. But it may mean that you have to rise above them and explain why the decision made sense to those who made it even though you find it distasteful.

- **Think globally and be a systemwide advocate.** If resources weren't limited and investors weren't demanding, you could afford to do without a continuing reassessment of expenditures and options. If you had an ER with excess capacity, you might not have to make triage decisions. Decisions like these put the Kathleens of the world in a tough position. Until the plug is pulled, they are expected to put their egos and their hearts into their projects and be articulate, passionate spokespeople. Then, when tough decisions are made, they are expected to shift their loyalties and explain the reasonableness of harsh decisions and dashed hopes. It's easy to lose sight of your systemwide responsibilities when you're passionate about your project or your department. But that's only half of the job for anyone in a position of leadership within the system.

- **Distinguish between the value of projects and the value of people.** Not every project is of equal value. That's a tough reality to accept, particularly for someone in a support or ancillary role. If you are asking someone to take a step back, as Kathleen was asked to do, that person may not feel affirmed or appreciated for the strengths and skills he brings to the party. That's particularly true if the person, time after time, is getting the second-tier projects and second-tier attention. Kathleen walked out of the director's office feeling devalued and disgraced rather than appreciated for everything she had done to rally her troops to give the project their best effort. If you're asking someone to take it on the chin, you've got to make sure he walks away feeling like a medal-worthy hero rather than expendable cannon fodder.

- **Insist that the institution do right by the people who are displaced.** When triage decisions are made and some people are asked to step to the side, everyone sees how those who make sacrifices are treated. Loyalty doesn't mean that you can offer employment for life or continue investing in projects that throw good money after bad. But it does mean that you can honor contractual and legal obligations, ease the transition, and treat people fairly. If you want people to trust the system, then the system has to behave in a way that is worthy of that trust.

Empowerment: The Courage to Let Go

Christina Lee was a brilliant first-generation Korean American engineer. From elementary school to graduate school, she had consistently outperformed her classmates in math, science, and engineering. Now that she was part of a major corporation, Christina was resentful about carrying the production planning and engineering team on her shoulders. It was unfair, she said, that the Anglo men got by on charm and personal relationships while she did the hard work. It was unfair that she worked nights and weekends to get the details right while her colleagues submitted reports and recommendations that were riddled with miscalculations and careless mistakes. It was unfair that she had to plead, cajole, and threaten to get her requests for data answered. It was unfair that many of her ideas were implemented too slowly to realize the cost savings and profits that could have been achieved if they had been implemented with a greater sense of urgency.

Christina was smarter than most of her colleagues. She was a harder worker. She was more attentive to detail. She was a more astute problem solver and a more clever and creative engineer. The vice president of production planning and engineering had a dilemma. For breakthrough new solutions, Christina was indispensable. He depended on her. But, despite her talent and her acute mind, no one wanted to work with her. By the time we met Christina, her open contempt and sharp tongue were about to derail her career. She had publicly humiliated the other engineers and several veteran plant managers. Even when she was right, no one wanted to admit it. No one wanted to embrace the conclusions or recommendations that she offered.

Our first team-building sessions with Christina and her colleagues were tense. There were accusations and counteraccusations. When the dust settled and we debriefed Christina afterward, we were pleased that three facts of life had become clearer to her than ever before.

- **You can't go it alone.** Even if you work more than a hundred hours a week and sacrifice your family and personal life, you can't do everything by yourself. Getting things done in a major corporation isn't like earning an A in a math or engineering class. The job is too complex for a solo performer. Like it or not, Christina needed help and support from the very co-workers she held in contempt. Without their voluntary cooperation, it would be impossible for her to accomplish any of her performance objectives or to put her new engineering concepts to work.

- **Other people can do some things better than you.** No one could provide technical leadership as well as Christina could. Everyone understood that. But getting things right on paper wasn't the same as getting change implemented in a real factory. Some of Christina's teammates had more patience and more of a knack for coaching, explaining, and hand holding. Staff members who were paid less than Christina could do routine tasks more cost effectively, even if it took them twice as long to set up the computer analyses.

- **You can't dictate every move or preprogram every decision.** When you rely on others, count on them to approach the job in their own style, with their own judgment and their own instincts. Count on them to follow a logic that's a little different from yours. Count on them to make their own mistakes, create their own dilemmas, and find their own way out of the difficulties they encounter. Sure, this will make you crazy and try your patience and indulgence—just as it did with Christina. You can teach others what you know, and you can show them the logic of your approach, but you can't make them into clones without stifling their initiative, judgment, and courage.

Under the best of circumstances, it isn't easy to entrust your performance objectives—and, quite possibly, your career—to someone else's judgment, initiative, care, and skill. It's even harder to back off and let go if you're a technical expert with high control needs. And these weren't the best of circumstances for Christina. She had encountered months of foot dragging, careless mistakes, and not taking her requests and recommendations seriously, even after senior management gave its approval.

It took a real leap of faith for Christina to make a fresh start and shift her mind-set from "expect the worst" to "trust and empower." She left the team-building session willing to take her colleagues at their word when they said they would give her more support and promised to advise her when problems first arose rather than after a deadline had passed.

But, as difficult as the conversations in the team-building session were, the real moments of truth didn't occur there. After all, the team-building session only required candor, not risk. A week after the session, back on the job, one of Christina's colleagues sent an e-mail message explaining why his group wasn't able to comply with the procedure Christina had designed and couldn't achieve the savings Christina had promised to senior management. At the end of his message he wrote, "I wanted you to know this as soon as I discovered we had a problem. After all, that's what we promised we'd do in our team-building session. Let's get together and find a better way forward."

The ball was now back in Christina's court. Her boss copied us on the e-mail exchange. He asked whether he should intervene with Christina, lest she become outraged and repeat the behavior that had brought his team to the brink of mutiny before the team-building workshop. We agreed that his coaching could be helpful to keep Christina on track. Here's what her boss recommended to Christina:

- **Control your outrage and disappointment.** Technically, you may be right, he told her. You may be smarter. And you may have the power to vent your outrage and expose your colleague's lack of follow-through to senior management. But the net effect of your outrage is guaranteed to be resistance, resentment, and passive-aggressive avoidance. It will not only inhibit risk but also erode candor, purpose, will, and rigor.

- **Schedule a face-to-face meeting.** It's cheaper and quicker to resolve issues like this by e-mail or telephone, particularly if, as in this case, your protagonist is based halfway around the globe. Spending extra nights away from home and incurring extra travel expenses may not be on your wish list. And it's not easy to turn on a dime and arrange an overseas trip on a moment's notice, even when the clock is ticking and the problem needs to be addressed right away. After trust is established, many technical problems can be addressed via teleconference, videoconference, or an exchange of e-mails. But when trust is low and you're trying to make a fresh start, it isn't enough to just work the technical problem. You need to raise the level of trust by spending quality time with the other person, getting to know each other and making a heartfelt commitment to invest in the relationship.

- **Act "as if."** It may not feel natural to rein in your outrage and give someone an undeserved benefit of the doubt. Indulging your emotions and acting out your feelings may be honest and authentic. But that doesn't mean it's the best way to build a foundation for risk. Research on expectations and self-fulfilling prophecies (Livingston, 1969; Rosenthal and Jacobson, 1996) confirms the warnings that Christina's boss offered. When you trust your colleagues, it's natural to be patient and understanding when they make mistakes or ask for help. When you don't trust them, it's natural to telegraph suspicion and negativity, however subtly, even when they follow through and do the right thing, as Christina's colleague did when he sent his e-mail message. If you know you are feeling suspicious and mistrustful, you may need to monitor your behavior and act "as if" you have a higher level of confidence, lest you destroy the trust you are trying to build.

Altruism: Once More with Feeling

The risks of helping others are almost always greater than the risks of doing whatever it takes to protect your own interests. This is true not only if you're a female Korean-American engineer relying on an Anglo male network but also in a department store chain or a national sales rep organization that fosters *chutzpah*. It's also true in cultures that reward people for acting with collective interests and the big-picture mission in mind.

In some communities throughout Nazi-controlled Europe, people risked their lives and their family fortunes to aid Jewish refugees. It didn't matter how many other families were also taking in refugees. With one indiscreet word from a neighbor or business rival, you and your family could be imprisoned or shot for treason. Despite the risks, many people displayed the courage to do the right thing. Three generations earlier, Quakers and others in eastern Canada and the United States also took tremendous risks. There were many who saw slavery as an abomination and helped escaped slaves get to Nova Scotia via the underground railroad. It's hard to imagine that apartheid would have ended in South Africa without intervention from communities who had more to gain from silence than outrage, or that Jewish refugees would have been allowed to emigrate to Israel from Ethiopia or the former Soviet Union without protests and financial contributions.

In business, the risks may not be matters of life and death, but nevertheless there are risks for those who choose to get involved and help others. If a co-worker is struggling to make his or her quota, offering to coach and mentor may eat into your own personal productivity. Some of the manufacturing department heads who pooled resources in the pharmaceutical company had their budgets and staff cut permanently. It can be risky to give someone else an opportunity when you are confident that you could do the job better by yourself. It's risky to empower someone to recover from a miscalculation or other mistake when you believe you could have prevented that mistake in the first place. It's risky to pay workers for time in training or time between projects, when they aren't generating an immediate profit, rather than lay them off and hope they'll be available and up to speed when you need them later.

We saw a dramatic example of altruistic behavior in a pharmaceutical sales organization shortly after the firm was acquired. The new compensation system, used by the acquiring corporation, was one that rewarded individual, rather than team, performance. It put members of the regional sales force in competition with one another for appointments with the same physicians and medical practices.

The new system created a dilemma for the teammates, particularly those presenting the hottest and most intriguing new treatment regimens. The question was, If a colleague is finding it difficult to make his or her numbers, should I get involved and help, knowing that my efforts will cost me part of my incentive bonus? Or should I mind my own business, keep plugging away, maximize my own numbers, and let my colleague fend for herself? Should I care about whether the time I spend with physicians is making it more difficult for another teammate to get an appointment with the same medical group or show them what we have to offer in other treatment areas—particularly when the company doesn't seem to want me to care?

After much heated discussion about the defects in the new compensation system, people sadly resigned themselves to the fact that the system wasn't going to change any time soon. The question was how they would work the new system, not how they would redesign it or revive the one they had had in the old company.

One of the more senior sales reps put a stake in the ground when he said, "I haven't spent ten years helping to build a team just to flush it all now. We have a choice today about what we want to build here and what we want to take to the new company with us. If anyone here is having trouble getting appointments with any of the physicians I'm seeing, I want to know about it. I'm promising you I'll do everything I can to get you in the door, whether it benefits me or not. Who knows? Maybe next year or the year after, I'll be calling you for help. But, whether I need help or not, I want to be part of a team on which people continue to look out for one another."

With his comment, there was a sigh of relief in the room. The discussion turned to how group members would continue to function as a team, despite the temptation to fend for oneself and ignore the needs of other sales reps in the region. The group took an oath to be altruistic rather than egoistic, in spite of the fact that the compensation system was explicitly designed to reward self-interest rather than collective interest. When we followed up a year later, the teammates hadn't broken that oath. Altruism, not egoism, was the team norm. The team believed it was no coincidence that they had posted the strongest performance of any region in the new company and had retained more talent than any other region in the company.

According to research by Batson (1991), people are more likely to choose the altruistic path if they believe that

- **They are the only ones in a position to help.** If other bystanders see the situation and don't offer help, why should I be the one who is obliged to offer help? If no one else is helping the sales reps with the least experience or the least exciting product lines to get appointments, why should I? The oath taken by the sales reps at the pharmaceutical company was "There will be no bystanders. Everyone gets involved."

- **The other person needs and wants help.** If a crime victim has the physical strength to fend off an attacker, for example, and I would only be in the way, what good would my help do? Sales reps who needed help had to ask for help, rather than maintain a macho front and go it alone. And they needed to be willing to accept help, even when it involved some feedback or guidance that was tough to hear.

- **Important goals are unattainable without help.** If the business will make it whether or not the person in need is successful, why bother to invest the time to help? Unless the company needed the profit from the less glamorous treatment regimens, one could argue that the reps who were responsible for those products could have been reassigned or their positions eliminated altogether.

- **The other person could suffer dire consequences without help.** If the other person couldn't be injured, for example, why should I bother to help him with safety equipment? It was clear, in the new system, that reps who failed to make their quotas would be in career jeopardy.

- **They have a kinship with the person who needs help.** If I can't identify or empathize with the person who needs help, why feel moved enough to get involved? It was also clear that the reps valued one another as professional colleagues. They believed that people were hard workers and that they weren't being asked to carry "dead wood" on the team.

- **Helping is a moral or religious imperative.** If I have to answer to a higher power for my moral acts or decisions not to act, how can I justify failing to do the right thing—whether or not I will receive a tangible personal benefit or reward?

According to Batson, there is a sharp difference between altruism and enlightened self-interest. With altruism, you're motivated by empathy for the person or group who needs your help, or by your commitment to the greater good of the enterprise, corporation, or community. With enlightened self-interest, you do the right thing to fulfill your own ambitions for recognition, power, or a long-term financial gain that wouldn't be possible if you didn't invest time and take a short-term risk.

With altruism, doing the right and just thing is its own reward. You may not receive any better care in the hospital because you saw that someone else needed attention sooner than your own child did. You won't receive a better seat or meal on the airplane because you didn't push to the front of the line. You may not receive a medal or reward for preventing a crime or testifying against the perpetrator. You may not earn more or get a faster promotion because you've coached a colleague who's having trouble with the new computer system. You do it because you care and because it's the right thing to do. You do it because you have given your word and have agreed to live by a code of honor. You do it because it perpetuates the values that sustain the organization, and not just because it's likely to bolster this quarter's stock price.

Enlightened self-interest is dangerous, Batson claims, because it masks the help giver's true intentions. As a result, those who are counting on help can find themselves betrayed or abandoned precisely when they need help the most. When the going got tough near the end of World War II, many Jewish refugees found themselves betrayed by the very families who had taken them in because the payments they were receiving were no longer worth the risks. The amazing fact about the team of pharmaceutical sales reps was not that they took an oath to support one another but that they kept that oath. If the motivation had been self-interest rather than altruism, those individuals who could have earned more by breaking rank would have said, "I'm sorry. I have a family to consider. Business is business."

In Summary

If the questions you've answered about the five courage factors tell you that risk needs to be increased, what steps can you take to create a different reality for your team?

1. Show empathy. Be willing to listen. Show you care when you are asking someone to make a sacrifice or make himself vulnerable. Understand the situation from the other person's vantage point, not only in terms of the objective reality, but also in terms of that person's personality style, professional training, and cultural conditioning.

2. Telegraph a belief that others are doing their best. Sharp accusations and blame aren't going to make someone willing to put aside self-interest and do whatever it takes to contribute to enterprisewide success.

3. Use objective criteria to make triage decisions. Be prepared to offer an explanation, and be prepared to justify your explanation if its fairness and reasonableness are challenged.

4. Be willing to talk and reassess the data as conditions change. Stay open to new facts and new realities. Make sure those who are waiting in the wings or making sacrifices understand that their voices can and should be heard and that their contributions are valued.

5. Don't exploit someone else's vulnerability as weakness. If you are an aggressive competitor, it may require all the self-restraint you can muster to rein in your killer instinct. Be clear on who your real competitors are, and go after them with all the skill and cunning you can. Be equally clear on who your allies are and what's required to help them and get them to help you.

6. View yourself as part of a community. Be willing to grow an enterprise, not just feather your own nest. If you can't see the value of this, there will be very little basis for risk, particularly when the system requires a sacrifice or triage decision.

7. Give others the benefit of the doubt. Show others that you will protect their reputations and their livelihoods. If there is criticism to deliver, do it in a way that preserves the other person's dignity and assumes that the other person is capable and honorable.

8. Make risk taking a requirement. If there is a code of honor that has to be preserved, don't allow excuses or contribution to the bottom line to compromise it. A code of honor is only as strong as its weakest link and falls apart if some people are exempt.

9. Measure and reward risk taking, and make heroes out of those who exemplify the honor code. Unsung and invisible heroes don't become models for others to follow. If you want to see risk taking, reward it and make positive examples of those who lead the charge.

10. Acknowledge the hurt and rise above it. When you are asked to make a sacrifice, don't close ranks and give "management speak." Be real. But don't make that an excuse for criticizing those who have put you in an awkward position.

11. Think globally and be a systemwide advocate. Explain the rationale of risks, vulnerability, and sacrifices from a systemwide perspective.

12. Distinguish between the value of projects and the value of people. Dignify the contributions and capabilities of individuals, even if you have to decide that some projects are more mission critical than others.

13. Insist that the institution do right by the people who are displaced. How you treat those who are put in vulnerable positions will signal to others how they can expect to be treated.

14. Don't act as if you can go it alone. You can't, even if you work more than a hundred hours a week and are more capable than anyone else.

15. Accept the fact that other people can do some things better than you. Recognize others for the strengths they bring to the party and be willing to rely on them for contributions, even if that gives them more visibility than you.

16. Don't try to dictate every move or preprogram every decision. Trust others to use their own judgment and put their own style, personality, and professionalism into the job.

17. Take initiative. Be proactive and earn the other party's confidence.

18. Create positive self-fulfilling prophecies with the climate you create, the input you provide, the output you expect of others, and the feedback you offer, both when things go right and when things go wrong.

19. Make the code of honor and willingness to sacrifice for the good of the whole a worthy end in itself rather than a means to an end. Don't allow some individuals to be exempt from the honor code, or you will compromise everyone's willingness to risk, trust, empower, and make their egos subservient to the success of the enterprise as a whole.

The
FIVE FACTORS
in Action

A FIVE-PART
FORMULA

Dealing with Conflict

*Leaders with courage don't take others where they already
wanted to go. They take people in a new direction, further and
faster than they would have chosen to go on their own.*
BOB GALVIN

Some moments of truth come with advance warning, giving us time
to prepare and rehearse. Others hit us by surprise and require a quick,
instinctive response. Whether we have time to prepare or are caught
off guard, risk is almost always the one courage factor that looms in
front of us. It requires that leap of faith that we take when we put ourselves on the line and hope others will come through for us.

We take risks any time we put aside what's required to "cover ourselves" and champion our ideas and proposals. We take a risk every
time we ask others for help, particularly if we don't know them well
and aren't sure if they'll come through. "Trust my judgment. Back me
up. Reassure me that I'm on the right path. Provide me with the time,
the resources, or the visibility that's needed to get the job done." All of
these requests require some measure of risk, both when we ask them

of others and when we tie our fortunes and reputations to the best efforts of others.

Resolving any conflict involves some measure of risk. If you work out a solution in which you will meet each other halfway, you are gambling that the other person will keep his or her word. The risk is higher still if the resolution requires you to give more than you receive, in the hope that you are contributing to a greater "win" for the enterprise, the customers, or the investors.

And that brings us to the paradox of applying the five-part courage formula. Risk is the first thing we want, yet it's the last thing we're prepared to give—unless there's a secure foundation and we know that we're dealing with people we can trust. Risk makes us painfully aware of how vulnerable we are and how much we've put today's success, and perhaps our entire careers, in the hands of other people. We can't be expected to put aside what's expedient or what serves our own self-interests in order to do what's right unless we have confidence that what we give we will also receive.

How does the application of the five courage factors ultimately lead to the risk we need to take to resolve conflicts in a way that contributes to the good of the enterprise?

By establishing a climate for candor—one in which we feel we can speak the truth and hear the truth from the other parties

By agreeing on a common purpose—so we are working together to achieve the same lofty and audacious goals

By generating goodwill—so we can face difficult issues and frustrations with optimism, spirit, and promise

By creating rigor—so we can trust the data, generate a full range of possibilities, weigh our options, and create know-how that will enable us to solve new problems

Only when these foundations have been established are we ready to put the last of the courage factors in place.

By taking risks—to provide the support, the opportunity, and the empowerment that our partners need and receiving the trust we deserve from them

Step One: Candor

It wasn't the first time Bob Harris had stormed into the boardroom and thrown the latest issue of the trade journal down on the conference table. A few of the executive vice presidents had seen the report already and knew the boss would be steamed that their conflicts were being aired in public.

It was a classic Bob Harris tirade. The VPs braced themselves. On one level, of course, Bob was right to be furious. "I don't know what's worse," Bob said. "Our differences should never find their way into the press, especially without a report on what we've done to move forward as a united team. And I shouldn't have to learn about conflicts and dissent from the press."

The differences cited in the trade journal never did get properly addressed. No one spoke in the meeting unless Bob asked a direct question. The tone was tense. Those who managed to stay out of the spotlight avoided Bob's wrath. Those who couldn't avoid the spotlight were grilled mercilessly and berated when they couldn't reply quickly enough. Bob took no hostages. Some of his attacks got quite personal.

Unfortunately, Bob's outrage and impatience, while perhaps warranted, did nothing to improve the situation. His behavior telegraphed a clear message: Tell the boss what he wants to hear, when he wants to hear it. Don't bring news that he's not ready to hear. Keep your head down. Stay invisible. Pretend to get along, even when you don't. Maintain harmony, at least on the surface. Court favor.

One brave soul approached Bob later that same day and asked whether he was satisfied with what they'd achieved at the meeting. Bob barked back in righteous indignation. "Whoa!" our brave soul said. "I'm not the enemy. I just wanted to know if the meeting accomplished what you set out to do."

Bob squirmed uneasily. His face turned red. "Look," he said, "I don't have time for games. If there's something you think I'm doing wrong, let me have it straight." Our brave hero complied and told Bob that the issues never did get discussed because no one was willing to raise them and deal with them straightforwardly. He told Bob that the climate in the meeting made people defensive about what was written in the trade journal and suspicious about where "the leak" had started. He didn't believe they'd developed a coherent strategy to do damage control and resolve the conflicts that were cited in the article.

Bob had a hard time taking any responsibility for the group's lack of candor. He thought he had called his executive team to action and had impressed on them the seriousness of the situation. He didn't think that reading them the riot act should have reduced their level of candor. "If we have wimps on our executive team who are afraid to open their mouths when the going gets tough," Bob said, in his trademark style, "let me know who they are and I'll gladly replace them with people who aren't afraid to tell me what they think, no matter how wrong they might be. At our next meeting, I'll ask, and we'll see if anyone is intimidated."

In a sarcastic and patronizing style, Bob opened the next meeting by asking if anyone felt too threatened to say what needed to be said. As usual, the members of the executive team averted their gaze and one of the VPs made a joke. "That's exactly what I thought," Bob said, feeling vindicated, and continued with the agenda.

With that, the team breathed a collective sigh. The collusion of silence had again been preserved. Bob Harris was, once again, oblivious to the impact of his "say what I want, hear what I want" tirades. And the rest of the team was oblivious to the fact that, one team member at a time, they too were making a semiconscious decision—to indulge their fear rather than rise above it and say what needed to be said.

The trade journal article raised a number of issues about the way the bank was building its franchise in the market niche they had carved out for themselves. They were issues that the executive team had pushed aside and failed to work through, largely because it was easier to either avoid the conflicts that the issues would provoke or look to Bob to adjudicate if they reached an impasse. The article said that Bob's bank talked innovatively but was doing little that was actually innovative. The article was right. If the team couldn't even talk openly enough to acknowledge that there were conflicts that needed to be addressed, how could they get to the level of risk taking that would be required for some departments and lines of business, such as trusts and the local retail banks, to relinquish their position of leadership to others, such as commercial lending and the newly created national marketing department?

We know how to advise Bob Harris about opening the lines of communication, drawing people out, and listening to important feedback even when it's news any top executive would rather not have to deal with. But what are *you* supposed to do, as a middle-level manager, if Bob won't even read our chapter on candor, let alone take the advice to heart? The answer lies in what you do with your own fear—and whether you can follow in the footsteps of the brave soul who approached Bob and said, "With all due respect, sir, we have a problem." The brave soul didn't expect Bob to say "Thank you." If it were easy to talk candidly in Bob's presence, it wouldn't take courage to speak the truth—or to acknowledge the fact that your own silence might be contributing to the problem.

Step Two: Purpose

In many of our workshops on courage and conflict resolution, we guide participants through an analysis of the events leading up to the catastrophic launch of NASA's space shuttle *Challenger* in 1985. There was no Bob Harris at the helm, inhibiting candor. A team of experts had assembled to make the decision. With so many tough-minded, get-it-done leaders representing so many different interests and agendas, it's not surprising that the tone became contentious and tense. Some would argue that the launch of the ill-fated *Challenger* on an unusually cold January day was a calculated risk, a risk that would have been applauded if the O-rings had held the rocket together. But what purpose did the risk serve? That was the question that wasn't discussed or resolved before the engineers put aside their concerns and gave the green light for the launch.

The dynamics of NASA's *Challenger* disaster have been replayed in many of the high-profile business scandals that have occurred in the recent past. While few of these resulted in the same loss of life that occurred in the explosion of the *Challenger*, many innocent people have lost their life savings. In each of the failures—ImClone, Enron, Arthur Andersen, WorldCom, the Maccabiah Games—there were experts who counseled the decision makers about the ethical and prudent actions to take. And in each case, the decision makers failed to heed their counsel.

What is most striking, as well as tragic, about these catastrophes (including the decision to launch the *Challenger*) isn't the fact that the decision makers failed to consider mission-critical data. It's the fact that they all took their eyes off the prize and were guided by a sense of purpose that put short-term gain and political expediency ahead of enterprisewide success and the trust that had enabled partners, investors, and customers to take risks and support the enterprise.

What was the "prize" that NASA sought in January 1985? It wasn't a shuttle launch. It was a public relations coup and a demonstration that the agency deserved an infusion of public money. What was the price for the Maccabiah Games? It wasn't a cheap bridge, constructed well under budget, on which the competing athletes could cross the Yarkon River in Tel Aviv. It wasn't even a gold medal in the competition. It was Jewish solidarity, showcasing and honoring Israel as a magnet for the best and brightest of the world Jewish community. Arthur Andersen lost sight of what was important, which was not pandering to greed but maintaining a reputation for scrupulous honesty and for asking the tough questions. WorldCom, ImClone, and a host of others forgot that, without investor trust and confidence, nothing else really mattered.

What was the prize that the members of Bob Harris's executive team sought to achieve, both as individuals and as a group, on the rare occasions when contentious issues actually surfaced? If the senior executives were most focused on scoring points with Bob, or at least avoiding his wrath, it's no wonder that the real issues couldn't be faced and the real conflicts couldn't be adequately resolved.

Each VP on Bob's team wanted to be recognized as "the hero" and sought to expand his or her sphere of control. They all wanted their own projects and interests to become flagship enterprises for the new financial services franchise. In an environment where who won and who got the credit were as important as what was actually achieved for the enterprise, it became almost impossible to separate personal agendas from business agendas. To not stand up in favor of someone's pet project was interpreted as a personal attack, which inevitably warranted personal retribution rather than a rational discussion about which investments would build the strongest franchise and the strongest foundation for growth. Backing off on a project you had been championing caused others to become suspicious of your "real motives," even if you explained why you felt something else was more mission critical.

Whose purposes should be served when conflicts are raised? If conflicts are moments of truth that you approach with a win-lose belief system, you will try to advance your agenda at the expense of others or allow them to advance their agenda at your expense. This was happening with Bob Harris's executives. The VPs were advancing their own agendas as cleverly and powerfully as possible and trying to keep as much control as possible, lest someone else advance at their expense. Neutral parties were lobbied to side with one group or another, either based on the merits of the issue or to preserve a political coalition. Such an adversarial approach assumes that each party will argue her case vigorously and that the winner will prevail with truth, logic, and compelling arguments.

A win-win belief system assumes that conflicts are best resolved by recognizing the legitimacy of both parties' needs and seeking solutions that will satisfy everyone's needs. If the issue is unimportant, resolution might be reached by compromise, with each party getting a portion of what it wants and ceding some ground to the other party. If the issue is important, the parties may need to find creative alternatives to work out a solution that will serve everyone's purposes. Such a non-adversarial approach assumes that both parties will benefit by working together rather than at cross-purposes and that there is more to be gained by finding mutually acceptable solutions than by competing to see who will win.

In today's environment, however, win-win solutions often are not enough. The real test isn't just whether we've each found a way to satisfy our competing interests and achieve our individual or parochial objectives. It's also whether we've done what's right. Asking whether we're doing the right thing—for the enterprise as a whole and for the good of our shareholders and the public we serve—imposes a different set of standards from asking whether "I've scratched your back and you've scratched mine."

Here's a practical example from Bob Harris's bank. It was the kind of win-win conflict resolution that looked good on the surface but made Bob Harris furious because the parties involved seemed to be looking out for their own competing interests but not for those of the enterprise as a whole. Bob learned that two highly profitable regions in contiguous media markets had agreed to pool their marketing resources and put together a media campaign. It seemed like a good solution for both since it allowed them to leverage their media spending. But it ignored the interests of a third region that had had its profits eroded by aggressive competition and therefore didn't have as much to invest in a marketing campaign of its own. Bob suggested a reallocation of the savings from the combined media campaign so the third region could increase its marketing budget. "Why couldn't the regional managers see this without me having to get involved?" Bob asked. The answer clearly was that the regional managers were each responsible for their own local business and not for the success of the enterprise.

For these reasons, we recommend a win-win-win approach to conflict resolution (see Figure 5), in which purpose is defined by answering these four questions:

- What are the higher interests of the enterprise and of the customers, investors, and partners who have placed their trust in the enterprise? Which of these higher interests absolutely must be achieved for the conflict to be resolved to preserve integrity and serve the long-term health of the enterprise?

- Who are the internal stakeholders who have competing interests?

- Which of these stakeholder interests cannot be compromised without putting the higher interests in jeopardy? Which of the interests can be compromised and by what margin?

- When all is said and done, how will you keep score—and gauge whether you, your counterparts, and the enterprise as a whole have actually "won"?

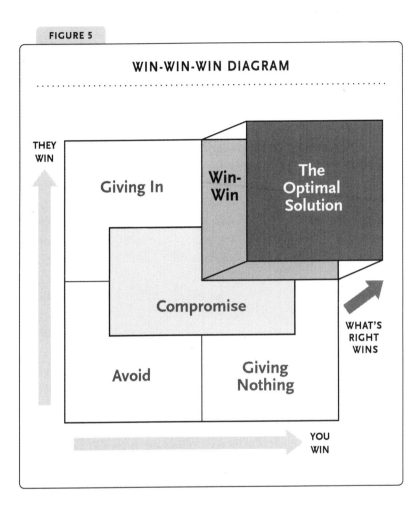

FIGURE 5

WIN-WIN-WIN DIAGRAM

THEY WIN

Giving In

Win-Win

The Optimal Solution

Compromise

WHAT'S RIGHT WINS

Avoid

Giving Nothing

YOU WIN

Clearly, these questions cannot be answered if the real interests aren't acknowledged, and there is little chance of that occurring without a high level of candor. A climate for candor, therefore, is a precondition for working out a good, shared, coherent definition of purpose.

But candor isn't enough. When Bob Harris was on vacation and didn't attend a few executive meetings, there was plenty of candor—but very little definition of shared purpose. Issues were raised, but discussions deteriorated into polarized debates and political dealing. There were no clear, visible criteria, just a lot of individual needs, and no basis for deciding what was mission-critical and what was not.

In any complex enterprise, so many goals have to be achieved that it's easy for executives to take their eyes off the prize. That's why savvy CEOs keep keep everyone talking about a few key goals, defined in clear, pithy terms. But at Bob Harris's bank, there were many individual and line-of-business goals to be achieved, with no clear consensus about what was mission critical.

Unless you keep a clear focus, like a beacon from the tower, it will be easy to get lost in the fog and crash on the rocks. And unless you make sure that your focus serves a higher purpose, you may be seduced by short-term performance objectives and bonus incentives, forgetting that it's more important to win the tournament than simply to score points. A clear, compelling, and lofty purpose helps keep everyone aligned and headed for the same goal.

Step Three: Will

When you're in a tough spot and there are difficult issues to sort out, you're bound to feel pressure and frustration. When resources are limited and there are more worthy opportunities than you can possibly pursue, those who are told to wait or make do with a meager allocation are bound to be disappointed.

If you truly define your purpose, you know that not every performance objective or project is of equal importance. It was easy to empathize with the frustration of an information technology manager in a pharmaceutical R&D organization who didn't like the fact that everyone fawned over the brightest medical chemists while taking his group's brilliant contributions for granted. But when the IT manager said, "We're every bit as important to this enterprise as a brilliant chemist," he was wrong. Medical chemistry drove his particular business.

Everyone knew Bob Harris would turn red in the face and begin ranting when he became frustrated. When he saw clear evidence that people were "getting with the program," his tension would ease and he'd become charming, witty, reassuring, and magnanimous. He gauged "getting with the program" by looking at pace and preparedness. When he saw what he was looking for, Bob relaxed, and when he didn't see it, his frustration grew—often to a level that was out of proportion to the problem.

People knew what would placate Bob, but not many knew what would get him truly energized and provide the lift to confront and overcome frustration. Even among those who knew what would give Bob a charge, few had the strength and determination to put themselves forward.

Bob liked to be pushed, challenged, confronted. He liked what he called a healthy argument, a vigorous debate. He did his best thinking when he was mentally down to the wire—down two points and just out of field goal range, with two minutes left in the game. At fifty-five, he still believed that his finest moments were playing college football. Unfortunately, he assumed that everyone else was programmed the same way.

It was a dramatic realization for Bob when he discovered that different people resonate to different things and get the energy to overcome frustration and adversity in different ways. Like many senior executives, he'd read market research on customer profiles and buying motives and on different ways to present the same financial services products. And recently he'd let his human resources department, along with an expensive outside consultant, talk him into a workshop on diversity. Still, he assumed, deep down, that all people were basically the same.

"You mean." he asked, "what builds my courage and gets my creative juices flowing might be the very same thing that inhibits someone else and makes them retreat from a challenge?" When Bob said this, the brave vice president who'd tried to talk with him about the tone at staff meetings gave a deep sigh of relief. "Yes, Bob," he said. "You've finally got it!" A few of his colleagues laughed heartily and hoped this would be the dawn of a new era at the bank—one in which being a clone of the guy at the top wasn't the only way to be viewed as a person who was able to meet a challenge.

Whether you are trying to energize individual teammates to make personal or professional improvements or are trying to infuse an entire team or organization with the will to persevere when encountering frustrations, you'll see little forward motion without a solid sense of purpose. Lofty and audacious goals will create some motivation for achievement-oriented teammates who buy into the purpose. But a sense of purpose alone doesn't restore hope or make people optimistic when they run into setbacks, frustrations, and conflicts that aren't resolved quickly and easily. Unless people have the will to stay in the game, conflicts can shut down the candor in a group and make its members wonder whether mission critical goals are achievable. A strong will keeps your stakeholders engaged and keeps them from settling for shortcuts that can damage your reputation when the straight and narrow seems too difficult.

Step Four: Rigor

Only now—with a foundation of candor, purpose, and will established—are your teammates ready to engage the rigors required to work out a win-win-win solution and a plan that will make it stick. What's needed is a clear plan that maps out the following:

- Who will be the sponsors to sign off on, approve, and fund the solutions that are agreed on?

- Who will be the expert advisors enlisted to share best practices, evaluate new technologies, and adapt tools and techniques to the situation at hand?

- Who will be the recipients of the solution—those who have to execute it, debug and refine it, and achieve the expected results?

- What is expected of each of these players—sponsors, expert advisors, and recipients?

- How will the efforts of each of the parties be coordinated and how will on-the-fly decisions be made when improvisation is required?

- What is the know-how that teammates already have that will enable them to execute the plan, and what is the know-how they need to acquire?

- What is the time frame for execution of the solution and the time frame in which expected results should be achieved?

There is no shortage of approaches to rational, data-driven problem solving. Engineers can assess work flows, and supply-chain experts can design the optimal inventory management system. Portfolio reviews and competitive market analyses are painstaking analytical processes but are not, by themselves, acts of courage. Technical specialists know how to

- Break a technical problem into its component parts
- Identify the givens and the time limits
- Brainstorm the possibilities until there is a wide array of options
- Apply rational criteria to narrow the list of possibilities
- Alpha and beta test the most promising solutions
- Pick the best option based on an assessment of costs, risks, and benefits
- Document the solutions with protocols and routines so they can be replicated as designed

There is a lot of hard work, but no real courage, in following protocols, using tools, and writing protocols. But it does take courage to make sure that you're tackling the right problems with the appropriate amount of rigor. It takes courage to admit that your business has changed, even if you are a third-generation bank executive, and to admit that your own level of know-how isn't yet adequate to solve a new set of problems. It takes courage to ask questions that have not been asked before or to say, "This doesn't make sense to me. Why do you do it this way?"

It takes courage to admit that there are constraints and that some of them are fixed and immovable. It's much easier to kill the messenger when he stops us and says there is a problem—and that it's a problem that has not been anticipated or seen before and that the organization is not yet equipped to address. "You're telling me what you need [to solve the problem]," a lead engineer told an impromptu design team in the movie that dramatized the flight of *Apollo 13*. "But I'm telling you what you have [to work with]. I'm not making this stuff up." It took courage to face the problem as it was, to get creative, and to not quit until a solution was found. It took courage to think creatively when there was no time to test the solution in the laboratory before rolling it out to the field.

On the *Apollo 13* flight, it was physically impossible to send a new shipment into space. What the astronauts had on board was all they had to keep them alive and get them back to Earth. The lines are less firm when it comes to legal and environmental codes, ethical standards, and accounting principles. So, when it's tempting to redraw the boundaries, it takes more, not less, courage to say, "There are some lines we just won't cross," and, "There are some standards we will never compromise." It isn't easy to act as if ethical standards are sacrosanct when you're being encouraged to look the other way or told they aren't important.

Most CEOs like Bob Harris get impatient with the details. They want to know what's possible and what course of action you recommend. If you assure them your plan will deliver the goods and if you've delivered the goods before, they may not dig into the details. When what you're proposing seems to be too much, too complex, and too expensive, they'll challenge you. They'll ask you to justify the rigorous plan you've proposed and may cite precedents that were quicker, simpler, and less costly. Or they may want assurance that the problems that occurred the last time won't recur and won't come back to haunt them later.

Does rigor really matter? Does an intimate knowledge of the details matter? It depends how much risk you are asking the other party to take when you say, "I need your support to solve this problem." If there is little at stake, little rigor is needed. But if you're asking someone to bet his savings on an investment opportunity, bet his career on a new opportunity, or bet his life on a new miracle cure, the stakes had better be backed up with rigor. And if that person will have to answer tough questions from others, you'd better make sure he has the facts straight and knows why a particular solution was chosen.

Step Five: Risk

Now we return to where we started. Your palms are sweating. Your heart is racing. Why are you being asked to take a risk and go out on a limb to support and trust someone else in your team? Perhaps

- Someone is asking for more support than you are comfortable offering or for an allocation of resources that you were counting on to achieve your own objectives

- The decision that was made in yesterday's meeting could jeopardize your bonus or your promotion unless it is revisited and revised

- Someone is claiming leadership in a domain that was supposed to be your area of authority and control

- A colleague wants you to communicate in a way that isn't your preferred style and is on the defensive because of the way you have approached her

- A colleague, customer, or outside consultant wants to talk directly with your boss or your direct reports, without inviting you to attend the meeting

- Someone is counting on you to do something that really isn't your job or that will require more nights, weekends, and personal sacrifices than you believe is fair

- Someone has made a mistake that will be costly to put right or will be embarrassing to you and your part of the organization

- Someone expects to be empowered to handle an assignment independently, and you aren't sure that she is up to the challenge

These risks and others represent moments of truth that will test your courage. Each of them will give you pause for concern. Even with a foundation of candor, purpose, will, and rigor, you may not be able to avoid the fact that you are still facing a risk. You may not be able to put the fear aside. But you can decide whether to let the fear stop you from doing what needs to be done or mobilize you to act.

"Courage," Mark Twain is credited with saying, "isn't the absence of fear; it is the mastery of fear." Courage may not stop your palms from sweating. It may not remove the nervous anticipation that you feel when you decide you need to make your voice heard. It may not make the other party more receptive when you raise a contentious issue. But the five-part formula can change how you build a foundation to act in the face of fear and can give you a road map for navigating through the resistance and opposition you might encounter when you say, "We've got to talk," or, "There's got to be a better way to approach this issue."

THE COACH

Imbuing Others with the Courage to Act

*One isn't necessarily born with courage, but one is born
with potential. Without courage, we cannot practice any
other virtue with consistency.*
MAYA ANGELOU

You can tell a lot about people from those who surround them, the
kind of offices they keep, how they look at you, what hangs on their
walls, how they dress, and how they talk to the staff. As you wait to be
ushered in for an appointment, it all forms a quick snapshot. It's a moment, frozen in time, that reveals everything, including how much
someone wishes to reveal or keep hidden.

When you walk into coach John Chaney's office in the basement
of the Temple University basketball complex, you immediately see three
things. First, of course, there are basketball players milling around—
talking easily, laughing—a trickling stream of young, energetic men
and women sprinkled with a few coaches and management types, all
flowing through a contained space. They appear to be a bit aimless, but
there is nothing accidental about their presence. Clearly, they mean to
be there.

Second, you can't help noticing the bold mottoes hanging on banners and scripted into each of the team pictures that hang prominently

on the wall. One motto says "BE THE DREAM." Another says "WIN-NING IS AN ATTITUDE." If you know anything about college basketball in the United States, you are familiar with Temple University. Temple isn't known for producing NBA superstars or for winning the coveted NCAA title, but they are known for being a scrappy contender that, year after year, finishes with a respectable win-loss record and that makes a good showing in the NCAA playoffs. Any college basketball aficionado will tell you that Temple is a team that knows how to pull together and win, not just blow a lot of smoke about winning.

Third, there is Besse, a mother if there ever was one, sweet talking the crowd, checking in with folks, bringing some kind of order to all that is going on. She is the keeper of the gate. Besse is a strong presence. Warm and loving, she sets the tone and is swept up in it as well. It's her face that lights the way in this place of hope. She's been part of Temple University for more than thirty years, well before John Chaney joined her and breathed new life into Temple basketball, well before he made winning an attitude.

Coach Chaney was a little late. He apologized, never mentioning that he had been with a friend who had been diagnosed with cancer, and it was up to John to provide hope, to lift him up and get him to transcend the blow that fate had dealt him, as John does with everyone. When you sit down with him, you see that he looks nothing like the wild-eyed sorcerer who's portrayed on national television. On the court, and certainly on the television screen, Chaney looks bigger than life—arms waving, shouting at the referees, goading his own players, a man possessed, a tad shy of being a maniac. He's a compelling figure in his rumpled white dress shirt, sleeves rolled up, eyes blazing, leaping up to defend his players or throw some advice that they should take to heart—now.

Here in the office, you see a different John Chaney. He is loose, comfortable in his own skin, not so large, in fact, a bit thin. He certainly doesn't look like someone to be feared, dressed down in his billed cap and a short-sleeved sport shirt. Surprisingly, Chaney's office is also dressed down, small and plain, not a throne room for the king. Out of respect and affection, he's called "Coach," but there's nothing distancing or regal about it. It's just part of his being. After all, John Chaney is the consummate head coach, a master at looking into the souls of human beings and sizing up their potential, long before they have the courage to actually "be the dream," rather than wishing it would magically come true.

Coach Chaney's door is open for all those who manage to get by Besse. He brought cookies—not for himself but for those who drop in and look like they need a special treat. Many times in the middle of our meeting, a face appeared at the door. Besse had said, "He'll be glad to see you." And he was. Coach stopped in midsentence, got up, introduced the person with great pride, and offered some outrageous, heartfelt compliment or an affectionate aside with enough truth to be believed. He was like a loving father welcoming a child who had been away for a time even though it might have been only a few days. The beginning or end of the brief interchange was often a hug, always with sincerity, never a throwaway.

We asked Besse what she found most memorable about Coach Chaney's leadership. She was amazed that the players come back to check in with him five, ten, twenty, or more years later. It might be an all-pro in the NBA or a rookie needing a bit of advice or support. They all come, knowing they will receive the same welcome they got on their first day. Coach is still Coach.

Indeed, in a little less than two hours, some fifteen people dropped in to see Coach Chaney. Each took a piece of him—unsolicited affection, advice, a small speech about studies, a humorous jab that said he knows more about your essence and your soul than he would ever tell about you. Or he might tell them a small story, chosen with care to implant a thought they could feed on after leaving his office.

Within minutes, or even seconds, we were struck by how well Coach Chaney knew each of his visitors. What he knew wasn't just their achievements on the basketball court, their athletic prowess, or the raw talent and potential that made Chaney want to recruit them for Temple in the first place. Of course, he knew all of that, and in an instant could recall specific incidents in specific games in which each player had exhibited the very best of his athletic potential. But he also knew far more. He knew each player's dreams, ambitions, and, equally important for these young men, fears and self-doubts that could trip them up and erase their courage to act. He understood the temptations that could tip the scales and the fine line between being successful and being a college basketball has-been, between doing your family proud and letting them down. He understood that it wasn't just their own dreams and ambitions that each of these young athletes carried into Temple and beyond with them, but the hopes and dreams of single mothers and extended families who had sacrificed dearly to give these young men a shot at a better life.

In the few hours we spent with Coach Chaney, we could see that each visitor wanted nothing more than just a moment of the Coach's, the father's, presence. There were, of course, the usual appreciations, gifts, and banter about old victories and old defeats. But mostly, as Besse said, each visitor simply wanted to be in the presence of someone who cared deeply for him and for whom he returned that love. Each needed to be touched by someone who could see deeply into his soul, who would help him stay focused on the dream, who would, with a single vignette or glance, help him rise above his fears and steer around the temptations.

The dance of visitors entering and leaving was spontaneous and unrehearsed, but it also had a smooth and natural rhythm. With a glance or a word, each visitor could tell that his moment had passed and that Coach had to get back to his conversation. Chaney didn't skip a beat. Once the visitor departed, he returned to his story or the point he had been making. There was no sense of interruption, no sign of annoyance, not the slightest indication that giving his time to whoever came to his door was anything but a sincere pleasure to him.

The first visitor to appear at the door was Greg, newly arrived from Jacksonville, a tall freshman, perhaps 6′7″, who was taking the toughest course load he could imagine—pre-engineering. He just stood there and the coach leaped up, hugged him, and began to talk about his size eighteen shoes, wondering just how big he would get. That introduction quickly passed on to news about his mother and his sister and then how he was getting along on campus. Then there was a word about being sure to hang with the kids who were good for him.

In a few clipped sentences, Coach had succeeded in providing lots of warmth, recognition, and support. The season didn't begin for a month, but Coach Chaney already knew Greg well and had connected at a very personal level. It didn't take more than two or three minutes for Coach to acknowledge that he understood Greg's fears and apprehensions and that he was confident Greg could rise above the newness and unfamiliarity of the university, being away from his family, and the temptation to hang out with kids who seemed like a lot of fun but would lead him away from the fulfillment of his dreams.

Alex was another of Coach Chaney's unexpected visitors. Coach used me as a platform to celebrate one of his "favorite sons." "Now here is the real thing, the best of the best, someone who really makes me proud," Coach fairly shouted, with unbridled enthusiasm. "Alex is a Prop 48,"* he explained. "He's never missed a class, never been in trouble. He helps the young players, tells the truth—such a good model. I'm really proud of him!"

With that speech, Coach grabbed Alex by the shoulder, twisted him around, and gave him a short hit on the arm and a kiss on the back of the neck as only a loving father could do. After Alex left the room, Chaney threw his hands up in wonder. He shared a personal story about Alex and his family, an anecdote that illustrated beyond any doubt that his concern for each player—and each player's potential—extended well beyond the limits of the basketball court.

Coach knew the very best of who each player was and the very best of what each one aspired to be. In Coach's eyes, each young man could see his full potential reflected and affirmed. It was out there, even before the player had the courage to be the dream, rather than merely talk about it in wistful, private conversations. In less than a minute, that's what Coach communicated to Alex, with an audience watching his public affirmation of the very best Alex could offer to himself and his team.

Every season, you can count on some sports writer to do a piece about the Temple Owls and Coach Chaney. After all, Chaney has earned a place in the Basketball Hall of Fame, even though his team has never actually won a national championship. The writers all cite the same facts. They talk about the 5:30 A.M. practices, the no-exceptions code of conduct, the high academic standards. They talk about the Temple magic and the stunning win-loss record—a record

*Proposition 48 was established among NCAA schools to provide opportunities for young athletes who otherwise might not be able to showcase their extraordinary talents or gain access to the educational opportunities afforded by these colleges and universities. Under Prop 48, each year a limited number of scholarships are provided to athletes who fail to meet the minimum academic qualifications of these schools and are perceived as "high-risk" candidates. At Temple University, a much larger percentage of these student athletes complete their four-year degrees than at most schools. This is the antithesis to the practice at some schools of using these athletes to build their athletic program with little expectation that they will succeed academically.

that would be impressive for any college team, but especially so for a group of kids who come from tough neighborhoods and broken homes, for whom basketball isn't a ticket to the NBA but a ticket to a college education and a chance at a better life and a more fulfilling dream.

Every sports writer poses the same questions, article after article, winning season after winning season. How does Chaney imbue these kids with the courage to overcome the challenges placed in front of them—kids who come from environments that maim and kill too many, where drugs run the streets, where single mothers try to keep their children from giving in to the pressures and temptations, and where a basketball is often the key to salvation? And, then, with the key in the lock—a place on the team and perhaps a scholarship—how does Chaney imbue each one, within the team, with the courage to let go of the individualism that got him this far and, instead, to become a selfless member of a team and develop the discipline to be a student in the midst of an ever-changing list of new temptations? How does such iron discipline resonate with kids who grew up in chaotic environments and who were used to getting whatever they wanted based on charm and athletic prowess? Every writer muses, and few of them are able to put their finger on the small but significant things that Coach Chaney does to give his players the courage to act, on and off the basketball court.

In a brief two-hour snapshot, we got a glimpse of the real Coach Chaney. It isn't the wild-eyed man on the basketball court or the despot who rules his charges with iron discipline. The real power and genius is in the compassionate, loving, tender father; in the preacher and teacher; in the confidant and cheerleader; and in the judge and jury. "Live the dream. Winning is an attitude." These aren't hollow words or a superficial mission statement. For Chaney, the secret of courage is about instilling hope, a belief that good can come from the relationships that evolve from the game. Winning isn't just about making it into the national championships or putting the ball through the hoop. It's about keeping the game in perspective, using it as a vehicle for getting to the dream—the dream of being the very best that each player is capable of being, for self, family, community, and a higher power.

Applying the Five Courage Factors

. . . .

What we saw of Coach was more powerful than anything he said to us about leadership, character, and courage. What we saw was the formula at work. And what we saw flawlessly and smoothly executed was every one of the five factors that we've described in this book, in rhythm and in sequence. It doesn't take hours or days of undivided attention to exhibit candor, purpose, will, rigor, and risk—or to evoke them not only in someone who is clearly in your charge but even in a casual visitor. But it does take practice, attention, and the willingness to give something of yourself.

CANDOR

Ask Coach for an opinion and you'll get it, straight up and undiluted. And if you don't ask, you'll get it the same way. Coach isn't concerned with the political consequences of speaking the truth. He isn't concerned about whether the other person likes him or likes what he has to say. Rather, he asks himself, is it truth that needs to be heard, to serve a higher purpose, to rekindle will, to strengthen rigor, to put people in a frame of mind to take the appropriate risks?

Coach also understands that he has little hope of making a real difference in his players' lives unless they also are willing to be candid with him. Not that he's open to changing the program to fit individual idiosyncrasies, needs, or egos. He's clear about that. Temple's basketball program isn't a democracy. But drop a hint to Coach that you're struggling with something and he's right there to listen—really listen—to what's said and what isn't said. He's patient and persistent with his questions. He reaches out to understand how the world looks from the perspective of a young man who's pushing himself to his personal limits and struggling to make a new place for himself.

There is little doubt that Coach Chaney's charisma, personal influence, and position can be daunting for those wishing to be completely open with him. After all, he fills multiple roles for many of his young players; he's a championship coach, surrogate father, counselor, advocate, and critic. He is able to help many overcome a quite natural anxiety by communicating his sincerity and compassion and, in many cases, love and respect for those with whom he speaks. What each of them can count on is that he will be honest with them and that whatever he says will, in his mind, be said with their personal interest as well as that of the team's in mind.

Candor doesn't start and stop with the relationship between Coach and his players. It's also a skill that Coach develops in his players; it's a virtue he watches for and nurtures so that teammates have the courage to tell the truth to one another. Candor is a large part of what it means for a model player like Alex to look out for the younger men in the program. In a world where it's easy for players to collude with one another in a good-natured but self-destructive conspiracy that puts egos and false pride ahead of genuine achievement, Chaney knows that candor doesn't come naturally. It takes work. It takes practice. It takes constant prodding. And it takes making heroes of players like Alex who are willing to stick their necks out and tell their teammates the truth, whether it's about something that will improve someone's play on the court or his win-loss record in life.

Chaney watches how his young players relate to one another. Colluding with someone who has broken training, for example, is almost as serious as doing the deed oneself. You're expected to confront a teammate and, if you can't get through to him, let a coach or tutor know so the other player can be helped. And, equally important, you're expected to accept feedback when it is offered. If another player, a coach, a tutor, or a friend offers a bit of advice or points out a transgression, it's not because he's a stool pigeon or a brownnoser. It's because he cares. If you can't take the feedback, you have a lot to learn before you can become a hero in John Chaney's book.

PURPOSE

Purpose, for John Chaney, is not about winning basketball games. Don't get us wrong. It's great to win, and Chaney's teams are winners. But winning is only a consequence of a much larger and more profound purpose built on discipline and heart. For Chaney, winning a game is a reflection of attempting to win the real game, which means cultivating the ability to be the dream every day. Chaney wants his players to understand that they can create their own destinies, and basketball is the catalyst for producing this understanding. Winning is about getting out of college with an education and with real options in life, with the sense that you can create your own life, even if, as is true for most of Chaney's players, fate hasn't dealt you a winning hand.

Winning, in Chaney's sense of it, means shifting the ambitions of many of these young men from the game that has rewarded them for so long toward something larger. It means putting the game in perspective and using it as the means to create more opportunities in their lives. Winning isn't about the glory of postseason play and competing in the Elite Eight or the Final Four. It's about life, a much more meaningful and lofty goal.

WILL

There's no doubt that Coach has passion—for life, for the game, and, most of all, for his players and the people who are close to him. The snapshots and cutaway video shots show Coach courtside, eyes wide open, arms waving, shouting sharply to the players and the refs, with a loosened tie and a shirt coming untucked. Coach *is* the wild-eyed Temple Owl with a never-say-die attitude.

Stories about Chaney's will are legendary. So, too, are the stories about what he does to inspire a winning attitude in those who have signed on to be part of his program. On the first day of practice, he shuts the doors and talks to his boys for three, four, even five hours. It is an indoctrination for some and a reinforcement for others.

Coach frames the challenge and throws down the gauntlet. It isn't about basketball; it's about winning at life. Chaney acknowledges that it isn't easy to reach for and be the dream. He cajoles and demands, shares his own story, and explains what it will take to reach their dreams, dreams that society would be just as happy to deny them. Coach is sympathetic without letting players off the hook or suggesting that anyone has a valid excuse to give up on himself and his dreams, on his coach, on his family at home, or on his brothers on the court. He talks of the young men who have proven themselves and who have stepped up to accept the mantle of courage and lead the team this year. In Coach's world, praise and respect are earned through hard work and a willingness to not give up, even when the going is tougher than anything his players might have bargained for.

For five days, Coach pushes, prods, beseeches, and tempts his men—individually and collectively—to believe that they can do what it will take to be one of the great John Chaney teams. He tells them that they are better than the temptations and the defeatism that can creep in and undermine all of their best possibilities. While they are captivated by his magic and his deep faith in the very best they can offer, Coach asks for a commitment that they will do whatever it takes to stay the course and not succumb to the lure of the easy path and provocations that await. And they know that commitment goes far beyond the indoctrination, far beyond the pep talk.

Whenever his players' energy wanes and frustration or impatience sets in, Coach is there, ready to remind them of the oath they took and of their commitment to self, family, and teammates. He knows that *will* cannot flourish or rejuvenate itself in isolation. And he is a master at orchestrating and using peer pressure to maintain the edge these young men need to overcome the adversities life has thrown their way—and will continue to throw their way because of the color of their skin, the absence of well-placed family connections, Spanish surnames, or the fact that they are so much larger than life that people assume they could not possibly have fears or doubts that chip away at the courage to act.

For Coach, nothing is done halfway. You either have the will to be the dream or you are giving up on yourself and everyone who's counting on you. He demands no less of himself, no less of his other coaches, tutors, managers, and staff. Even Besse feels Chaney's strong will and shares in perpetuating and amplifying it. The process is never ending. Coach says unabashedly that he has never given up on a kid. He can be tough, but, if his young men show him their resolve, he will work with them and keep at it until they get it. Every day Coach has a theme, a message that supports people's growing dreams, their belief that they can live their dreams and that those willing to do what it takes are going to make it. Every day, he looks into their eyes and sees whether they have the attitude and are capable of inspiring it in others—or whether he needs to get under their wings and give them some lift.

RIGOR

From the beginning, Coach makes it clear to the players that the program has rules—rules they may not understand and may not always like, but that they have to embrace and respect as a condition of staying on the team. This is a new thing for many of the talented young men who come to Temple to play basketball. Before signing on with Chaney, most of these young men have been able to do things their own way. They've been able to smile and get by on their talent and charm. They could act as if the rules don't apply to them.

But part of the contract with Chaney is that no one is above the rules. The honor code and the disciplines apply to everyone, every day. It doesn't matter how hot you are on the court or how desperately the team needs you to advance to the next playoff round. It doesn't matter how important the game is or who is watching from the stands.

Coach's rigorous training starts at 5:30 A.M., every morning, with a two- to three-hour practice, which finishes early enough so the players can get to class on time. Coach knows who will find it difficult to get up and get to practice on time. With one young man, he started asking three weeks before the first scheduled practice if he was setting his alarm and getting up early to start the day. By the time the first day of practice arrived, Chaney wanted the young man to be ready—with no excuses.

That's the way it works on if you sign on with John Chaney. Coach is there to drill, practice, and rehearse. And when the moment of truth comes, there are no excuses. You're either with the program or you're not.

The same discipline applies to the players' academic studies. It's one thing to talk about being an engineer, to aspire and dream. It's quite another to be the dream—to dig in, crack the books, and make the grade instead of coasting, partying, and impressing friends and admirers. Four days a week every player meets with a tutor, regardless of grades or performance in class. There are no exceptions, no free rides, no options. As a result, Coach knows exactly how each player is doing and what needs to be done to provide the help and support that he needs to make the grade. In life, as on the court, Coach sets out to make doing what is right a habit, so ingrained that it requires no thinking.

He speaks of muscle memory that can be obtained only by making a shot correctly, over and over, until the memory is in the muscle and the player doesn't need to think about it. Coach knows that having the right habits will prevent problems, which then will not have to be corrected later.

Study habits and grades aren't the only things covered by Coach's rules. The on-the-road dress code includes shirts and ties, of course. After all, his players represent the university, the team, their parents, and themselves, and each deserves to be seen looking good. There is a curfew. There is a code of good conduct that is fiercely enforced. And there is a code of honor for play on the court as well—such as passing to the open man rather than shooting the ball yourself, always putting the team ahead of your own ego and your own statistics.

Rigor doesn't require a system of cops and robbers, bureaucracy and audits. But it does require a system of controls and consequences. Breach the rules and the consequences might be doing laps, not playing in a game, or being suspended. Even worse, Coach could call home and talk with your mother. Coach knows that most of his players come from homes where Mom sacrificed and worked hard to give her son a shot at a college education and a chance to be something in life. Most players know that Mom would be even less tolerant than Coach if she thought her son was squandering the opportunity and showing disrespect for her sacrifice.

Coach understands that there will always be another game and another season. But a breach of the honor code cannot be undone. It's when the temptation to bend the rules is the greatest that discipline is truly put to the test. In a game with Duke, before the largest crowd in Philadelphia's basketball history, things were going badly and a talented young player was grousing about not getting playing time. The game was on the line, and many of his family were members in the stands. With ten minutes to go, he finally got his chance. He grabbed an offensive rebound and, with his back to the basket, instead of pushing the ball out to a teammate for an open three-point attempt, he drove to the basket, dribbling through traffic, and made a spectacular layup. The crowd roared. But Coach was incensed. Within thirty seconds, the player was pulled from the game and, in humiliation, was told to sit on the bench. Coach had no patience or tolerance for a hotshot who offered little more than lame excuses after forgetting the rule about seeking the open man rather than going for personal glory.

If the guiding principle is that basketball is the ticket to a world-class education—rather than a free ride through the system, exempt from the rules that apply to everyone else—the honor code can't be something that you turn on and turn off at will. It can't be something that you strive for 70 percent or 85 percent of the time. If star players are exempt, Chaney knows, there is no code. The code was more important than the game with Duke, the ego of the man who made a brilliant solo play, the roar of the crowd, and the vocal protests of the player's family members and fans, who didn't understand why Coach had benched their favorite son for the rest of the game.

RISK

Temple often wins basketball games by putting together a tenacious defense. Watch a John Chaney team play at its best and you won't see the explosive showmanship of a few heroic superstars supported by a cadre of secondary players. You'll see a relentless, united wall that forces an opponent to work for every point. A Temple team is only as strong as its weakest link. No one can be at the top of his game all the time, so the key to success has to be selfless playing, being familiar with the strengths and weaknesses of other team members, and being able, on the spur of the moment, to fill in for and support one another.

There's a world of difference between being a local playground star and a true team player in the way that's essential to Chaney's team. According to Coach, not everyone can learn to make the switch from soloist to team player. Chaney believes he can look into a prospect's eyes and determine whether he has the potential to risk for the team, to put his pride and ego aside for the good of the group. That potential, Chaney explains patiently, starts with humility. Humility may sound like the antithesis of courage, but it isn't. Humility doesn't mean that a player won't act with candor, purpose, will, and rigor. It just means that, when he does, he'll think of more than himself, more than "me first." If a player has humility, Coach explains, the rest can be learned. Without it, he believes, a player becomes more of a liability than an asset, no matter how talented he is.

Risk—the willingness to put team ahead of self and reach out to give someone else an opportunity to score when you could make the play and bask in the glory of the spotlight—isn't something that most of Chaney's players have learned. Many of his recruits were raised in an environment in which respect for others' property is irrelevant, telling the truth is for sissies, and doing as little as possible is the sign of being smart rather than successful in the classroom.

For Chaney, signs of humility provide a starting point for the re-education that he knows must occur for his team to succeed. His players must learn to be willing to pass up a good shot for the possibility of a better one by a teammate, to have the points spread across five balanced players instead of a few stars, to have low-scoring games that they win become more important than high-scoring games that they lose. Risk is for the good of the team. And what's good for the team, these players have to learn, ultimately is what's good for each individual as well.

The magic of basketball is that each game provides several hundred, sometimes several thousand, moments of truth that test a player's willingness to risk—for one another, for the team as a whole, for the spectators, and even for the players on the opposing team. After all, Coach knows, there's a difference between being a classy winner and someone who gloats and uses his victory to tear down the courage of the other guy, so his players also have to learn how to win. In basketball, you can walk away from an opponent and never see him again. But in life, Chaney knows, you'll have to face the same opponents day after day, month after month, and opponents who have courage are far more rational, far more willing to negotiate, and far more forgiving than opponents who are fearful and mistrusting.

Work Teams and Athletic Teams

If you've ever been on a truly great team, you will never forget the experience. It doesn't matter if it was a basketball team, a scientific research group, or an account team that was at the top of its game when you presented your proposal. When everything clicks on such a team, it looks and feels like magic. But, as any magician will tell you, magic is an art that requires know-how and practice, as well as a few masters who can show you how the tricks are performed. John Chaney is such a master.

Business is not sports, you might say. And you'd be right. John Chaney himself would agree, despite the fact that he's the consummate sports figure, a national hero who was inducted into the Basketball Hall of Fame—not for winning championships but for teaching players to be champions.

In the world of business, there's a thin veneer of civility, but the competition is fierce and the killer instinct is vicious. And in business, unlike sports, the game isn't over after thirty, forty, or sixty minutes of play. You can't suffer a humiliating defeat today, and then walk onto the court tomorrow and make a fresh start, with the clock and the scoreboard reset to zero.

And there are differences, no doubt, between your talent pool and John Chaney's recruits. Coach has drawn his players from the playgrounds of a hundred cities, from a thousand broken homes where poverty rules and education takes a backseat to almost everything. Your recruits may be better educated, may come from nicer neighborhoods and more intact families, and may start with life skills that are light-years ahead of the work habits and study skills that Chaney's players bring to Temple University. Some of your recruits may have Ph.D.s, engineering degrees, and solid track records. They may have already arrived and already tasted what it is to be the dream. Now the challenge is getting them to share a dream or muster the courage to act in a different way from what was required in the old marketplace, the old technical environment, the old company.

If there are lessons that your teammates have already learned and mastered—aspects of candor, purpose, will, rigor, and risk that are already part of their character—there are parts of the Chaney formula that you may be able to ignore, like any coach who tailors the practice regimen to the strengths and learning needs of the players. But just because your players start in a different class doesn't mean you don't have to pay as much attention to the five courage factors as Chaney does.

After all, a hotshot engineer who powers down the court to rush for the best projects and pushes colleagues out of the way to slam-dunk her solution isn't very different from the hotshots that John Chaney might bench, even when they score the winning points. The careless but brilliant account executive who creates a stream of unnecessary work for others by failing to respect protocols may erode your profits or drive up your costs without being aware of the financial impact of his thoughtlessness. The manager who talks about the dream of being politically correct but in private dismisses or denigrates the mission statement isn't going to help you be the dream. And, in an era when business teams form and disband weekly, when the ink never dries on the organization chart, when performance and knowledge count for more than loyalty and seniority, and when the next merger is being planned even before you've integrated the operations of the last merger, risk doesn't come naturally.

Winning, Chaney will tell you, is more than a set of numbers and statistics—not that he doesn't have numbers that would be the envy of any head coach. He does, having taken his Temple Owls to the NCAA playoffs nineteen times in twenty years and having posted equally impressive win-loss records as the head coach at Chaney State College and before that at Gratz High School, an inner-city school in a tough Philadelphia neighborhood. Nonetheless, he'll tell you that winning is about attitude—and courage. Without the right attitude, winning is an accident of fate. It's easy to rest on your laurels and get beaten by tougher competition or unexpected adversity tomorrow. The right attitude is what makes winning happen consistently and what makes it look like magic.

Chaney's "Be the dream" motto suggests a focus on doing your very best in the moment—and that is the dream and a player's hope for now. Doing his very best allows each player to look ahead while living intensely in the present. It is the essence of a self-correcting team, of one that values best practices and looks toward solutions rather than excuses. And because being the dream involves great focus, it requires discipline as well as idealism.

During our visit, Coach Chaney pulled out a greeting card with the photographs of four young African American boys on the front. Inside was an excerpt from a poem that said

I, being poor, have only my dreams;
I have spread my dreams under your feet;
Tread softly because you just might tread on my dreams.

One of the real secrets of Chaney's success is, of course, that his brand of courage doesn't tread on the dreams of his players. Instead, it's built on understanding their dreams and providing the lift they need to get there. And it's built on an understanding that one player's dreams don't have to come at the expense of someone else's—even if, for the good of the team, you have to put the advancement of your own individual dreams on hold for a little while.

MOMENTS OF TRUTH

. . . .

The Challenge of Courage

Courage is rightly esteemed the first of human virtues because it is the virtue which guarantees all others, particularly when people are stretched to their breaking point.
WINSTON CHURCHILL

You've read all but the last chapter of the book. You understand the concept of courage and the five factors of courage that build on one another—first candor, then purpose, followed by will, rigor, and, after the foundations are in place, risk. But there's one lingering problem. You can't build courage by reading a book, watching a video, or simply understanding the concept in theory.

Courage isn't reflected in what you know or what you can recognize when you see it in others. Courage is reflected in what you do when you are put to the test and face real moments of truth.

The "mBa" Formula

· ·

When we face trying or troublesome moments of truth, we usually don't stop to think. We respond—sometimes by seizing the opportunity and acting, and sometimes by waiting and failing to act. Our response feels automatic. If we're challenged about how we acted, we'll say, "I did what I needed to do. I had no choice. The situation confronted me, and I simply responded."

We see evidence of this kind of conditioning all the time. When Bob Harris is critical and demeaning, the group shuts down, even when key people know there are issues that need to be raised. When no one defines Mission One, we each pursue our individual agendas. When the mood is tense and pessimistic, we feel our own enthusiasm and optimism wane. If no one else is following agreed-to disciplines, why should I? And if I have no assurance that risk will be recognized, let alone rewarded, I back off when I should be forthcoming with help or resources.

But conditioning, and feeling that we are victims of conditioning, ignores a fundamental reality. We choose how to respond to the moments of truth that confront us. That's where the "B" in the mBa formula comes in—and where training has to focus. The "B" stands for *beliefs*. If we believe that courage is built from the top down, we will wait for those at the top to act and will resent it when they don't. If we believe that courage shouldn't be required at all, and that a well-run organization should engineer out the moments of truth that test our mettle, we'll resent it when we hear the call. If we believe that our colleagues should already know better, we'll be stunned and exasperated when we discover that they don't. And none of these beliefs will help.

What training has to do, if it is going to build courage, is to reshape beliefs that inhibit courage and inculcate beliefs that build candor, purpose, will, rigor, and risk, in sequence. Some of us are already imbued with the emotional intelligence, the optimism, and the sensitivity to be in a league with John Chaney. Others of us have to learn to recognize and answer the call.

Given a choice, of course, most of us would prefer to be in a situation in which we don't have to hear the call. Our first instinct is to find someone to blame, rather than to find a solution to the problems that confront us. That's why Peter Jennings, on the evening of September 11, 2001, asked Shimon Peres whether Israel owed an apology to the people of the United States. It's why, when we face frustration, ambiguity, or any other conflict-prone realities, we demand to know who put us in harm's way. It is easier to blame and walk away than it is to face up to the moment of truth and act.

In her book *Danger in the Comfort Zone*, psychiatry professor Judith Bardwick explains that most reasonable people would prefer a work environment that offers entitlement and comfort to one that serves up adversity and requires accountability. In a later article (1997), Bardwick added that the choice is analogous to asking someone whether they would prefer to live in peacetime or wartime. You already know the answer.

But what makes some people stay rather than flee, along with their loved ones and prized possessions, when they suddenly find themselves under attack, thrust into a situation they didn't want and apparently didn't create? It comes down to beliefs. We choose to stay and deal with adversity if we

- Believe there is no viable or attractive way out

- Believe the cause is worth fighting for and the war can be won

- Believe that others are counting on us and do not wish to desert comrades who are choosing to stay

- Believe that the spoils of battle will be worth the indignities and hardships we will have to endure

- Believe that staying upholds a personal honor code

Stress Point in the System

In a building, it's clear that some parts of the physical structure have to absorb more of the weight, the stress, and the sway than other parts do. Some buildings are exposed to strong winds, extreme temperatures, ocean waves, and earthquakes. The same is true of team-based organizational structures.

Take, as an example, the customer service department of a large electronics company that designed and sold switches, control boxes, and "head-end" computerized controls to cable television operators. The job of the staff in this department, officially, was to answer calls from the technicians who worked for the cable television operators who had purchased their systems, check on the status of orders, and refer technical problems that they couldn't answer to the systems engineers. Unofficially, however, members of this staff were also responsible for placating irate and impatient customers whose systems had gone down and determining which requests were merely urgent and which were *really* urgent. They also were responsible for following up with the engineers and being advocates and ombudspeople for their customers, a responsibility that some of the engineers found demeaning and insulting. No one had to explain the need for courage to the service representatives who were at the stress point of this structure, even though some of the systems engineers and field engineers didn't feel the same stress that they felt.

Or consider the safety engineers in a property and casualty insurance company who are expected to inspect policyholders' factories and warehouses and assess the risks of fire, flood, and business interruption. They aren't paid nearly as much as the account executives who sell the policies or the underwriters who set the rates, but they are responsible for crucial information that affects the insurance company's profit-loss ratios. They are also responsible for enforcing the conditions of insurance that were written into the policy, including conditions that the risk manager who purchased the coverage may believe are irrational. These safety engineers are going to feel more stress than teammates who don't feel the same pinch of the conflict-prone realities.

Physical structures are designed so that the stress points have greater strength and greater resilience than the rest of the structure. But in a physical structure, a wall or column isn't going to say, "This isn't fair," or, "I should be paid more." In a human structure, it's clear that some parts of the system do tougher duty than others—and that the ones doing the toughest duty aren't necessarily the ones getting the most pay, the most perks, or the most recognition. If you're in a stress-point role, some of the beliefs that you have to manage may involve your sense of self-worth, pride, and value; others aren't necessarily going to say, "Thanks. I needed that. Good job." If you're not in a stress-point role, you may need beliefs that help you cope with the indignation, attitude, or impatience that those who are working under stress might exhibit.

The Few, the Proud

Boot camp in the United States Marine Corps has been called the greatest team-building and leadership training program on earth (Freedman, 1998). Recruits come in with varying levels of courage and come out with

- Directness and the candor to say what needs to be said and to listen when others level with them

- A strong sense of purpose and dedication to country, corps, unit, and self

- An indefatigable will and the ability to lift the will of others

- A respect for discipline and rigor that makes it possible to spot a marine long after he has left the corps

- A commitment to risk for comrades in need and/or in danger

The same is true of the Israeli Air Force. Recruits come in fresh out of high school, from diverse backgrounds, with varying degrees of skill, valor, and courage. The lessons they learn in the air force do more than prepare them to fly successful missions or support those missions from the ground, where the enemy is only five to twenty minutes away by fighter jet or missile and where seconds and split seconds count.

More than anything else, Freedman said, it is the active nature of the U.S. Marine Corps and the Israeli Air Force training experience that makes it so effective. Recruits don't just read a book, watch experienced role models, and memorize a code of honor and values. They do all of that, to be sure, but they do much more. They act. They face adversity, challenges, dilemmas, and problems—and act. Action is what defines courage. And it's what enables people to learn it.

The Principles of Courage

....

The U.S. Marine Corps and the Israeli Air Force are highly selective and elite groups. Not everyone is cut out to be a marine. Not everyone makes the cut and is accepted into the Israeli Air Force. But the principles of learning through action can be applied to our organizations and lives and can help us and those around us master the courage to act.

ACTION LEARNING PRINCIPLE #1: KNOW WHAT YOU'RE PREPARING FOR

Before training starts, you should know what the moments of truth are that will test the team's courage. You should know the conflict-prone realities that the team will have to face. You should know where the pressure points are in the system and who will have to withstand more of the strain and take up more of the slack than others. Sure, the marines train in the basics: running, climbing, and handling weapons. Air force recruits learn the basics of aeronautics. But neither of them trains without mapping the terrain for which they are training and without learning how a teammate's mettle will be tested once he is asked to rise to a challenge and answer the call.

ACTION LEARNING PRINCIPLE #2: APPLY IT

Be pragmatic. Assume that, in the sanctity of the workshop or learning laboratory you design, your teammates will get the point and master the five courage factors. What should they do with this newfound knowledge? Where should they apply it? In the absence of a real battlefield, the marine corps stages military exercises. The Israeli Air Force stages sorties. But, presumably, you are raising the level of courage to do more than create preparedness. You have real challenges to meet.

So before you invite people to the training session, and before you design the training, think about the applications that you want to see. Form task forces to engineer the rigors that have to be implemented. Convene project teams to execute change. Raise the bar on performance standards for an account team or an engineering team. If there isn't a return on the investment in training, it will be hard for your management to support it, even if you are building an essential competence like courage. If there isn't an application, training will be an event or a motivational speech rather than the creation of a lasting upgrade in skills.

ACTION LEARNING PRINCIPLE #3: PROVIDE FEEDBACK

Courage is personal, so the feedback has to be personal as well. Individuals need to know what they already do well and where they need to improve. They need personal development plans, with goals, time lines, and benchmarks. And they need to be acutely aware of how they affect the courage of others around them, for better and for worse. For this reason, 360-degree feedback is an indispensable part of any training program that purports to build courage. If you don't know how your actions and reactions affect the courage of those who look to you for leadership, as well as your peers, your higher-ups, and your customers, how can you possibly know where you can contribute to better performance when your team faces a moment of truth?

Candor, the foundation element of courage, requires more than surveys and written development plans. Teammates need to know how to level with one another in the heat of the moment of truth. They need to know how to give feedback crisply and directly and how to accept constructive criticism on the spot, without getting defensive. This skill is practiced over and over in nearly every U.S. Marine Corps and Israeli Air Force drill. It can be humbling. It's also part of the magic that brings these teams together.

ACTION LEARNING PRINCIPLE #4: MAKE IT ACTIVE AND INTERACTIVE

Courage isn't learned from a textbook. It's learned through action. Simulations, structured problems, and practice drills get people up and involved, and they hold the attention of impatient participants with low boredom thresholds. If the simulations or drills are properly selected and customized, they can replicate and dramatize the types of difficult situations that the team will actually have to face. Properly designed, they make it possible to see the impact of team decisions in a matter of minutes or hours, rather than weeks or years.

Not every simulation will be an experience of success for the participants. In fact, some of the most powerful learning occurs when a team has to analyze why a solution was elusive, why important cues were missed, or why certain risks weren't taken. It may be tricky for the facilitators who are running the training program to have to stage simulations that they know will end in failure unless and until the team masters the five-factor formula. Learning from failure and regrouping to try again is one of the biggest differences between military and civilian training. "When I left the navy and took my first civilian job as a training officer," a retired captain told us, "I had to learn that I didn't own my trainees twenty-four hours a day and couldn't push them to the same limits that we pushed our navy trainees. I also had to learn that I wasn't dealing with people who all had the same rank and the same willingness to suppress their egos in order to stretch and learn."

ACTION LEARNING PRINCIPLE #5: VALUE, HONOR, AND BRIDGE DIVERSITY

Like life, training isn't a level playing field in which everyone brings the same skills and strengths to the problem at hand. People don't play the same roles in a simulation or find the answers at the same time. The test of courage often comes when those with more insight or more strength have to work with those who don't see the solutions as quickly or who are lacking in the strengths or the knowledge that's mission-critical to solve a particular problem.

Give a team a treasure hunt, for example. Some teammates may walk with a faster gait than others. And some may not be able to walk at all. Or give them a throwing and catching exercise or a series of mathematical problems. How do teammates bridge their physical, mental, and other differences? How do they show respect without denying that people have different abilities and different aptitudes?

Put a team under time pressure or resource constraints and not everyone will react the same way. Differing cultural backgrounds, personality types, and professional training will make teammates respond differently to the same moments of truth. How do teammates recognize the differences and succeed because of, rather than in spite of, their unique qualities?

ACTION LEARNING PRINCIPLE #6:
BUILD A CODE OF HONOR

To the French, a *code d'honneur*, or code of honor, is what separates a good, upstanding person from a scoundrel. You may not go to jail if you give your word and then violate your code of honor, but you definitely will bring shame on yourself, your family, and anyone who continues to hold you in high esteem. The code is not just a set of principles or guidelines that you can abide by when it's convenient and abandon when it's more trouble than it's worth. It's an ethical and moral imperative that has to be lived.

"The code," as U.S. Marines call it, is inviolate. Similarly, one lapse in judgment or an adolescent prank can cost an Israeli Air Force candidate his or her wings or eligibility for this elite group. Why? With lives at stake, there's simply no room for people you can't trust to uphold the highest moral and ethical standards.

The code also cements the beliefs that create, nurture, and perpetuate courage. "The difficult thing about dealing with pessimists," psychologist Martin Seligman (1998) wrote, "is that they are usually right. They have assessed the moments of truth accurately and know that the cards are stacked against them. Optimists, on the other hand, have a healthy defence against reality which enables them to see possibilities that don't yet exist." A code of honor shares that healthy defense against reality with others. To stay the course and work toward a vision of success that doesn't yet exist requires a shared delusion; a code of honor is part of what makes it possible to sustain that delusion, despite overwhelming evidence to the contrary.

ACTION LEARNING PRINCIPLE #7:
MAKE LEARNING FUN

It's easier to raise tough issues and stick with the discussion when you're able to laugh at the dilemma and see the humor in the situation. It's easier to persevere when you're having fun. And it's easier to get people to drop their defenses and act naturally when they lighten up.

Part of making learning fun is a mental trick, like the one Tom Sawyer used to trick his friends into painting the fence on a hot summer day. It's in the tone that the facilitators set, whether the learning is in a workshop, a team meeting, or a demonstration on the factory floor. And part of making learning fun involves the mix of activities and simulations that you include in the program, the way you use time pressure and resource constraints, and the way you use videos, music, and other media.

"Courage," according to author Mary Anne Radmacher, "doesn't always roar. Sometimes it's the small voice at the end of the day that says, 'I'll try again tomorrow.'" Make it enjoyable to face moments of truth, both in the simulated world of training and in the real world of conflict-prone organizations, and you'll be more likely to amplify, rather than stifle, that small voice. And with that voice as your beacon, you'll keep the courage to continue to live the dream. We wish you success in that adventure.

REFERENCES

Bardwick, J. M. *Danger in the Comfort Zone: From Boardroom to Mailroom—How to Break the Entitlement Habit That's Killing American Business.* New York: AMACOM, 1991.

———. "Cadillacs and Steak Knives." Presentation to The Master's Forum, 1997.

———. *Seeking the Calm in the Storm: Managing Chaos in Your Business Life.* New York: Prentice Hall Financial Times, 2002.

Bar-On, R., and J. D. A. Parker, eds. *The Handbook of Emotional Intelligence: Theory, Development, Assessment, and Application at Home, School, and in the Workplace.* Foreword by D. Goleman. San Francisco: Jossey-Bass, 2000.

Batson, C. D. *The Altruism Question: Toward a Social-Psychological Answer.* New York: Lawrence Erlbaum, 1991.

Cooke, R. A. *Organizational Culture Inventory Manual.* Plymouth, Mich.: Human Synergistics, 1994.

Cooperrider, D., P. Sorensen Jr., D. Whitney, and T. Yaeger. *Appreciative Inquiry: Rethinking Human Organization Toward a Positive Theory of Change.* Champaign, Ill.: Stipes Publishing, 1998.

Dell, D., and J. Kickey. *Sustaining the Talent Quest: Getting and Keeping the Best People in Volatile Times.* New York: Conference Board, 2002.

Farley, C. J. *The King's Secret: The Legend of King Sejong.* Illustrated by R. Jew. Seoul: International Circle of Korean Linguistics, 1997.

Freedman, D. H. "Corps Values." *Inc.* (April 1, 1998).

Fried, E. *Active-Passive: The Crucial Psychological Dimension.* New York: Harper-Collins, 1985.

Gal, R. *A Portrait of the Israeli Soldier: Contributions in Military Studies.* Westport, Conn.: Greenwood Publishing Group, 1986.

Goleman, D. P. *Working with Emotional Intelligence.* New York: Bantam Books, 1998.

Goleman, D. P., A. McKee, and R. E. Boyatzis. *Primal Leadership: Realizing the Power of Emotional Intelligence.* Cambridge, Mass.: Harvard Business School Press, 2002.

Harlow, H. F. *Learning to Love*. New York: Aronson, 1971.

Harvey, J. B. *The Abilene Paradox and Other Meditations on Management*. San Francisco: Jossey-Bass, 1999.

Janis, I. L. *Groupthink: Psychological Studies of Policy Decisions and Fiascos*. Boston: Houghton-Mifflin, 1982.

————. *Crucial Decisions: Leadership in Policymaking and Crisis Management*. New York: Simon & Schuster, 1989.

Key, Y., and K. Renaud. *King Sejong the Great: The Light of Fifteenth-Century Korea*. New York: Lothrop, Lee, and Shepard, 1991.

Kleiner, A. "Corporate Culture in Internet Time." *Strategy and Business* (Q1 2000) 18:2-8.

Kohn, A. *Punished by Rewards: The Trouble with Gold Stars, Incentive Plans, A's, Praise, and Other Bribes*. Boston: Houghton-Mifflin, 1999.

Kotter, J. *Leading Change*. Cambridge, Mass.: Harvard Business School Press, 1996.

Kriegel, R., and M. H. Kriegel. *Peak Performance Under Pressure*. New York: Doubleday, 1984.

Lewin, K. Field *Theory in Social Science: Selected Theoretical Papers*. Westport, Conn.: Greenwood Publishing Group, 1975.

Livingston, J. S. *Pygmalion in Management*. Cambridge, Mass.: Harvard Business Review, 1969.

Peters, T. J., and R. H. Waterman. *In Search of Excellence: Lessons from America's Best-Run Companies*. New York: HarperCollins, 1982.

Rosenthal, R., and L. Jacobson. *Pygmalion in the Classroom: Teacher Expectation and Pupils' Intellectual Development*. Irvington, N. J.: Irvington Press, 1996.

Rotter, J. B. *Development and Application of Social Learning Theory: Selected Papers*. New York: Praeger, 1982.

Seligman, M. E. P. *Learned Optimism: How to Change Your Mind and Your Life*. New York: Pocket Books, 1984.

Authors' Note: References to Joe Neubauer, Bill Leonard, and Mission One at ARAMARK are proprietary information and used with permission.

INDEX